**LONDON, NEW YORK, MELBOURNE,
MUNICH, AND DELHI**

Senior Editor **Alastair Dougall**
Design Manager **Robert Perry**
Designers **Nick Avery, Owen Bennett, Jon Hall**
Managing Editor **Catherine Saunders**
Art Director **Lisa Lanzarini**
Publishing Manager **Simon Beecroft**
Category Publisher **Alex Allan**
Production Editor **Siu Chan**
Production Controller **Nick Seston**

First published in Great Britain in 2010
by Dorling Kindersley Limited,
80 Strand, London WC2R ORL
A Penguin Company

10 11 12 13 14 10 9 8 7 6 5 4 3 2 1
176239—10/09

A CIP catalogue record for this book is available from the British Library.

ISBN: 978-1-4053-4851-5

Colour reproduction by Alta Image, UK
Printed and bound in China by Hung Hing Printing

**Discover more at
www.dk.com**

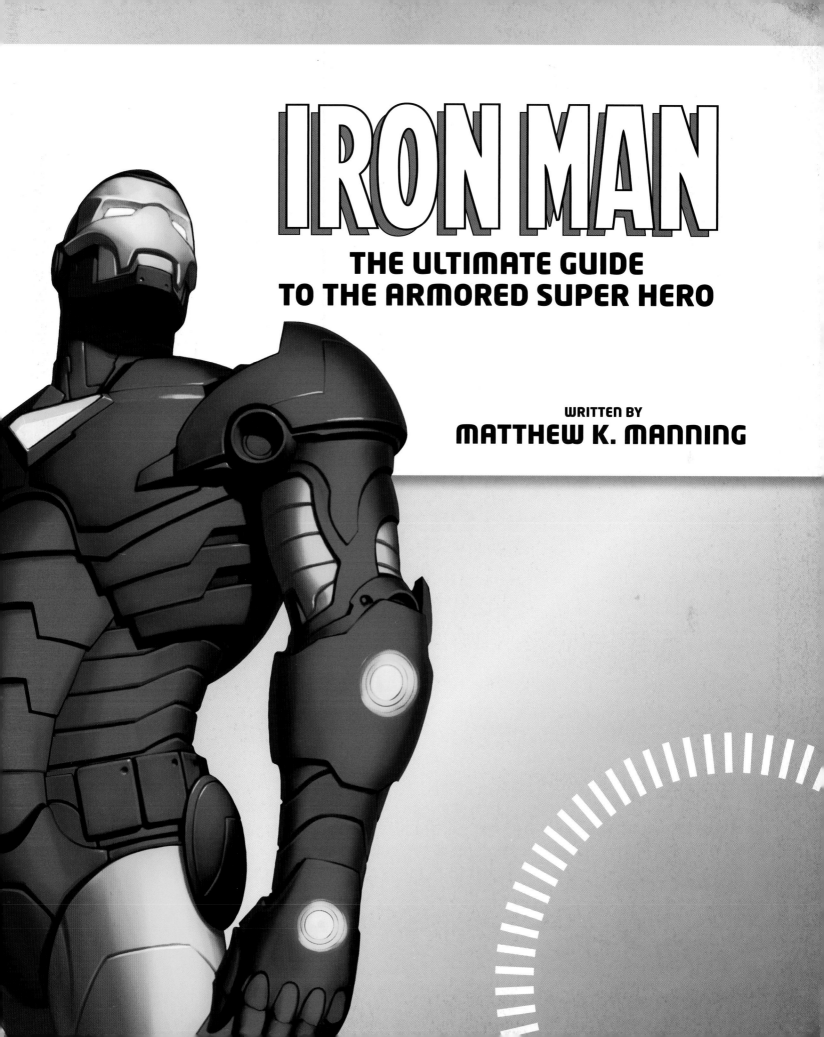

IRON MAN

THE ULTIMATE GUIDE
TO THE ARMORED SUPER HERO

WRITTEN BY
MATTHEW K. MANNING

CONTENTS

Foreword by Matt Fraction	6	Hulkbuster!	70
Introducing Iron Man	8	Cold War Threats	72
The Birth of Iron Man	10	Mandarin	74
Key Issue: *Tales of Suspense #39*	12	Key Issue: *Tales of Suspense #62*	76
The Suit's Powers	14	Madame Masque	78
The Suit	16	Iron Man & S.H.I.E.L.D.	80
The Armor: 1963 to 1988	18	The 1970s	82
The Armor: 1993 to 2000	20	Demon in a Bottle	86
The Armor: the 21st Century	22	Key Issue: *Iron Man #128*	88
Tony Stark	24	Justin Hammer	90
The Wit and Wisdom of Tony Stark	26	Doctor Doom	92
Stark Industries	28	The 1980s	94
A Troubled Hero	30	Alcohol Relapse	98
Friends & Allies	32	Key Issue: *Iron Man #182*	100
Pepper Potts	34	Iron Man II [James Rhodes]	102
Happy Hogan	36	Secret Wars	104
Rhodey	38	Obadiah Stane	106
Girls, Girls, Girls!	40	West Coast Avengers	108
Bethany Cabe	42	Armor Wars	110
Main Enemies	44	Key Issue: *Iron Man #232*	112
Other Foes	46	Armor Wars II	114
Avengers Assemble!	48	The 1990s	116
Team-Ups	50	Dragon Seed Saga	120
Other Iron Men	52	Operation: Galactic Storm	122
Timeline	54	The Coming of War Machine	124
The 1960s	60	Going Solo	126
Key Issue: *Tales of Suspense #48*	64	War Machine Weapon Spec	128
Captain America	66	Force Works	130
Iron Man Versus Hulk	68	Timeslide	132

Heroes Reborn	134
Heroes Return	136
Key Issue: *Iron Man Vol. 3 #1*	138
Avengers Assembled	140
2000s and on…	142
Secretary of Defense	146
Avengers Disassembled	148
House of M	150
The New Avengers	152
Iron Lad & The Young Avengers	154
Extremis	156
Key Issue: *Iron Man Vol. 4 #5*	158
Illuminati	160
Civil War	162
Key Issue: *Civil War: The Confession #1*	164
Iron Man and Spider-Man	166
Tony Stark: Director of S.H.I.E.L.D.	168
The Mighty Avengers	170
50-State Initiative	172
The Order	174
World War Hulk	176
Ezekiel Stane	178
Secret Invasion	180
Iron Patriot	182
Iron Man: Fugitive	184
Key Issue: *Iron Man Vol. 5 #10*	186
Alternative Realities	188
Ultimate Iron Man	190
Through the Decades	192
Afterword by Matthew K. Manning	194
Index	196
Acknowledgments	200

Paco Roca

FOREWORD

I like Iron Man, but I love Tony Stark. I'm not sure if the good luck and great time I've had writing *The Invincible Iron Man* has anything to do with that fact, but I suspect so.

Inspired by Howard Hughes and premiering in *Tales of Suspense* in April '63, Stark was the character that Stan Lee always claimed got the most fan mail from women. In 1966, when Grantray-Lawrence Animation made the *The Marvel Super Heroes* daily animated series (which aired *The Invincible Iron Man* on Wednesday afternoons) (by "animated," I mean "almost-animated via moving various art elements from the original art from the comics around on-screen"), the *Iron Man* theme song started off with the couplet, "Tony Stark makes you feel/He's a cool exec with a heart of steel..." The jingle itself began with Stark—not Iron Man.

Here's my thing. In the book—even in my own pages of the book—you can put different people inside the armor and still call the comic and the character Iron Man and it pretty much still flies. He—or she—still has the helmet, the circle or triangle doodad on the chest, light-up palms, sometimes even rocket-skates in the boots. Flying, that's important. It's fine. It's fun. It works.

Because the suit is the future and that's always fun to watch. Tony is its test pilot. Its inventor. And that combo resonates like a tuning fork deep within us.

There's a thing I think we all relate to in Super Hero stories, no matter what media they come to us wrapped in, that helps explain their enduring popularity. I believe "Super Heroes" endure because of the *transformative* moment—the instant where our hero becomes something *more*.

Name for me a single Super Hero—in comics, film, TV, wherever—where, the whole time they're running around in their Super Hero guise there's a part of you waiting the alter ego to go away so they can return to their civilian life. I can't really think of anybody *other* than Tony Stark who, depending on the day, is at least as interesting and fun to watch as Iron Man. You can't *wait* for Robert Downey Jr. to get back on screen and, if an *Iron Man* creative team is doing its job right, you shouldn't have to wait long for Tony Stark to get back on-panel, either.

This isn't the most original thought of the world, but I think that the common link in all the great stories and myths and characters that resonate with us is *transformation*. I believe that every great and lasting myth, legend, fable, film, pulp, or pop fiction that's ever captured popular imagination did so because, at its root, someone or something starts off in the story as one thing that we recognize with some degree of shame, regret, or empathy and, through crisis and resolution, becomes something *greater than*, and we, the audience, on some level, take at best inspiration and at worst are entertained by that transformative journey. All the stories we love are, in some ways, aspirational or cautionary tales of transformation. Of evolution. And I think Super Hero stories hit us the way they do because we literally *see* the transformation. It's not a wound being healed, it's not a wrong being righted—it's a man becoming superman. Or Superman or Spider-Man or Iron Man as the case may be. We are witness to the miraculous transformation and it just sends us.

Throw in a dash of danger—a sense of rescue to it all—of flesh and blood people digging deep and fighting back—and you've got yourself some mythic resonance.

Tony Stark is a man rescuing his fellow man, a man transforming himself, a man taking the reins of evolution in his teeth and forcing it to go where he wants it to go.

And he looks amazing in a tuxedo.

Here's to you, Tony.

MATT FRACTION
WRITER OF *THE INVINCIBLE IRON MAN*

Portland, Oregon
September 2009

INTRODUCING
IRON MAN

Iron Man has always looked towards the future. From his debut in the pages of *Tales of Suspense #39*, to the most recent issue of his fifth ongoing comic series, his billionaire alter ego Tony Stark has been in a constant state of reinvention. Stark's goal? To stay one step ahead of the competition, and to lead by heroic example.

When he first appeared on the scene, Tony clad himself in a bulky gray armor with all the style and panache of an fire hydrant. His evolution into a hero was just beginning. His look soon transformed into that of an atomic knight in golden shining armor and then to the robotic equivalent of a hot rod. Flash with substance. The idea of piloting their own Iron Man armor became a daydream for thousands of readers. But Tony Stark was just getting warmed up.

Over the years, Iron Man has remained on the cutting edge of technology, adapting to the future almost before its arrival. Tony Stark has been a war profiteer, a playboy, a Super Hero financier, an electronics pioneer, a humanitarian, a business consultant, a computer technician, a super-spy and even the US Secretary of Defense. But always at his core, Tony Stark has been Iron Man, a visual symbol of heroism, change and faith in science to shape a better world.

He's Iron Man. The Golden Avenger. Shellhead. But most importantly, he's Tony Stark, one of the greatest minds of his generation.

THE BIRTH OF IRON MAN

The brainchild of some of the most creative individuals ever to work in the comic book medium, Iron Man made his dramatic debut on the cover to *Tales of Suspense #39*.

By March of 1963, comic book writer and editor Stan Lee was getting pretty sure of himself. And by all accounts, he had every right to be. Working alongside already legendary artists like Jack Kirby and Steve Ditko, Lee had ushered in what was to be known as the Marvel Age of comics. Just a few short months earlier, in November of 1961, Lee and Kirby had introduced the world to the Fantastic Four, in their title's premier issue. They followed up that hit with the debut of the Hulk in May of the following year. Then, teaming with Ditko, Lee introduced Spider-Man that September in the pages of *Amazing Fantasy*'s 15th and final issue. With the introduction of Thor and Ant-Man soon to follow, Lee had a string of runaway successes on his hands, and he felt that practically anything he touched would turn to gold.

So he set out to test that theory. In an increasingly idealistic, anti-establishment age of Civil Rights and anti-Vietnam War protest, Lee decided to create a character that the readership wouldn't readily identify with. He created a weapons designer who worked for the government, rather than rebelling against it. Instead of an everyman character like Spider-Man, who gained instant sympathy from his readers due to his identifiable problems and inner conflicts, Lee created a millionaire playboy, aloof from society's ills and immune to any financial concerns. Despite all these apparent handicaps, Iron Man was a hit with the public—just as Lee had suspected all along.

Lee understood that like all great characters, Tony Stark just needed a touch of tragedy to humanize him. By making Tony injured in a wartime attack and forced to wear a metal chest plate in order to survive, Lee created sympathy for an otherwise detached character. In an unprecedented occurrence in Lee's experience, Iron Man began to receive more mail from female readers than any of his other popular titles, a fact Lee attributed to an inborn maternal instinct to take care of this romantically tragic figure.

Stan Lee had once more created a hero with a lasting fan base and media legacy. Iron Man first appeared sporting a gray suit of armor; as if to reflect Lee's own Midas touch, by Iron Man's second appearance, the color of his armor had turned to gold.

At the time, keeping a consistent shade of gray was a troublesome challenge for a newsprint press. To remedy the situation, Stan Lee decided to have Iron Man paint his armor gold (which conveniently printed as yellow) in his second appearance.

"Here you have this character, who on the outside is invulnerable, I mean, just can't be touched, but inside is this wounded figure. Stan made it very much an in-your-face wound, you know, his heart was broken,

literally broken."

Iron Man writer Gerry Conway

THE CREATORS

STAN LEE
The creator behind hundreds of Marvel characters, Stan "The Man" Lee not only helped to usher in Marvel's rise to fame in the 1960s, but also served as a guiding force behind the company for years in a myriad of forms, including writer, editor, president, and chairman. Lee wrote nearly all of Iron Man's original adventures, inventing a gallery of villains for the hero, including the Mandarin and the Crimson Dynamo, as well as many supporting characters, such as Tony's longtime allies Pepper Potts and Happy Hogan. Legendary for his enthusiasm as a spokesman for all things Marvel, Stan even made a cameo in the 2008 Iron Man feature film, playing a Hugh Hefner-like playboy bachelor.

LARRY LIEBER
Stan Lee's younger brother, writer Larry Lieber opted not to alter the family name as his brother had done. A newspaper cartoonist as well as a scribe, Lieber's main claim to fame was his scripting Iron Man's first appearance in *Tales of Suspense # 39*. With Stan only providing the plot of Iron Man's legendary origin, Larry provided the dialog over Don Heck's pencils. It was Larry who conceived the name Tony Stark, as Stan was in the habit of giving characters first and last names that began with the same letter, just to make them more memorable in his own mind.

DON HECK
Although he didn't design the Iron Man armor itself, Don Heck did just about everything else to bring Tony Stark's adventures to life. The interior artist for *Tales of Suspense #39*, as well as most of Iron Man's other early exploits, Don Heck created the dramatic pacing that kept readers coming back for more. Designing the look of millionaire Tony Stark based on Stan Lee's suggestion of a Howard Hughes-type personality, Heck gave the character a trademark mustache, adding a dash of famous swashbuckling actor Errol Flynn to Tony's appearance. Over the years, Heck would design many other characters in Shellhead's life, including Pepper Potts and Happy Hogan.

JACK KIRBY
The guiding force behind Marvel Comics' trademark look in the 1960s, Jack "the King" Kirby's work is as popular today as it was 40 years ago. Always experimenting with his craft and pushing the boundaries of forced perspective and dynamic storytelling, Kirby had already co-created dozens of Marvel icons, from Captain America to the Fantastic Four. Knowing Kirby's flair for creating characters that resonated with readers, Lee tasked Jack with designing Iron Man for the cover of the all-important *Tales of Suspense #39*. While Iron Man's look has evolved and changed many times over the years, Kirby's vision of a robotic suit of armor is still fondly remembered by fans as a symbol of the classic Marvel Age.

This original art for the splash page for *Tales of Suspense #70* showcases Stan Lee's lighthearted credit box, which was one of his trademarks. Lee always made sure his staff were acknowledged for their work, something rarely seen at the time.

TALES OF #39 SUSPENSE

"**You are not facing a wounded, dying man now… or an aged, gentle professor! This is Iron Man who opposes you, and all you stand for!**"

IRON MAN

MAIN CHARACTERS: Iron Man; Wong-Chu; Professor Yinsen
SUPPORTING CHARACTERS: An unnamed general and US government employees; female socialites; prisoners and soldiers of Wong-Chu's camp
LOCATIONS: Stark Industries; Wong-Chu's South Vietnam camp; US military camp in South Vietnam

PUBLICATION DATE
March 1963

EDITOR-IN-CHIEF
Stan Lee

COVER ARTIST
Jack Kirby and Don Heck

PLOTTER
Stan Lee

SCRIPTER
Larry Lieber

PENCILER/INKER
Don Heck

LETTERER
Art Simek

BACKGROUND

It was all told in a mere 13 pages. Despite having his landmark debut crammed into an anthology comic with a few other science fiction stories, there was no question that Iron Man was the true star of *Tales of Suspense* #39. Not only was this fledgling hero given the lead story feature, his top billing was also touted on the cover, with a blurb proclaiming that Iron Man had sprung from the same creative well as Spider-Man and the Fantastic Four. And for the most part, he did. Iron Man was Stan Lee's brainchild, but when the time came to actually pen his initial tale, Lee's busy schedule didn't permit him to script the hero's first outing. Lee plotted the adventure and handed the story summary to artist Don Heck. The dialog chores found their way to the desk of Larry Lieber, Stan's younger brother, and co-conspirator on another Marvel icon, the mighty Thor. The result was another certified success for Marvel, and Iron Man remained at the helm of *Tales of Suspense* for the rest of the title's lifespan.

The Story...

Millionaire Tony Stark suffers a debilitating injury and is taken captive by communist forces, only to escape by creating a new identity as Iron Man.

Tony Stark was always a bit of a showboat. A millionaire munitions manufacturer, well regarded for his brilliant technological innovations that were often employed by the US military, Tony lived a life of luxury and acclaim. He had a girl hanging on his arm at every party, and a prospective client hanging on his every word at any business meeting. He had just wowed one of his military associates with a demonstration of his newest invention: high-powered miniature transistors **(1)**. By attaching one of these small devices to a normal everyday magnet, Stark was able to rip a thick, steel door right off its hinges **(2)**. The demonstration was more than enough to impress the general in charge, and Tony was given a contract to help aid US forces in Vietnam.

Meanwhile, in the heart of the jungles of that war-torn country, communist leader Wong-Chu **(3)** was enjoying his own exhibition. The unscrupulous commander of a band of guerrillas, Wong-Chu had just added another conquered village to his fiefdom and, as was his custom, had issued a challenge to the male inhabitants. If one of them could best him in a wrestling match, he would set the entire village free. Several villagers accepted Wong-Chu's challenge, but the tyrant dispatched each one with ease. Once again, Wong-Chu was victorious.

Tony Stark's arrival in Vietnam threatened to change that. Unable to transport heavy artillery through the jungle, the heads of a US military base near Wong-Chu's latest camp were testing Stark's new miniature transistors in hand-held mortars. Tony wanted to see the action firsthand **(4)**. But when he accidentally set off a booby-trapped trip wire **(5)**, he was knocked unconscious by the resulting explosion, with a piece of shrapnel lodged dangerously near his heart. To make matters worse, the helpless businessman was soon captured by the communist forces and brought back to Wong-Chu's camp.

Fortunately, like most of the civilized world, Wong-Chu had heard of Tony Stark. So rather than kill the brilliant inventor outright, the communist leader instead instructed Tony to build a weapon that would help in combating the American forces **(6)**. In exchange, Wong-Chu promised to have his finest surgeon see to Tony's heart and cure him of his condition. Knowing that Wong-Chu had no intention of giving him any medical treatment, Tony agreed to the terrorist's terms, and set out with his own agenda. He would build a suit of armor that would not only help sustain his life, but would also be his means of escape.

With the aid of Professor Yinsen **(7)**, a fellow prisoner and brilliant physicist whom the world at large believed dead, Stark constructed an iron suit of armor, powered by his experimental transistors. Donning the armor just as his heart began to fail, Stark lay down on a table, waiting for the suit to fully charge and for its electronic transistors to save his life **(8)**. In order to stall Wong-Chu's approaching troops, Professor Yinsen ran madly into the hallway only to be gunned down by the tyrant's men. The momentary diversion was all Stark needed, and as Iron Man, he made his escape from his living quarters.

Later, as Wong-Chu dispatched yet another hopeful in a wrestling match, a new challenger called to him from the crowd. While Wong-Chu gawked in disbelief at the metal marvel standing before him, Iron Man attacked his foe, and easily bested him **(9)**. Fighting through a hail of bullets, Iron Man took down Chu's entire camp, before defeating the fleeing tyrant himself by trapping him in an explosion of a nearby ammunition shed **(10)**. Trapped inside his iron shell and alone in the Vietnamese jungle, Iron Man disappeared into the wilderness, pondering where this new life of his would take him next **(11)**.

"I know I've only days to live, but my last act will be to defeat this grinning, smirking, red terrorist!"

THE SUIT'S POWERS

They say the clothes make the man, and Tony Stark would have no reason to argue. Iron Man's actions make him a hero, but his armor is what gets the job done.

CHEST PLATE

The Iron Man chest plate has been of special importance to Tony Stark ever since he first donned his armor. Originally structured to keep his injured heart beating through the use of a magnetic-field generator, the chest piece was soon adapted to serve as one of the many offensive tools in Iron Man's arsenal. While he no longer needs the armor to keep himself alive, Iron Man frequently relies on his chest plate's powerful unibeam in battle.

Capable of firing a blast similar to that of his repulsors, the unibeam can also function as a searchlight able to project in nearly every spectrum, even infrared and ultraviolet. The unibeam can also produce a local electro-magnetic pulse, a laser beam, holographic images, and a wavelength scanner.

REPULSORS

Tony's magnetic repulsor beams have always been the cornerstones of his Iron Man technology. Originally utilizing high-powered transistorized magnets capable of localized repelling force, Stark soon refined the tech into his modern-day repulsor blasts. Essentially a powerful particle beam, the ray can be focused to a narrow area, or be dispersed to cover a wider range. When fired from his gauntlets at an enemy target, the repulsors have the ability to repel energy and physical attacks alike.

In addition, the Iron Man armor allows Tony to switch to pulse bolts, which are also focused through his palm apertures. Segmented flashes of energy, the pulse bolts actually grow stronger and more powerful the longer the distance they travel, giving Iron Man the perfect weapon for long-range attacks against particularly daunting foes.

JET BOOTS

Also utilizing repulsor technology, Iron Man's jet boots have often played a vital part in his adventures. Powered by scramjet and air-jet propulsion systems as well as afterburner thrust, the jet boots are the armor's main utility for transportation and can fly at speeds of up to Mach 8. In addition, when Iron Man wants to take things a bit slower, perhaps to survey an enemy installation, the boots take advantage of a localized gravity field, granting the armor hovering capabilities. Combining the boots' raw power with the usage of Tony's in-flight computer and built-in gyroscope, Iron Man is able to maintain his balance and follow any trajectory of his choosing. In earlier models, Tony installed magnetic suction cups in his boots to allow him to do his best impression of Spider-Man and adhere to flat surfaces.

THE SUIT

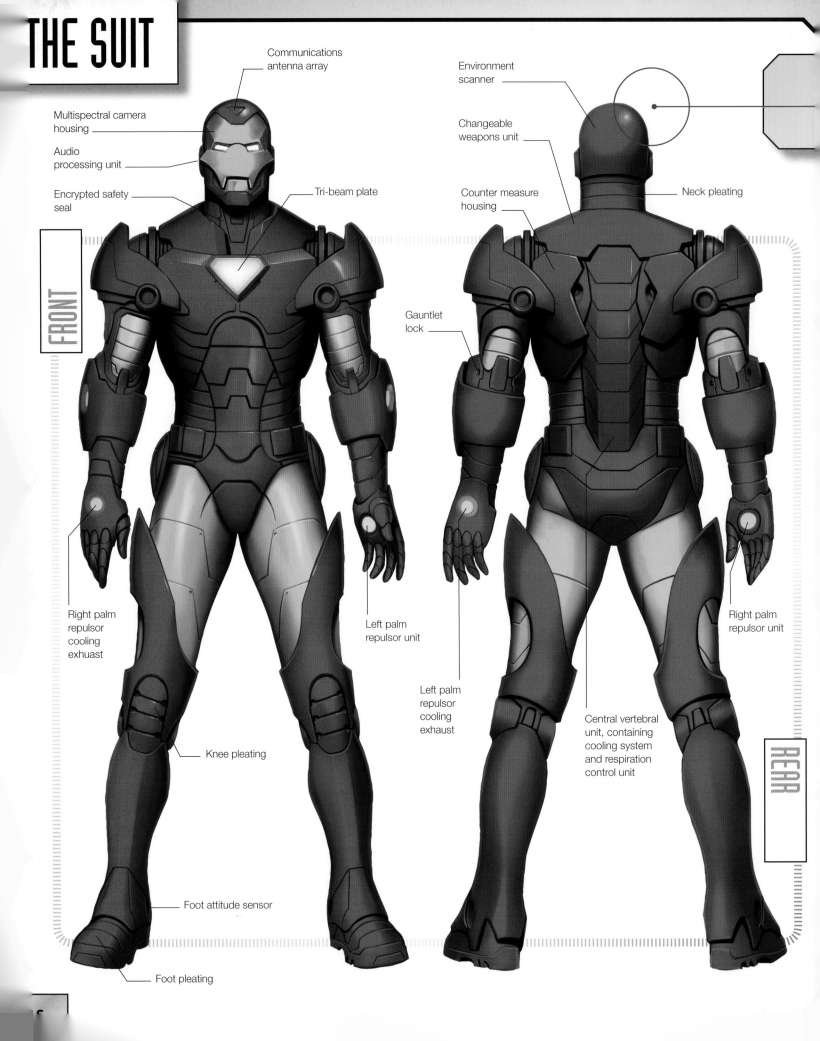

FRONT

REAR

Communications antenna array

Multispectral camera housing

Audio processing unit

Encrypted safety seal

Tri-beam plate

Right palm repulsor cooling exhuast

Left palm repulsor unit

Knee pleating

Foot attitude sensor

Foot pleating

Environment scanner

Changeable weapons unit

Counter measure housing

Neck pleating

Gauntlet lock

Left palm repulsor cooling exhaust

Right palm repulsor unit

Central vertebral unit, containing cooling system and respiration control unit

HEADPIECE DETAILING

Originally constructed in three separate pieces, Tony Stark upgraded his helmet so that it could slip on over his head in a single motion.

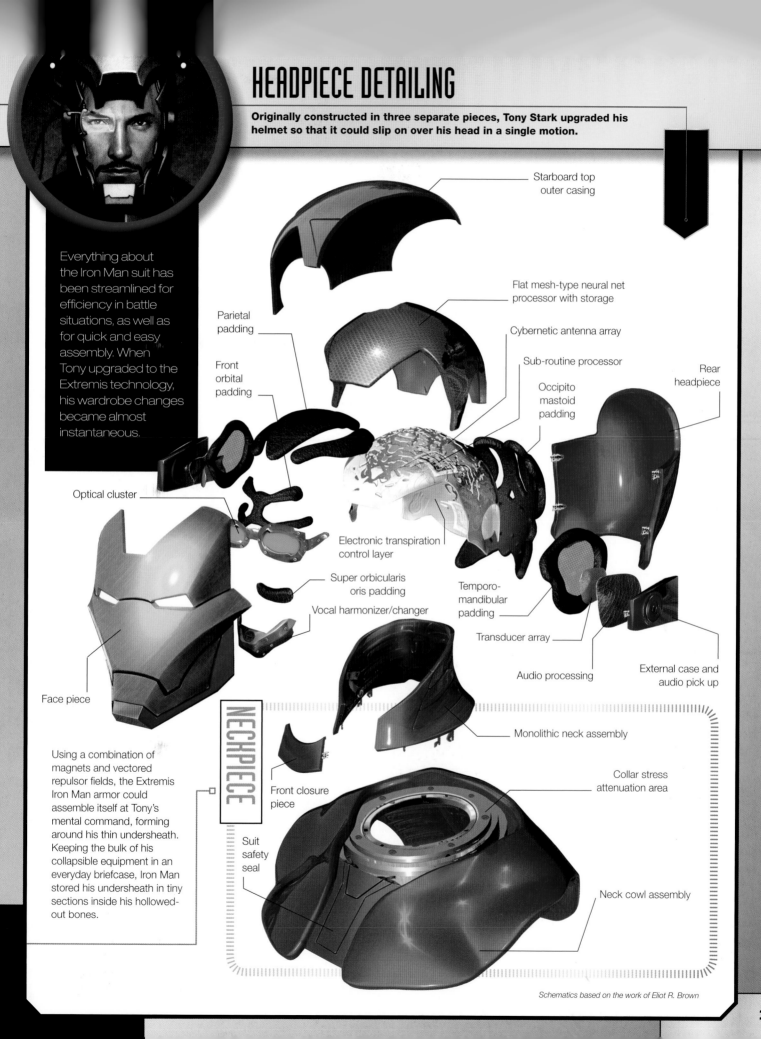

Everything about the Iron Man suit has been streamlined for efficiency in battle situations, as well as for quick and easy assembly. When Tony upgraded to the Extremis technology, his wardrobe changes became almost instantaneous.

Using a combination of magnets and vectored repulsor fields, the Extremis Iron Man armor could assemble itself at Tony's mental command, forming around his thin undersheath. Keeping the bulk of his collapsible equipment in an everyday briefcase, Iron Man stored his undersheath in tiny sections inside his hollowed-out bones.

Starboard top outer casing

Flat mesh-type neural net processor with storage

Cybernetic antenna array

Sub-routine processor

Rear headpiece

Occipito mastoid padding

Parietal padding

Front orbital padding

Optical cluster

Electronic transpiration control layer

Super orbicularis oris padding

Vocal harmonizer/changer

Temporo-mandibular padding

Transducer array

Audio processing

External case and audio pick up

Face piece

NECKPIECE

Front closure piece

Monolithic neck assembly

Collar stress attenuation area

Suit safety seal

Neck cowl assembly

Schematics based on the work of Eliot R. Brown

THE ARMOR

1963 to 1988

Tony Stark has gone through dozens of Iron Man suits since his first explosive heroic debut, improving and refining his armor each and every time.

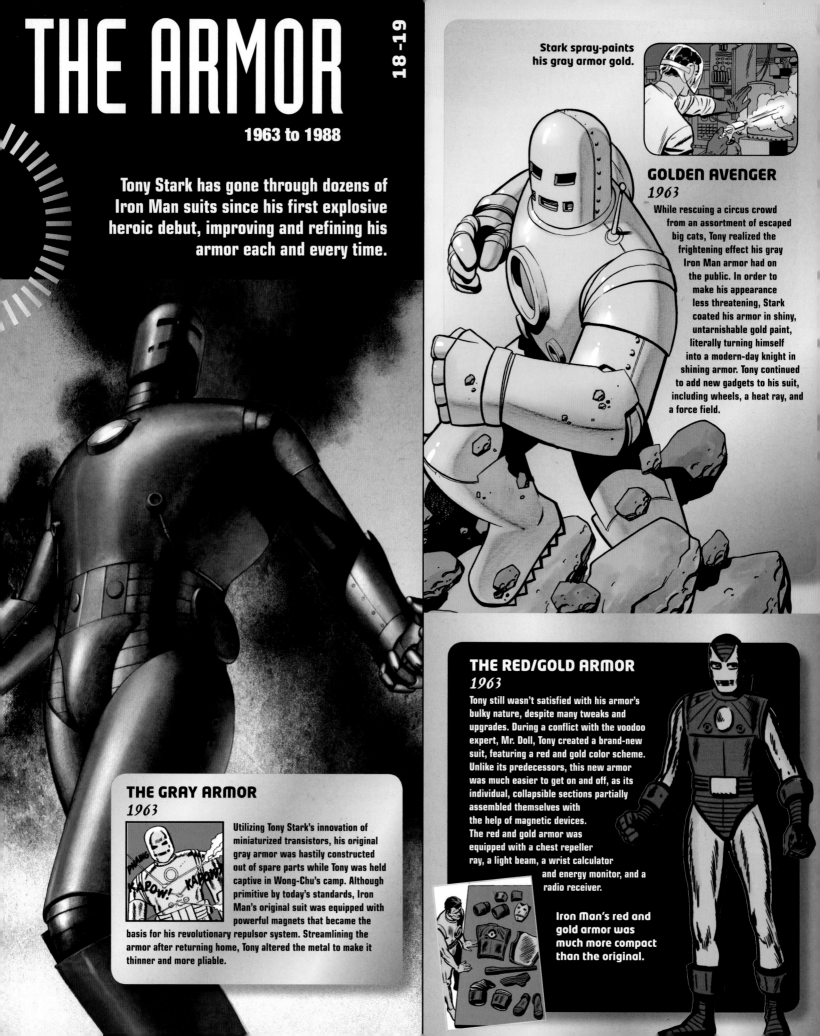

Stark spray-paints his gray armor gold.

GOLDEN AVENGER
1963

While rescuing a circus crowd from an assortment of escaped big cats, Tony realized the frightening effect his gray Iron Man armor had on the public. In order to make his appearance less threatening, Stark coated his armor in shiny, untarnishable gold paint, literally turning himself into a modern-day knight in shining armor. Tony continued to add new gadgets to his suit, including wheels, a heat ray, and a force field.

THE GRAY ARMOR
1963

Utilizing Tony Stark's innovation of miniaturized transistors, his original gray armor was hastily constructed out of spare parts while Tony was held captive in Wong-Chu's camp. Although primitive by today's standards, Iron Man's original suit was equipped with powerful magnets that became the basis for his revolutionary repulsor system. Streamlining the armor after returning home, Tony altered the metal to make it thinner and more pliable.

THE RED/GOLD ARMOR
1963

Tony still wasn't satisfied with his armor's bulky nature, despite many tweaks and upgrades. During a conflict with the voodoo expert, Mr. Doll, Tony created a brand-new suit, featuring a red and gold color scheme. Unlike its predecessors, this new armor was much easier to get on and off, as its individual, collapsible sections partially assembled themselves with the help of magnetic devices. The red and gold armor was equipped with a chest repeller ray, a light beam, a wrist calculator and energy monitor, and a radio receiver.

Iron Man's red and gold armor was much more compact than the original.

SPACE ARMOR MK 1
1981

A visit to a satellite owned by the corrupt Roxxon Oil company, provided Iron Man with the ideal opportunity to test his new space armor. Armed with jet-powered rocket boots, nuclear thrusters, a radar scanner, a vario-beam, and gauntlets capable of being disengaged and remote controlled, Iron Man's space armor could handle the rigors and challenges of an airless vacuum with ease.

RECOVERY ARMOR
1985

After Tony had temporarily handed his heroic Iron Man duties over to Jim Rhodes, he still found himself tinkering with armor designs. As a result, Tony created his recovery armor, a close replica to his original gray design, but with a few improvements here and there.

STEALTH ARMOR
1981

While on a rescue mission in Germany, Tony put his dark stealth armor to use for the first time. Constructed of polarized metal-mesh, Iron Man's stealth armor was built with only the most minor of defenses, in order to make room for espionage equipment like sound-dampened boot jets, a radar-bending wave modifier, a sonic scanning device, and a miniature spy camera.

SILVER CENTURION
1985

To finally overcome the machinations of the villainous Obadiah Stane, Iron Man unleashed a new, more powerful version of his armor. With a built-in navigational computer, radar invisibility, holographic camouflage, energy absorption and redistribution capabilities, powerful pulse bolts, a protection field, and the ability to fly into Earth's upper atmosphere, the Silver Centurion armor truly made Iron Man a force to be reckoned with.

THE ICONIC ARMOR
1964

It's in Tony Stark's nature to constantly design and redesign. Thus Iron Man's most memorable look was more the result of a series of improvements than one dramatic overhaul. After streamlining his mask during a battle with the Mandarin, Tony continued to experiment with design and function, improving every aspect of his armor's performance, from its repulsor rays to its roller wheels. Iron Man's suit soon possessed numerous gadgets, such as a reverser ray, a black-light tracer, a built-in generator, a chemical spray, explosive darts, and a diamond-tipped blade. In addition, Iron Man was able to seal his armor for brief under-water travel, utilizing a back-up air supply.

NEO CLASSIC
1988

While waging his infamous Armor Wars, Tony constructed a new suit of armor that improved on all his past designs. Built to trick the world into thinking a new man was piloting the Iron Man suit, his new red and gold design was armed with a gauntlet-projected energy shield, a more powerful pulse bolt, enhanced speed, rapid-fire sequencing, and an electromagnetic pulse beam.

HYDRO ARMOR MK 1
1987

Built for long expeditions under water, Iron Man's first attempt at deep-sea armor was equipped with several hours worth of oxygen, enabling the wearer to travel miles while submerged. Able to withstand even the strongest pressures found at the ocean floor, Iron Man's hydro armor also had a searchlight and a sonar system.

1993–2000

NEUROMIMETIC TELEPRESENCE UNIT
1993

Tony Stark had been experimenting with encephalo-circuits in his helmet that could control a suit of Iron Man armor by remote control. He was soon forced to put this new technology to practical use. Experimental surgery to equip his body with an artificial nervous system had just saved his life, but Tony awoke from the operation to find that he was completely paralyzed. With the help of his old friend Abe Zimmer and a neural interface headpiece, Tony was able to create a new and improved remote-controlled armor operated by his brainwaves and voice commands.

Early remote-controlled armor.

VR Mask

WAR MACHINE ARMOR
1992

Tony Stark secretly designed the War Machine armor with his friend Jim Rhodes' combat skills in mind. Iron Man first wore the War Machine suit into battle when facing the ninjas known as the Masters of Silence. Later, when circumstances forced Tony to fake his own death, he bequeathed this silver suit of armor to Rhodey, asking him to carry on his legacy as Iron Man in his absence. Rhodey agreed, but later changed his name to War Machine in a bid for independence when he discovered that Tony's death was a sham.

MODULAR ARMOR
1994

Once Tony Stark regained full control over his muscles, it didn't take him long to jump back into battle as Iron Man. With the help of his computer program HOMER, Tony manufactured an innovative new design that re-examined the basic construction of Iron Man. Instead of a single integrated unit, Tony created a modular component system that could be reconfigured by swapping out various sub-systems such as boots, gloves, or helmets. This allowed Iron Man to "dress for the occasion," bringing only the equipment each adventure called for.

HULKBUSTER MK 1
1994

As part of his modular armor system, Tony created the Hulkbuster suit, with impact-resistant carbon-composites and a magno-hydraulic pseudomusculature rated at 175 tons. This armor was tough enough to handle even the fiercest battle with the green goliath known as the Incredible Hulk.

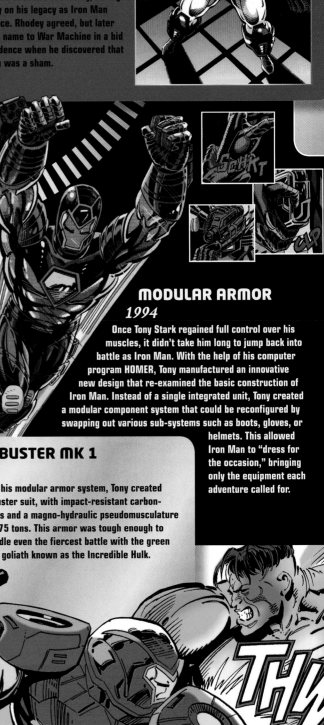

THE CROSSING
1995

Corrupted by the power of the time-spanning villain Immortus, Iron Man slowly began to lose control of his faculties. Under Immortus' thrall, Tony Stark set up shop in a remote Arctic fortress, and designed a blue and white snowsuit to aid his travel to and from his new base. Soon Tony designed another new look to fit his personality shift; this new, highly sophisticated armor possessed prototype teleportation abilities.

YOUNG TONY MK 1
1996

After being recruited from the past to fight the Iron Man he was destined to become, a younger version of Tony Stark was forced to don an unused Iron Man suit in order to do battle with his older counterpart. With the Avengers by his side, young Tony's new armor stood up against Iron Man's every attack, until the older Tony unleashed a near-fatal blow that crippled the young boy's fragile heart.

YOUNG TONY MK 2
1996

Built from a variety of spare parts found around Avengers Mansion, including an everyday kitchen blender and toaster, young Tony invented his own Iron Man suit. He used the notes of his now-deceased elder to guide him along the way. A work in progress, just like many other versions of the armor, young Tony's suit included hyper-thrust boot propulsion, therma-screen shielding, built-in gyro-stabilizers, and a variety of lasers.

PROMETHEUM ARMOR
1996

Stranded in a pocket universe with no memory of his past, Tony found himself once again reinventing the wheel as he created his prometheum Iron Man armor. Equipped with a wide array of sensory input, repulsor housings, a chest laser, tractor beam, and advanced life-support technology, the prometheum armor withstood the ferocity of a rampaging Hulk.

RETRO ARMOR
1998

Back in his proper dimension, Iron Man began a new era in his life. Accordingly, he unveiled a new suit of armor. This version showcased various favorite battle-tested inventions, including boot jets, radio and police bands, and balancing gyros. Iron Man's new retro armor also offered a number of improved features, such as computerized target locking and firing, inertia dampening fields, advanced scanners, nightvision capabilities, and miniature explosive charges.

SENTIENT ARMOR
2000

Once in a while, Tony Stark's scientific genius threatened to make his armor too advanced. Constantly adding to the capabilities of his new armor, he finally went too far. Compact enough to be transformed into a small, metal backpack-like case, Tony's latest Iron Man costume was brought to life in a Frankensteinesque manner by a stray bolt of lightning. Tony's suit proceeded to battle its inventor for control. It possessed both sentience and a desire for independent life as strong as that of any animal. However, the man finally overcame the machine.

Sentient foldaway mode.

THE ARMOR

The 21st Century

TIN MAN ARMOR
2002

Signifying a return to basics, Iron Man's tin man armor resembled older tried and tested armor models with less of an emphasis on cutting-edge tech. Still containing a wide variety of weapons and surveillance gear, the tin man armor incorporated Tony's own personal secretary of sorts into its circuitry. Called Friday, this computer program was capable of doing everything from analyzing rare poisons to holding unwanted telephone calls.

SPACE ARMOR
2000

Iron Man got the chance to test his newest suit outfitted for an outer space environment when he was forced to confront Justin Hammer onboard the criminal's satellite base. With a thin layer of compression gel protecting his body from the elements, the newly improved space armor was much slimmer than previous models. It also offered detachable solid fuel boosters, compressed gas maneuvering pods, and a solar sail capable of automatic piloting during reentry.

STEALTH ARMOR MK 3
2002

When tracking down the seemingly renegade Black Panther, Iron Man utilized his latest-model stealth armor. Composed of advanced composite ceramics, the armor was capable of projecting holograms onto its surface and making the wearer virtually invisible. Ideal for espionage missions, the suit also had an innovative noise-reduction engine, but only possessed the ability to fire three repulsor shots. The armor contained absolutely no metal, and instead was built with experimental bio-neural gel-pack circuitry.

THORBUSTER ARMOR
2003

When Iron Man was forced to battle Thor, he adapted magical armor powered by the same enchantment that gives Thor's famous magic hammer Mjölnir its strength. Combining the strength of Thor with his own power, Iron Man gave the thunder god a run for his money.

SKIN ARMOR
2001

Acquiring new technology from Manhattan's Askew Labs, Iron Man constructed his SKIN armor using revolutionary liquid metal circuitry that shaped around Iron Man's body in a nearly unbreakable shell. Yet when not in use, the substance could be compacted to the size of a baseball. To augment this impressive armor, Tony added smart bomb probes, an energy blade that could extend into a shield, chameleon-like capabilities, and a holographic projector.

ABLATIVE ARMOR
2003

When facing an alien entity that had the ability to adhere to electronics and animate them with artificial life, Tony decided to give his ablative armor a test run. Layered with thousands of high-impact polymer tiles, this suit was designed to shed tiles in the event of damage. When an enemy missile hit the armor, the damaged tiles would simply pop off. Meanwhile, a polymer kiln on the back of the suit produced more tiles, which the armor's force field locked in place.

EXTREMIS ARMOR
2005

The Extremis armor is Iron Man's most advanced to date. Tony utilized Extremis virus technology to literally rewrite his body's own functions into a superior fusion of man and machine. With Extremis tech in his system, Tony could link with satellites or any other technological device, simply with the power of thought.

HYPERVELOCITY ARMOR
2007

With awe-inspiring computing capabilities and storage—enough to house the entire catalog of Tony Stark's memories—the Hypervelocity armor also contained superior firepower. Possessing long arms with waldo extensions, multiple-mode boot jets, and a telescoping supercavitation induction spike with a compressed-air bubblefeed that allowed for near-supersonic speeds of underwater travel, the armor was aptly nicknamed Tony 2.0.

The Tony 2.0 armor had amazing underwater capabilities.

HIGH-G ARMOR
2006

Bulky and heavy, similar to his three previous outer space suits, Tony's High-G (high-gravity) armor was constructed with stability very much in mind. With magnetic and jet compensators and advanced health readings at his fingertips, the High-G suit allowed Iron Man to survive and stay oriented while being rocketed through space, and even withstand an impromptu battle with Titanium Man.

HULKBUSTER MK 2 ARMOR
2007

When Tony Stark helped exile the Hulk into outer space, he had planned for the contingency that the Green Goliath might somehow return to Earth. Wearing his largest, most protective suit of armor, Iron Man challenged the Hulk to a physical confrontation above Manhattan, while simultaneously broadcasting an inspiring address to the nation. Despite the Hulkbuster armor's remarkable durability and firepower, the Hulk made short work of Iron Man's impressive new toy.

HYDRO ARMOR MK2
2006

When pursuing a convict to the undersea kingdom of Atlantis, X-Men member Wolverine recruited help from his fellow New Avenger Iron Man. Using one of Tony Stark's new deep-sea diving suits, Wolverine was able to stand the untold pressure extremes of the ocean's floor and continue to hunt down his prey.

Tony Stark was a dreamer. Unfortunately, that was a quality he and his father didn't share. While young Tony built model iron men out of erector sets and fantasized about the ancient tales of King Arthur and knights in shining armor, his father Howard found his escape from the stress of running weapons manufacturer Stark Industries at the bottom of a whisky bottle. Tony had a genius-level IQ and an imaginative mind but as a boy never seemed to take life seriously enough for his overbearing father. When Tony turned seven years old, despite the protests of his wife Maria, Howard shipped Tony off to boarding school in an attempt to instill him with discipline. There, Tony excelled at his studies, and eventually grew to be a well-rounded young man, despite his shy nature. Graduating from college at an extremely young age, Tony became his father's right-hand man. Although he could knock off a radical innovative weapons design in less time than it took him to get ready for a night on the town, Tony's heart was never truly in his work. He preferred the life of a young playboy—which only served to distance the two Stark men even further.

TONY STARK

At age 15, he enrolled in MIT. By 21, he was running one of the largest companies in North America. Anthony "Tony" Stark has always been ahead of the pack, the curve, and his time.

When Howard and Maria Stark were killed in a car accident, Tony found himself at the head of their multibillion-dollar company. After learning that his parents had died owing to a construction fault in their automobile, Tony's first act as head of Stark Industries was to purchase the car company responsible and overhaul their entire approach to brake design. To this day, Tony is still unaware that the "accident" was actually engineered by a group of industry competitors who would later found the corrupt organization Roxxon Oil.

After a year or two spent grappling with the complexities of running a massive business such as Stark Industries, Tony grew into the man his father had always wanted him to be. Working tirelessly to expand the company into a multi-national corporation, Tony's drive to succeed only increased following his injury in an explosion in Afghanistan and the commencement of his double life as the armored avenger Iron Man. Witnessing the terrible destructive power of his weapons firsthand, and realizing that the tide of public opinion was turning against those seen as war profiteers, Tony altered Stark Industries' focus from weapons manufacturing to a variety of other technological innovations, establishing his father's company as a true leader of the industrial world.

Growing up in the family mansion near New York's Central Park, Tony has a penchant for prime real estate. His luxury homes include a plush penthouse at Stark International's Long Island headquarters, and apartments in Manhattan's Stark Tower skyscraper, as well as atop Stark Enterprises in California.

KEY DATA

FULL NAME Anthony Edward "Tony" Stark

ALIASES Iron Man; also known as Shellhead and the Golden Avenger

HIGHT 6 ft 1 in **WEIGHT** 225 lbs
EYES Blue **HAIR** Black

KNOWN RELATIVES Maria Collins Carbonell Stark and Howard Anthony Stark (parents, deceased), Morgan Stark (cousin), Edward Stark (uncle, deceased), Isaac Stark, Sr., Isaac Stark, Jr. (ancestors, deceased)

OCCUPATION Adventurer, CEO of Stark Industries, former Director of SHIELD, former head of the Initiative, founder of the Maria Stark Foundation, former CEO of Stark International, Stark Solutions, Stark Enterprises, Circuits Maximus, former US Secretary of Defense, former technician for Askew Electronics

Tony's social exploits have run a close race with his adventures as Iron Man. Perhaps he has been overcompensating for school days spent alone with his head buried in various scientific journals and works of fiction. Tony, for years one of the world's most sought-after bachelors, is often spotted at exclusive parties and events with a new girl on his arm—much to the annoyance of his longtime personal assistant Pepper Potts.

Despite his ridiculously busy schedule, Tony still manages regular exercise, realizing that his brain isn't the only muscle he needs to flex daily. Whether training with his fellow Avengers or just starting his day with a morning jog, physical fitness is a key part of Tony's everyday routine.

Much like the modern computer, the Iron Man armor is a work in progress. Tony is constantly adding innovations and streamlining aspects of his suit in order to remain at the forefront of cutting-edge technology. As a result, he manages to keep one step ahead of the corrupt men and women that his life of crime-fighting pits him against. Though Tony is more at home in his lab tinkering with new ideas than at the end of a boardroom table at a business meeting, he still finds time to juggle both, only allowing a select few trusted friends, such as James Rhodes and Pepper Potts, to aid him on either front.

The Wit and Wisdom of Tony Stark

All of those who've wondered why **Iron Man** risks his life time and time again… if they could feel the indescribable **exhilaration** of flying in an armored suit, they'd wonder **no more!**

Two can play the game of gadgets, rabbit ears! On the other hand, there's a classic **simplicity** to a good **right hand jab** that's not to be denied!

All right, Doom, you've won that round. But that's only *check*… not check-*mate!*

If you want to *remain* saved, get back out of the line of fire.

Head butting like this could get me thrown out of most wrestling bouts—but I'm not fighting for trophies here! I'm fighting for my *life!*

No one has the right to defy the wishes of his government… not even Iron Man!

My appearance terrifies women and children as if I were a **monster!** I'm a frightening sight to the very people I want to aid and protect!

But could I have married Janice? Would it have been fair with a heart like mine?

Firebrand, you've come up with a *costume* that has powers and protection nearly *equal* to mine... How can you so insanely *misuse* it?!

What about **my** cause? What is it **I'm** fighting for? Whatever it **is**, I must **live** for it… and **die** for it.

I went from being a man trapped in an iron suit to being a man freed by it.

There is a pollution crisis in the world, but it can't be solved by taking the first **hysterical action!**

I don't deal in weapons any more... I'm more interested in creating the future than blowing it up.

Being a man in a metal suit doesn't solve any problems... It just gives you a whole lot of new ones to think about.

You can't let somebody else do your suffering for you.

Can I have a personal relationship with anyone and continue to function as Iron Man should?

I won't waste time defending the *past* or arguing about the present while a man's in *danger!*

I guess, in the final *reckoning*, it does add up... the life of a Super Hero has *meaning*... and *purpose*.

Hiding? Is that what it's **come** to? Hiding my feelings, my **life**—behind an iron **mask?**

This is the most **sophisticated**, most astonishing invention I've ever constructed! But that's the precise reason... why it has to be **destroyed!**

With all the pain and sorrow my other armor caused, I shudder to think what could happen if this fell into evil hands.

I've learned that free will isn't a gift—it's a muscle which needs to be exercised—and only when it's in peak condition—is a man truly awake.

STARK INDUSTRIES

> "Am I an arms dealer? No. Did I start out as a weapons designer? Yes. Do I intend to die as one? No." **Tony Stark**

Stark Industries has undergone many changes over the years—different names, different policies, different locations—its fluctuating fortunes mirroring those of its presiding genius, the endlessly inventive Tony Stark.

A Family Business

The brainchild of Isaac Stark Sr., Stark Industries was an engineering manufacturing business formed in the 19th century. The company continued to be a family-run organization, with the position of president and CEO being passed down through generations of Stark men. In modern times, Stark Industries began to focus on weapons manufacturing, relying on government contracts for the bulk of its income. When owned by Howard Stark, the corporation flourished until Howard and his wife Maria died in a car crash. Control of the company then passed to the couple's reluctant son, Tony. Despite being responsible for designing many of Stark Industries' technological innovations, Tony wasn't sure he was ready for the responsibility of running such a large business. However, with the help of his executive assistant Pepper Potts, Tony grew into the role, and soon learned to embrace his family's legacy, raising Stark profits to an all-time high. Since then, Tony has continued to put his own stamp on the company and led it through many varied incarnations.

STARK INDUSTRIES
When Tony first inherited the company, Stark Industries was primarily a weapons manufacturer. After his injury and his subsequent transformation into Iron Man, Tony began to have serious ethical misgivings about his deadly creations, and led the company away from weapons and into technologies more likely to benefit humanity.

STARK INTERNATIONAL
A futurist at heart, Tony decided to alter the name of his company to reflect its presence on the global market. With subsidiaries in all parts of the world, and a growing interest in research, Stark decided that the new moniker Stark International better signified the changing times.

CIRCUITS MAXIMUS
During Tony's relapse into alcoholism, Obadiah Stane staged an extremely hostile takeover of Stark's company, changing the name to Stane International and returning to weapons manufacturing. After getting clean once more, Tony decided to move to California and start from scratch with a new electronics firm.

STARK ENTERPRISES
Not satisfied with chasing Stark out of his own business, Obadiah Stane began to sabotage Circuits Maximus, destroying the fledgling company in an explosion. After confronting Stane in a battle that led to Obadiah's death, Tony distanced himself from Stane's corrupt life by forming the Los Angeles-based Stark Enterprises.

STARK-FUJIKAWA
After later reacquiring Stane International and eradicating its illegal practices, Tony seemingly perished while fighting Immortus as Iron Man. During the time of his absence, the foreign conglomerate Fujikawa staged a takeover of Stark Enterprises, one they maintained even after Tony's miraculous resurrection and return.

STARK SOLUTIONS
Instead of attempting to fight to regain his old company, Tony created the consulting firm, Stark Solutions. Offering his services to anyone willing to pay his high price tag, Tony put Stark Solutions in place largely to donate much of the profits to his charitable Maria Stark Foundation.

STARK INDUSTRIES 2
After becoming romantically involved with Rumiko Fujikawa, Tony Stark was able to regain controlling stock in his own company. He decided to return full circle and rename the corporation Stark Industries. The company has since been hit hard by a technological virus introduced by the Skrull aliens, and by destruction caused by Ezekiel Stane. Despite Stark's best intentions, his family's legacy is now on the brink of bankruptcy.

STAFF
Besides his friends Pepper Potts, Happy Hogan, and Jim Rhodes, Tony has gone to great lengths to hire the best of the best.

MRS. BAMBI ARBOGAST
Tony's sassy executive assistant for many years, Mrs. Arbogast proved time and time again that she could handle herself in a crisis, even standing up to the Melter on one occasion.

MARCY PEARSON
Public Relations head of Stark Enterprises, Marcy took over briefly as CEO when Stark was shot and on his deathbed. Her ambitions later got the best of her, forcing Jim Rhodes to terminate her employment.

KEVIN O'BRIEN
A researcher at the first incarnation of Stark Industries, O'Brien helped Tony develop the sophisticated Guardsman armor. Driven insane by a flaw in the equipment design, Kevin battled Iron Man and died in the melee.

ABRAHAM KLEIN
A former engineering professor of Tony's, Abe petitioned for a job from his former student. Working undercover for the villain Mordecai Midas, Abe sabotaged the company from the inside for his notorious boss.

ARTEMUS PITHINS
Former PR head of Stark International, Pithins resigned from his position during Stane's takeover. He and Tony were later reunited when Pithins served as the White House press secretary to Tony's Secretary of Defense.

MORLEY ERWIN
Becoming Rhodey's trusted confidant and technical assistant when Jim first became Iron Man, Morley soon made the move to Circuits Maximus along with his sister and Tony, until his untimely death in an explosion.

CLYTEMNESTRA ERWIN
Morley's sister, and a technological genius in her own right, Clytemnestra was one of the founders of Circuits Maximus. Blaming Tony for her brother's death, she betrayed him to AIM, and was killed in the resulting battle.

ABE ZIMMER
Tony first met Abe when purchasing the company Accutech. Zimmer soon earned his place in Tony's trusted inner circle, and used his computer wizardry to help Tony several times, even sacrificing his life for his boss.

JOCASTA
An artificial intelligence and former Avenger, Jocasta downloaded herself into Iron Man's armor in order to maintain her survival during a battle. She served for a time as a trusted component of Stark's computer systems.

INVENTIONS
Tony Stark's ever-evolving Iron Man armor is just one of his amazing inventions.

S.H.I.E.L.D. HELICARRIER
As one of the brilliant minds behind the international peacekeeping force SHIELD, Tony Stark designed weapons systems and technology for the agency for years, before he changed his company's focus to less lethal innovations. Working with director Nick Fury, Mr. Fantastic of the Fantastic Four, and X-Men member Forge, Tony created one of the SHIELD's most lauded innovations, the helicarrier, a flying aircraft carrier. With room for up to 1,000 crewmen, and utilizing revolutionary vortex-beam technology, the helicarrier served as the mobile headquarters for SHIELD's operations.

MANDROIDS
Built by Tony Stark to protect SHIELD soldiers from superhuman attacks, the armored Mandroids were first employed against the Avengers.

HAWKEYE'S ARROWS
Although most of Avenger Hawkeye's trick arrows are designed by the archer himself, some of his more technological arrows were devised by Tony Stark.

CAP'S SHIELD
When the government stripped him of his title, Steve Rogers asked Tony to build him a replacement shield.

THE QUINJET
The Quinjet, the Avengers' efficient shuttle, was originally designed by T'Challa, the Black Panther, and has since been redesigned by Tony Stark for use by the New Avengers and the Mighty Avengers. The jet is capable of vertical takeoff and can reach speeds of more than Mach 2.

MISCELLANEOUS INVENTIONS

- Particle beam torpedo
- Evader personal protection unit
- Friday: a virtual personal assistant
- HOMER (Heuristically Operative Matrix Emulation Rostrum) computer system
- The Works: State-of-the-art "smart building"
- Guardsmen armor
- Plato (Piezo-Electrical Logistic Analytic Tactical Operator) artificial intelligence
- Flying Prowler (and other flying automobiles)
- Vroom Room: Virtual reality training center
- Sentinel landmine
- Uranus II rocket
- Jupiter Landing Vehicle
- Anti-missile Missile Gun
- SK-1 stealth jet
- Experimental Sea Tank
- Hex Ships *Pegasus* and *Chimera*
- SHIELD satellite
- Life Model Decoys
- Armor negator packs
- Transistorized blast gun
- Iron Spider armor
- Holo-Communicator
- Encephalo-circuitry
- Transistor-powered roller skates
- Warwagon tank

Behind his playboy persona and his charming, carefree wit, Tony Stark is a man tortured by past mistakes and future concerns. He lives a life of extremes, a life that has led him to battle potentially crippling health problems and a chronic addiction to alcohol.

A TROUBLED HERO

CRISIS OF CONSCIENCE

Tony Stark's entire fortune was founded on death. Although he has tried to see it from some other perspective, there's no avoiding the facts. His father was a weapons manufacturer, selling brilliant and efficient killing machines to the US government to aid their various war efforts. When Tony took over his father's business, he too became little more than a glorified arms dealer. Tony improved upon his father's ideas and Stark Industries reaped the benefits.

It wasn't until Tony witnessed firsthand the destructive might of his terrible creations that he began to have serious misgivings about his life's work. After a near-fatal injury caused by one of his own Stark landmines, Tony began to appreciate the consequences of his creations. It took time, paperwork, and wading through miles of red tape, before Tony was able to cease all Stark weapons manufacturing once and for all. He now fights as Iron Man trying to make amends for his past by protecting the people of the present. But the fact that he can never bring back the many thousands of lives destroyed by his company's inventions weighs heavily upon him.

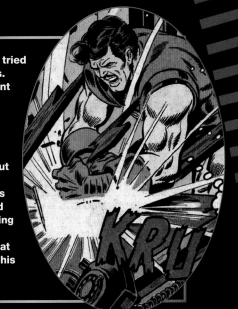

THE CONSTANT DEMON

Tony Stark's greatest fear is that he'll lose control again. Struggling with alcoholism nearly his entire adult life, Tony has hit rock bottom on more than one occasion. Alcohol is a persistent threat looming in the darkest recessses of his mind—a threat that some of Tony's enemies have ruthlessly exploited. Hardly a day goes by that Tony doesn't do battle with the demon in the bottle.

UNLUCKY IN LOVE

High-octane exotic beauties, female teammates with excess personal baggage, charismatic but fatally flawed Super Villains: Tony hasn't had the best of luck when it comes to romance. Bad choices combined with his own guilt complex and secretive ways, has resulted in one unworkable relationship after another. To Tony, true love seems an elusive prize indeed. But there are some that feel that what he's looking for has been right under his nose all the while.

BROKEN BODY

While the armor he's created seems to be nearly invulnerable, the man who wears it has proven to be anything but. From the very beginning of Iron Man's career, Tony has struggled with a near-fatal heart condition, brought on by shrapnel lodged close to his heart. Originally Tony was forced to wear his life-saving Iron Man chest plate at all times, just to keep his frail heart beating. He has undergone a heart transplant to cure this condition, but over the years has fallen victim to other ills, such as a shattered spine and a bout of total paralysis.

FRIENDS & ALLIES

If a man can be judged by his friends alone, Iron Man certainly has nothing to worry about. Earning allies both in the boardroom and the battlefield, Tony Stark always has someone to call on in a crisis.

Nick Fury

As one of the backers of the peacekeeping force SHIELD, Tony Stark helped appoint Nick Fury as the organization's director. Stark has continued to aid SHIELD in both of his identities, even after Fury tried to stage a hostile takeover of Stark International back when Tony pledged to end its weapon production. In fact, immediately after Tony foiled Fury's attempt, the two fought side by side against the towering automaton Dreadnought.

Dum Dum Dugan

Nick Fury's right-hand man, and a fine leader in his own right, Timothy "Dum Dum" Dugan began working for Stark when Tony was named the Director of SHIELD. However, during the events of the Secret Invasion (see pp.180–181) by the alien, shapeshifting Skrulls, it was revealed that Tony had not been working with Dugan at all, but a Skrull impersonating the loyal soldier.

Eddie March

A boxer inspired by Iron Man's crime-busting adventures, Eddie March was groomed by Tony Stark to replace him as Iron Man. Worried about his failing health, Tony enthusiastically trained Eddie to take over for him, only to discover that March's life was secretly threatened by a blood clot. However, after Tony reclaimed his role as a Super Hero, he and Eddie continued their friendship, and March subsequently joined Stark's charitable Iron Man Foundation.

Scott Lang

The second hero to call himself Ant-Man (the first was scientist and original Avenger Henry Pym), Scott Lang worked for Stark International for years. Often trusted to help his employer out in a pinch, Lang was willing to go the extra mile for Tony, on one occasion even breaking into prison on his behalf to interrogate an inmate. Lang was tragically killed during the rampage of the unbalanced Avenger Scarlet Witch.

Pepper Potts

Although perhaps the most loyal friend Tony Stark has ever had, his executive assistant Pepper Potts hasn't always got on well with her eccentric boss. When she first met Tony, she found him to be a bit sexist. And years later, when she married Happy Hogan, Pepper wanted little to do with Tony Stark, knowing the trouble he always brought into their lives. Regardless, Pepper is always drawn back to Tony, and probably always will be.

Abe Zimmer

Tony first met computer technician Abe Zimmer when Stark Enterprises was looking to purchase the research firm Accutech. After hearing Zimmer's informative account of the Ghost saboteur, the two started a working relationship that budded into a true friendship. Zimmer helped Stark hack into foreign computers during his "Armor Wars." He proved his loyalty to Tony when he died at the hand of the villainous Stockpile to keep Tony's secrets safe.

Jim Rhodes

Their friendship forged in the heat of battle, Rhodey and Stark have seen the best and the worst in each other's nature, but still managed to maintain their original bond. Treating him him like his own brother, Tony even gave Jim a set of armor, a gesture reserved only for a chosen few.

Bethany Cabe

One of Tony's former lovers, and the main reason he first overcame his alcohol dependency, the charismatic Bethany Cabe keeps appearing and reappearing in Stark's life. From working as his head of security, to taking over as commander of his War Machine project, Bethany has remained loyal to her old flame.

Happy Hogan

Many people have claimed they would be willing to take a bullet for Tony, but Happy Hogan actually proved it. On more than one occasion, Happy saved his employer's life. But it was the last instance that proved fatal for him, when he stopped the Spymaster from assassinating Iron Man.

Maria Hill

Nick Fury's original replacement as director of SHIELD, Maria Hill stepped down to allow Stark to lead the organization, and proved fiercely loyal to him. Fired alongside Tony when SHIELD merged with the HAMMER organization led by the villainous Norman Osborn, Maria and Tony shared a fling while on the run.

Guardsman

After his mind was skewed by the circuitry in Tony's Guardsman armor, his former ally Kevin O'Brien became Iron Man's newest enemy. Long after Kevin tragically died in battle, Stark International usurper Obadiah Stane sold the Guardsman armor design to the prison known as the Vault, to better arm its security staff.

Edwin Jarvis

Tony's childhood butler and a staunch friend of the Stark family, Edwin Jarvis had the opportunity to watch Tony grow up into the man he is today. He then became the Avengers' butler. Jarvis was replaced by a Skrull during the Secret Invasion.

Ho Yinsen

A brilliant pioneer of medical science, and a futurist just like Tony Stark himself, Ho Yinsen was taken captive by the warmonger Wong-Chu. After being forced to examine alien rings at the behest of the Mandarin, Yinsen later sacrificed his life to ensure Tony's freedom.

Sal Kennedy

A modern-day hippy and proponent of casual drug use, Sal Kennedy's unorthodox thinking led Tony to make Sal his SHIELD advisor and unofficial mentor. He challenged Tony's ethics on a few occasions, but grew to hate his SHIELD position. Sal was killed during a viral attack on the SHIELD helicarrier orchestrated by the Mandarin.

Jack of Hearts

When his scientist father was murdered before his eyes, young Jack Hart was exposed to zero-fluid, which endowed him with superpowers. Hart became the crime-fighter Jack of Hearts. He was a protegé of Iron Man, before graduating to full Avengers membership.

Guardsman II

Michael O'Brien was the second man to don the Guardsman armor, and the second to be corrupted by its circuitry into fighting Iron Man. He later became a friend of Iron Man and filled in for him on occasion, even pitting his skills against the Mandarin.

Force

Laboratory assistant Clayton Wilson stole a force-field projector and embarked on a life of crime as Force. After having second thoughts about this career move, with the help of Tony Stark, Clay turned his life around and started over. To conceal his past, he changed his name to Carl Walker.

Henry Hellrung

He's not a hero, he just plays one on TV. Famous for his role as television's Iron Man, Henry Hellrung became drinking buddies with the real Tony Stark. Years later, when they had both beaten their drinking problems, he was Tony's sponsor at Alcoholics Anonymous, before accepting a role as the hero Anthem in the Order.

Pepper Potts

Pepper Potts is the one reason Stark Industries didn't crash and burn ages ago. She's been Tony's right-hand woman for more years than either of them would like to admit. Infatuated with her boss almost from the first, Pepper has been flirting with Tony for as long as Iron Man has been flirting with disaster.

Pepper in Peril

Unfortunately for Pepper, being Tony Stark's Girl Friday means she is constantly put in harm's way. Tony rescued her from the secretarial pool after Pepper caught and corrected an error that would have cost his company hundreds of thousands of dollars. However, Pepper's promotion to his executive assistant has made her the target of every Super Villain with a grudge against the Golden Avenger.

In Good Hands

When Pepper first took over as Tony's assistant, she saw her workload increase tenfold. But soon Tony started to realize the importance of his job as head of Stark Industries, and the two became a solid team, even as their romantic tensions grew. Pepper helped Stark on all fronts and even saved Iron Man's life on more than one occasion.

KEY DATA

FULL NAME Virginia "Pepper" Potts

ALIASES Rescue, Hera, formerly Pepper Hogan

RELATIVES Harold "Happy" Hogan (husband, deceased), unidentified foster son and daughter, Clay Hogan (brother-in-law), unidentified grandfather-in-law

OCCUPATION Executive assistant, former coordinator of the Order

AFFILIATIONS The Order, Stark Industries

Bomb Victim

Despite their frequent flirtations, Pepper and Tony were never quite able to spark up a full-fledged romance. Tony worried about the state of his injured heart, while Pepper worried about Tony's reluctance to settle down with any one woman. It wasn't until Pepper was caught in a deadly blast while attending a gala with Tony that he truly realized how important she was to him. With shrapnel imbedded in her chest near her heart, Tony was forced to equip Pepper with repulsor technology to keep her alive.

Despite her quick recovery and miraculous new lease on life, Pepper was wary of having one of Tony's weapons inside her body.

However, the mag-field in Pepper's chest was created as a battery, not a weapon. The good news left Pepper literally walking on air.

Goodbye Kiss

When Tony was fired from his position as head of SHIELD and replaced by the current media darling, Norman Osborn, he refused to share classified information with the supposedly reformed Green Goblin. As a wanted man for his principled stand, Tony gave Pepper a parting kiss before going on the run.

Rescue

But the kiss wasn't Tony's last gift to his loyal assistant. While finishing up some final paperwork for the now bankrupt Stark Industries, Pepper stumbled upon a secret chamber that housed a suit of armor designed specifically for her. Equipped only with life-saving technology and run by a familiar computer program called JARVIS (Just Another Rather Very Intelligent System), the armor was a perfect fit for Pepper, who eagerly adopted it, renaming herself Rescue.

HAPPY HOGAN

"He needs a chauffeur like a hole in the head! What does he keep me around for, anyway?"

More worried about injuring his opponents than winning a title, boxer Harold "Happy" Hogan never found much success in the ring. Retiring from the fight game and taking a job at Stark Industries as Tony Stark's personal chauffeur, Happy thought he'd put his days of violence behind him. Instead, his life became a powder keg, where any workday could be his last.

The Rescue
When Tony was racing a custom stock car at the Indianapolis Speedway, he forgot to recharge his Iron Man chest plate that, at that time, kept his injured heart beating. Losing control of his car, Tony crashed into an embankment, and was pulled out of the flames by spectator Happy Hogan.

Happy-Go-Lucky
Even after Tony Stark offered him a cushy job as his chauffeur as reward for his valiant act on the racetrack, Happy rarely dropped his trademark scowl— hence his "Happy" nickname.

Mr. and Mrs. Hogan
Although Happy and Tony Stark's personal assistant Pepper Potts did not hit it off at first, they soon became friends. Happy's attempts to be *more* than just a friend to Pepper were unsuccessful at first— she seemed to have eyes only for Tony. However, his persistence finally paid off when Pepper gave up pining over the seemingly unreceptive Stark, and married the devoted former boxer.

Love Triangle
From virtually the first time they met, Tony had feelings for Pepper. But because of his heart condition and his desire to keep his Iron Man identity secret, Tony distanced himself from her. However, the two still experienced the occasional romantic spark.

Secret Itentitty
When he was severely injured during Iron Man's televised fight with the Titanium Man, Happy revealed to Tony that he had figured out his secret identity as Iron Man some time ago.

Happy Becomes the Freak

In an attempt to heal the wounds Happy acquired at the hands of the Titanium Man, Tony subjected his friend to his experimental Enervation Intensifier, a device that could channel energy into its subject. Although Happy's injuries were healed, he was transformed for a time into a hulking shell of his former self called the Freak. He ran amok and terrified Pepper Potts. When transformed back, Happy retained no memory of becoming a monster.

BUT... HE'S SO GROTESQUE... SO HORRIBLE !! AND... THERE'S NO PLACE TO RUN... I... I'M TRAPPED...!

"You know something, Hap? You're the only guy I ever met who can make me feel like a moron."
Tony Stark

fine Let's go

Soon's I finish my drink

Breaking Up, Making Up...

Pepper Potts was all Happy ever wanted. When the two eloped and decided to quit their jobs at Stark Industries to pursue their dreams, Happy thought everything was finally going his way. But when their relationship became strained due to the loss of their adopted foster children, their marriage ended in divorce. However, fate would bring them back together under Stark's employ, and the two eventually reconciled and remarried.

But the truth is, there's no cure for the one thing that's wrong with our marriage.

which is?

The couple would still have their share of problems. A rift again grew between them when Pepper had a miscarriage.

Taking a Bullet

Instead of telling her husband about her miscarriage, Pepper confided in Tony Stark. When Tony revealed the news to a drunken Happy, the shock was overshadowed by an even bigger surprise: a sniper's bullet meant for Tony. Tony got Happy to a hospital, and with all their secrets out in the open, Pepper and Happy reunited once more.

BLAM

A Hero's Death

Despite his slow demeanor, it was never a good idea to underestimate Happy Hogan. The Spymaster made the mistake of doing just that when he attempted to use Happy as bait to lure Iron Man into a trap. Happy struggled valiantly, knocking the Spymaster and himself off of a catwalk to stop the attack. Happy's injuries left him in a coma. With no hope of his recovery, Pepper begged Tony to use his Extremis link to pull the plug on her husband's life-support machine and end his suffering.

JAMES RHODES

"RHODEY"

He's Iron Man's right-hand man and the first person Tony Stark turns to for help. Despite the occasional difference of opinion, Jim "Rhodey" Rhodes has never let Iron Man down.

APOCALYPSE THEN...

It's surprising James Rhodes and Tony Stark ever became friends at all (1). After all, the first time Rhodes ever laid eyes on Tony Stark he shot at him with a machine gun. Few close friendships begin in a hail of gunfire, but it was somehow appropriate for Tony and Jim.

James Rhodes was born in a poor neighborhood in South Philadelphia. Seeking to make a name for himself and rise above his background, Rhodes enlisted in the US Marines and was assigned to a tour of duty overseas. A superb helicopter pilot, Rhodes was nevertheless shot down, crash-landing his prized bird right in the middle of enemy territory. To make matters worse, as he was repairing his craft, a strange armored man came out of the surrounding jungle and approached him. Jim opened fire on this mysterious threat (2), but his bullets couldn't penetrate his target's metal hide. The armored man was, of course, Tony Stark in his very first Iron Man suit. Tony had just escaped from Wong-Chu's prison camp and was seeking Rhodey's help.

After jumpstarting Jim's helicopter (3), and routing another camp of enemy soldiers (4), Tony and Rhodey flew back to a nearby US military outpost. This shared combat experience helped form a lasting bond (5).

Always there...

After changing out of his secret Iron Man identity, Tony offered Rhodey a job as his personal pilot right after their first adventure. Not wishing to pass up such a tremendous opportunity, Rhodey accepted, as soon as his tour of duty came to a close. As Stark's pilot, Rhodey now traveled the world with his jet-setting boss, and the two formed a close friendship that rivaled any in either of their lives. On several occasions, Rhodey went above and beyond the call of duty and saved Tony's life—a debt Tony repaid as Iron Man at every available opportunity.

When Tony's alcoholism made it impossible for him to handle his duties as a Super Hero, Rhodey nervously stepped up to the proverbial plate and took his piloting skills to the next level as the new Iron Man for a while. Even though the armor caused him pain and mental torment, Rhodey wore it proudly. He also donned the Iron Man armor on a few subsequent occasions to save his friend's life.

When Tony Stark seemingly lay on his deathbed, and asked Rhodey to resume Iron Man duties full time and also take over as Stark Industries' CEO, Jim didn't back down from the challenge. Only when Rhodes discovered that Tony had faked his death without telling him, did the two have a falling out, one that time and a bit of good old-fashioned armored combat finally mended.

Since Rhodey first donned the Iron Man armor in an emergency, it was never tuned to his particular brainwaves, causing him headaches and even shifts in his personality.

"I'm handlin' the hero chores these days... you might want to write that down somewhere—so you remember it."

RHODEY IN LOVE

Like Tony, Jim Rhodes never shied away from a pretty face. No stranger to romance ever since he first kissed his childhood sweetheart, Glenda Sandoval, Rhodey has been known to flirt with attractive women even while in a committed relationship. While in his Iron Man identity, Rhodes even tried to hit on the female Captain Marvel, but had no luck winning her affections.

One of Rhodes's most serious relationships was with former Stark public relations representative, Marcy Pearson. But when her ruthless career ambitions began to overshadow her romantic feelings, he ended their relationship and fired her at the same time. Rhodey also dated Tony's ex-fling Rae LaCoste for a time. Despite being more serious about each other than she and Stark ever were, Rae and Rhodey could never really make it work.

Marcy Pearson

War Machine

When Tony faked his death (see pp. 124–125), he bequeathed an Iron Man suit to Rhodey that was tailor-made for his combat strengths. When Tony revealed his deception, Rhodey renamed the suit War Machine and, furious with Tony for not letting him in on the secret earlier, briefly cut all ties with him. Joining the West Coast Avengers, and then the human-rights organization Worldwatch, Rhodey carved out his own place in the world. He later lost his original War Machine suit during a time-travel mission, but gained new alien armor to continue his war against crime.

Through it all, Rhodey never forgot the man he owed his career to, and when Tony truly needed him, he was always there. He later sacrificed his alien armor, all the power he had in the world, to protect the secrets of Tony's armory when the Fujikawa company staged a hostile takeover of Stark Enterprises.

Rhodey had no desire to reclaim his role as Iron Man, but his loyalty to his friend compelled him.

INTO THE FUTURE

"HOLD BACK AND WAIT FOR THE BLEED OUT..."

"SORRY SOLDIER... BUT RHODEY DON'T BLEED!"

Jim Rhodes was always destined to be a soldier. Bouncing around careers such as working for the government by manning their giant robotic Sentinels, to commanding the training facility for Super Heroes at the 50 State Initiative's Camp Hammond, Rhodey seemed only happy when fighting the good fight. But when his body was horrifically injured during an attack on a military base in Dubai, it seemed like Jim had finally seen his last bit of action. A quadriplegic with half his face missing, Rhodey was rebuilt by Stark's War Machine facility and given a new lease on life. Now a true living weapon, Rhodey walks his own path, yet is still always only a phone call away if Tony needs his help.

GIRLS, GIRLS, GIRLS!

Tony Stark's social activities have given new meaning to the term "playboy." A favorite hobby of his, equal to tinkering in his workshop, Tony has spent countless hours romancing society's most beautiful women.

Marion
One of the many gorgeous socialites Tony has dated, Marion retained a special place in his heart, even if he couldn't quite remember her last name. After all, it was Marion who suggested that Iron Man paint his armor gold, in order to appear less threatening.

Meredith McCall
His high-school sweetheart and first love, Meredith was forbidden by her father from seeing Tony, the son of a hated business competitor. Meredith became a college professor and later married Dr. Sloane Alden, the future villain Frostbite. She then encountered a younger Tony Stark from an alternate timeline.

Natalia Romanova
One of the many beautiful women that helped occupy Tony's evenings during Iron Man's early days, Natalia Romanova was secretly a Soviet secret agent known as the Black Widow. Now a hero and an Avenger, on rare occasions Natalia and Tony have rekindled the passions of those former nights.

Marianne Rodgers
The possessor of latent telepathic abilities, Marianne Rodgers was plagued with visions while she dated Tony. Although the two became serious about each other and even got engaged, Marianne's disturbing premonitions led to her keeping her distance, inducing Tony to call off their wedding.

Whitney Frost
Born Countess Giulietta Nefaria, Whitney Frost didn't gain Tony's affections until her face was scarred in a horrible accident. Hiding behind a golden mask and renaming herself Madame Masque, Whitney fell for Tony when he showed her kindness despite her appearance. Though their romance died when Whitney chose crime over love, she remains obsessed with Tony to this day.

Joanna Nivena
Before his life-changing imprisonment by Wong-Chu, Tony had decided to settle down and marry his girlfriend Joanna. But when he returned from captivity reborn as the crime-fighter Iron Man, Joanna knew she could never be a part of his life.

Janice Cord
The daughter of one of Tony's business rivals and the object of the affections of Crimson Dynamo Alex Nevsky, Janice Cord still attempted to date Tony despite the odds stacked against them. Unfortunately, during a battle between Iron Man, Titanium Man, and the Crimson Dynamo, she was accidentally killed.

Sunset Bain
Dating Tony while he was still in college, Sunset Bain turned out to be more interested in acquiring Stark Industries' secrets than Tony's love. At the helm of the Baintronics company, sly Sunset later attempted to use stolen War Machine technology to sabotage a Stark Solutions deal in order to gain Tony's aid for her own corporation.

Bethany Cabe
A complex woman with a life scarred by tragedy, Bethany nursed Tony back to health when he first realized that he was an alcoholic. But as quickly as she built Tony up, she tore him back down again when she left him in order to attempt a reconciliation with her husband, whom she had believed was dead.

Janet Van Dyne
Years ago, when Janet Van Dyne, alias the Avenger Wasp, didn't know that Tony Stark was also her teammate Iron Man, she and Tony had a brief fling. Although they began to develop serious feelings for one another, the relationship ended when Tony revealed his double identity to Janet. No matter how she felt about Tony, the Wasp couldn't continue to be in a relationship with someone who was good friends with her ex-husband, Hank Pym.

Indries Moomji
When Obadiah Stane set out to destroy Tony's life, he employed the services of the exotic Indries Moomji. Meeting Tony by seeming happenstance, Moomji instantly won the playboy's affections. She broke Tony's heart when he was at his lowest and needed her the most in a calculated and successful effort to drive him back to alcoholism.

Roxanne Gilbert
A political activist and the sister of the volatile extremist Gary Gilbert (better known as the original criminal Firebrand), Roxanne dated Tony briefly before their relationship cooled.

Heather Glenn
She was the wrong woman at the wrong time. Heather was an alcoholic and party girl, a terrible influence on Tony when, owing to Obadiah Stane's manipulations, he relapsed into his old drinking habits.

Brie Daniels
An actress dying to break into the business any way she could, Brie gatecrashed a party held at Tony's Los Angeles home hoping to hobnob with the rich and famous. Her scheme was discovered, but Tony was taken by her beauty and the two began dating.

Rae LaCoste
Although she and Tony were never serious about one another, Rae was one of the many women whose company Tony enjoyed on more than one occasion. Their frivolous affair evolved into a genuine friendship when Tony was paralyzed and Rae was able to overlook his disability.

Kathleen Dare
She wouldn't take no for an answer. Their short-lived relationship ended due to Kathy's jealousy. The chemically-imbalanced Dare then snuck into Tony's California home and shot her former lover. Later, when Tony seemingly died, Kathy took her own life out of grief.

Dr Su Yin
Beautiful and gifted, Dr. Su Yin had little difficulty winning Tony's heart when he visited her native China to arrest a sudden rapid decline in his health. Unfortunately for Tony, not only could Yin not cure him, she was already married.

Rumiko Fujikawa
The image of a spoiled party girl concealed a highly intelligent woman. Rumiko met Tony on the island of Isla Suerte, and the two began to date, despite a few rough patches caused by Tony's double life as Iron Man. Tony was sure Rumiko was the one for him and bought her an engagement ring. Tragically, Rumiko was killed by a corporate rival wearing an Iron Man suit.

Veronica Benning
After cheating death, Tony worked his way back to health from a state of complete paralysis. Overcoming the odds with the help of his physical therapist Veronica Benning, Tony soon began to see her in a new light, and the two began a short-lived romance.

Countess Stephanie De La Spirosa
A pretty face from Iron Man's early years, the Countess was reunited with Tony when she hired his services during his days at Stark Solutions. The two managed to rekindle their romance in the brief pauses between Iron Man's battles.

Calista Hancock
When Tony briefly retired from his life as a multi-millionaire industrialist and took on the identity of humble computer technician Hogan Potts, he engaged in a brief affair with his boss Calista Hancock. Their fling ended when he resumed his former life as Tony Stark.

She-Hulk
For Tony, one of the advantages of being Director of Shield, was coming into close contact with She-Hulk Jennifer Walters. The all-action heroine was every bit as keen on mixing pleasure with business as Tony. It wasn't long before the two found themselves in each other's arms—and later at each other's throats.

Maya Hansen
A longtime friend of Tony's after meeting him at a technology conference, Maya Hansen went on to become a scientific pioneer. They met again when Tony was dramatically transformed by her Extremis serum (see pp. 156–7). Their relationship blossomed and they even moved in together for a while. Her commitment to her scientific career led her to end the affair by faking her own death.

Pepper Potts
After years of flirting and dodging around the issue, Tony and his prized executive assistant Virginia "Pepper" Potts finally decided to curb their romantic feelings and just be friends. However, that decision was made just after they shared a passionate kiss. The fact remains that no matter how much they may deny it, Pepper and Tony share a connection that simply refuses to be held at bay forever.

And always...

KEY DATA

FULL NAME Bethany Cabe

ALIAS War Machine 2.0

OCCUPATION War Machine project director, former CEO of Stark Enterprises, security chief, bodyguard

AFFILIATIONS Formerly Iron Legion, formerly partner in Cabe & McPherson, Security Specialists

POWERS/ABILITIES Expert hand to hand combatant, expert marksman

With a past as unusual as her career choice, perhaps no woman has challenged Tony Stark as much as...

Bethany Cabe

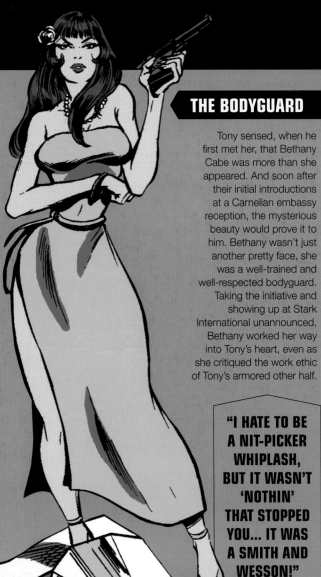

THE BODYGUARD

Tony sensed, when he first met her, that Bethany Cabe was more than she appeared. And soon after their initial introductions at a Carnelian embassy reception, the mysterious beauty would prove it to him. Bethany wasn't just another pretty face, she was a well-trained and well-respected bodyguard. Taking the initiative and showing up at Stark International unannounced, Bethany worked her way into Tony's heart, even as she critiqued the work ethic of Tony's armored other half.

> "I HATE TO BE A NIT-PICKER WHIPLASH, BUT IT WASN'T 'NOTHIN' THAT STOPPED YOU... IT WAS A SMITH AND WESSON!"

ALIVE!

Bethany was a woman of many secrets, and one of them was her marriage. At a young age, Cabe had married Alex van Tilberg, a German diplomat who, years ago, had seemingly died in a car crash caused by his addiction to pills.

Discovering that her husband was still alive, but a prisoner, Bethany traveled to East Germany and was also taken captive. Tony helped them both escape and also revealed his dual identity to his love.

Safely back in America, Bethany was torn between her past and her present, ultimately choosing her husband over Tony.

SECURITY CHIEF

Bethany had lived a hard life and, in time, she bounced back from the heartbreak she had experienced with Tony. When fate brought them together once more, Bethany was able to keep a professional demeanor, at first anyway. While Tony was recovering from a drastic surgical procedure, Jim Rhodes, alias War Machine, formed an "Iron Legion" in order to mount an assault on the extra-terrestrial Ultimo. Alongside men with previous experience piloting Iron Men suits, Rhodes enlisted Bethany Cabe. Outfitted with old Iron Man suits, Rhodes led the team into battle. As Ultimo threatened to gain the upper hand, Tony Stark arrived in his new modular armor to help save the day. Afterwards, he offered Bethany the job of head of Stark Security, a position she eagerly accepted. Their romance was soon rekindled, only to be cut short again when Tony seemingly died under the control of the villain, Immortus. He posthumously promoted Bethany to co-CEO in his stead, but this role was taken away from her when the foreign company Fujikawa International mounted a successful hostile takeover.

"TELL ME TONY... WHO'S GOING TO PROTECT YOU TONIGHT? MRS. ARBOGAST?"

MIND SWAP

Shortly before Tony Stark first developed his silver centurion armor, Bethany was taken captive by his chief rival, Obadiah Stane. There she underwent an experimental procedure created by Dr. Theron Atlanta in which her personality was switched into the body of a clone of the villain Madame Masque. This new "Bethany" attempted to assassinate Tony, and the real Bethany was forced to come to his rescue in the form of Madame Masque. Fortunately, Tony managed to see through the deception and helped restore Bethany to her own body.

WAR MACHINE RESEARCH DEPARTMENT

Iron Man was her past. War Machine would be her future.

Years after Tony's return from the grave, Bethany once again found employment at Stark Industries. When Jim Rhodes was critically wounded during an explosion at a military complex, Bethany was placed in charge of his rehabilitation and unfortunate transformation into a cyborg. Working as Rhodey's researcher from her Colorado base, Bethany became instrumental in War Machine's missions. She even went so far as to don a set of armor to destroy a Roxxon facility as War Machine 2.0.

Bethany helped coordinate War Machine's attack on mercenaries belonging to private defense contractor Eaglestar International.

MAIN ENEMIES

As Iron Man, Tony Stark has faced down more criminals than he cares to remember. From violent fanatics clad in high-tech battlesuits, to moneyed masterminds who rarely leave the comfort of their plush offices, Iron Man has battled them all, and overcome every obstacle they have put in his way. But a select few of Iron Man's adversaries have proved relentless thorns in his armored side, and worthy opponents for the heroic Golden Avenger.

The Mandarin

Believed to be the descendant of Genghis Khan, the warlord known only as the Mandarin considers himself destined to rule the world. A brilliant martial artist and strategist, the Mandarin continually plots to take over his native China and utilizes ten alien rings of almost limitless power to enforce his will. One of the Mandarin's least successful schemes involved the capture of Tony Stark by the warlord Wong-Chu. In the process, the Mandarin unwittingly helped create his nemesis: Iron Man.

Obadiah Stane

Obadiah Stane was not one to let bygones be bygones. When Tony Stark interfered with Stane's illegal business affairs, Obadiah dedicated his life to destroying Tony. Over time, Stane manipulated Stark into becoming a drunk, acquired Stark International, destroyed Tony's new company Circuits Maximus, and purloined Iron Man technology to forge his own Iron Monger armor. Only after losing a physical battle to Iron Man, did Stane finally admit defeat. Rather than live with this failure, he committed suicide.

Justin Hammer

The unscrupulous entrepreneur behind Hammer Industries, Justin Hammer has been an enemy of Iron Man's for years, constantly striking at Tony Stark from behind the scenes. Hammer's notoriety in the underworld first blossomed when he created his own network of Super Villains. Providing his amoral clients with enhanced technology in exchange for a cut of their profits, Hammer remained beyond the law's reach in his floating island hideout in international waters. Eventually, following a battle with Iron Man, Hammer was set adrift in space, frozen in a block of ice.

Titanium Man

A Russian citizen and fanatical political activist, Boris Bullski's giant stature is only equaled by his unswerving adherence to outdated Marxist communist beliefs. Years ago, during the Cold War, Boris believed he had found a way to stand out from all other Soviet military personnel. He arranged to fight Iron Man, who in Boris' eyes symbolized the corrupt capitalist system, on live television. Boris lost the bout, despite bending the rules to suit his purposes, and developed an unquenchable hatred for his American counterpart.

Blizzard

A disgruntled Stark Industries scientist, Gregor Shapanka attempted to rob the company's vaults but was foiled by Iron Man. Fired and humiliated, Gregor swore revenge on his former employer. Developing advanced freezing technology, Shapanka adopted the name Jack Frost, and set out as a career criminal, one destined to meet defeat at the hands of Iron Man. Later changing his name to Blizzard, Gregor was killed during a battle with an Iron Man from a possible future. He was later replaced by a new Blizzard, Donald Gill, who had been granted advanced freezing weaponry by another Iron Man archfoe, Justin Hammer.

Fin Fang Foom

One of an alien race of dragon-like creatures from the peaceful planet Kakaranathara, Fin Fang Foom traveled the stars only to crash land with the rest of his crew on Earth. The true owner of one of the ten energy rings exploited by the villain Mandarin, Foom was awoken from a deep sleep by that selfsame warlord. These days, Fin Fang Foom has emerged into the world as if to perform the role of rampaging dragon to Iron Man's modern-day knight in shining armor.

Spymaster

Three men have gone by the moniker Spymaster. The first, whose identity was never discovered, was a master of industrial espionage, targeting Stark Industries on many of his missions. Often working for Justin Hammer, he was murdered by the Ghost during an encounter with Iron Man. The second Spymaster was Nathan Lemon, a pupil of the criminal Taskmaster. He was killed on the orders of the newest Spymaster, supposed humanitarian Sinclair Abbott.

Whiplash

A weapons designer with an eye for a quick buck, Mark Scarlotti became the mercenary Whiplash. Armed with cybernetically controlled whips of his own design, Whiplash (sometimes called Blacklash) sought assignments from various employers, including Justin Hammer. Despite upgrading his weaponry several times, even adding a flying platform to his arsenal, Whiplash was defeated by Iron Man on most occasions. When Iron Man's armor briefly gained sentience, Whiplash was killed by the artificially intelligent being. Recently, a new Whiplash has been spotted alongside a female partner named Blacklash.

Crimson Dynamo

The product of scientific experiments dating back to the 1960s, the Crimson Dynamo is Russia's answer to Iron Man. Frequently reinvented over the years, the Crimson Dynamo armor has been worn by at least eight different individuals. The armor was originally invented by Anton Vanko, who was forced to attack Stark Industries by the Soviet government. After Vanko defected to the US, he died while opposing his successor as the Crimson Dynamo, Boris Turgenov. Today, the armor is usually piloted by Dimitri Bukharin, whose rivalry with Stark has developed into true friendship.

OTHER FOES

Kang the Conqueror

Nathaniel Richards, the time-traveling despot Kang, has wrought havoc in the life of Tony Stark. In fact, Kang's alternate future self, Immortus, was the one villain to truly defeat Iron Man, turning him into a murderer. Ironically, the teenaged Kang rebelled against his future destiny and decided to become the heroic Young Avenger Iron Lad.

Unicorn

Using a power horn developed by Anton Vanko (the original Crimson Dynamo), Milos Masaryk became the saboteur Unicorn. He crossed Iron Man's path when on a mission to attack a Stark Industries plant that was manufacturing weapons for the US government. The unstable Unicorn is much more dangerous than his moniker might suggest.

Firepower

The end result of a combination of stolen Stark technology and the devious mind of businessman Edwin Cord, Firepower was a destructive juggernaut without equal. Operated by mercenary Jack Taggert, Firepower seemed unbeatable until Iron Man redesigned his own armor specifically to take down the two-ton walking tank.

The Melter

When industrialist Bruno Horgan was discovered to be using inferior materials in his construction of weaponry for the US government, his contracts were awarded to Tony Stark. Swearing revenge, Bruno became the Melter, utilizing a ray capable of reducing Iron Man's armor to dripping slag.

Firebrand

Picking up his criminal career where the previous Firebrand, political zealot Gary Gilbert, left off, Rick Dennison, was even more hotheaded than his fiery predecessor. In his mutated form, Firebrand attacked an island business retreat, but was eventually defeated by the quick thinking of Iron Man.

Count Nefaria

The birth father of Whitney Frost and the reason for her descent into a life of crime as Madame Masque, crime boss Luchino Nefaria has battled the Avengers and Iron Man more times than either care to remember. Believed dead for many years, Nefaria returned to wage a calculated assault on Iron Man's life.

The Controller

Crippled in a lab accident, scientist Basil Sandhurst created an exoskeleton for himself and turned to a life of crime as the mind-manipulating Controller. Using his "slave discs" to control his unwitting pawns, the Controller has set up many illegitimate businesses to drain them of their energies.

M.O.D.O.K.

The crowning achievement of the terrorist organization AIM, MODOK is the mutated form of George Tarleton. An acronym for Mobile Organism Designed Only for Killing, MODOK is bent on mass destruction, but so far his plans have been foiled by Iron Man, Captain America, and the Avengers.

Wong-Chu

The heartless commander of the prison camp that unwittingly birthed Iron Man, Wong-Chu survived his first encounter with Stark only to plague him as a ruthless drug lord years later. Disfigured from his first encounter with Tony, Wong-Chu has seemingly perished, perhaps for good.

Living Laser

Scientist Arthur Parks used his miniaturized laser weapons to embark on a life of crime. An accident involving Iron Man turned him into a much deadlier being composed of pure photons.

A.I.M.

Iron Man has been thwarting the terrorist organization Advanced Idea Mechanics (AIM) for years. He recently put an end to a splinter faction called Advanced Genocide Mechanics.

Ezekiel Stane

The son of one of Stark's greatest rivals, Obadiah Stane, Ezekiel followed in his father's footsteps and used pirated Stark technology to wage war against Tony.

Sunturion

Iron Man and Arthur Dearborn, the energy-absorbing Sunturion, were enemies, until Sunturion realized his Roxxon employers were corrupt. He nearly gave his life for Iron Man's cause.

Temujin

Son of the Mandarin, Temujin inherited his father's enemies when Mandarin was thought dead. Temujin clashed with Iron Man, relying on martial arts as much as on his father's rings.

Morcedai Midas

The gold-obsessed crime boss has hired the likes of Madame Masque and Morgan Stark to do his bidding. Midas has set his greedy sights on Stark Industries many times.

Iron Patriot

Former Green Goblin Norman Osborn commandeered one of Tony's Iron Man suits, repainting it and publicly declaring himself a hero, despite his evil intentions.

Scarecrow

A contortionist by trade, Ebenezer Laughton left the stage behind when a chance encounter with Iron Man inspired him to become the flexible thief known as the Scarecrow.

Doctor Doom

Iron Man's equal and opposite number, Victor Von Doom has used his brilliant scientific mind and advanced battlesuit not for the good of mankind, but to further his own selfish agenda.

Madame Masque

Her scarred features reflect her disturbed mind. Whitney Frost has been Iron Man's lover, ally, and enemy. Her obsession with Tony Stark has grown to a near-fatal attraction.

Ghost

Tony Stark first encountered the enigmatic saboteur the Ghost when Stark Enterprises was purchasing the electronics company Accutech. A frequent opponent of Iron Man's, the Ghost joined Norman Osborn's Thunderbolts team, after using his intangibility to help Osborn steal an Iron Man suit.

Ultimo

A giant robot from outer space, Ultimo was unearthed by the Mandarin. Able to adapt to avoid defeat, Ultimo later merged with Tony's cousin Morgan Stark while battling War Machine.

Raiders

A trio of high-tech thieves using stolen Stark technology and financed by Edwin Cord, the Raiders have recently upgraded and now work as enforcers for the Chinese government.

L.M.D.

When an explosion brought a robotic duplicate of Tony Stark (known as a Life Model Decoy or LMD) to life, the android set out to replace the man he was created to serve. The LMD donned Iron Man's armor and battled his creator until he was destroyed in a vat of molten metal.

Vibro

Seismologist Alton Vibereaux gained power over earthquakes and became the unstable criminal Vibro. He fought and lost to both Tony Stark and Jim Rhodes during their Iron Man terms.

AVENGERS ASSEMBLE!

THOR

"And there came a day, a day unlike any other, when Earth's mightiest heroes and heroines found themselves united against a common threat. On that day, the Avengers were born—to fight the foes no single Super Hero could withstand! Through the years, their roster has prospered, changing many times, but their glory has never been denied! Heed the call, then—for now, the Avengers Assemble!"

HULK

ANT-MAN

THE BEGINNING

Thor's brother Loki was up to his old tricks again. Despite being imprisoned on a barren island in the mystical dimension of Asgard by his brother Thor, the Norse god of thunder, Loki still had access to his magical abilities. After manipulating the Hulk into attempting to wreck a passenger train, Loki diverted a radio call requesting help to Thor's civilian identity of Dr. Donald Blake. However, Loki's ploy worked a little too well. He successfully lured Thor into a battle with the Hulk, but he also accidentally summoned Iron Man, as well as Ant-Man and the Wasp. Discovering Loki's ruse, the newly formed team of heroes defeated the god of mischief. As they celebrated their triumph, they realized that working together certainly had its advantages. And so the Avengers, Earth's mightiest hero team, was born.

WASP

IRON MAN

It wasn't long before the Avengers set up shop in Tony Stark's childhood mansion and began to hold regular meetings. Bankrolled by Stark's seemingly limitless funds, the fledgling team soon faced a scheming alien dubbed the Space Phantom. Unfortunately, the battle bred more suspicion against the team's loose cannon, the incredible Hulk. Tired of the evident mistrust of heroes that were supposed to be his teammates, the Hulk quit the Avengers' ranks. In the Avengers very next adventure, the Hulk joined forces with Namor the Sub-Mariner and ruler of the undersea kingdom of Atlantis to battle the team. Fighting these two powerhouses to a standstill, the Avengers were unable to prevent Namor's escape. While searching for the disgruntled sea king, they chanced upon a body frozen in ice—and realized they had found the comatose form of the long-lost World War II icon, Captain America.

Reviving the fallen war hero, the Avengers soon accepted Cap to their ranks. The inspiration of an entire generation, Captain America naturally gravitated towards a leadership position, and cemented the team's reputation as the Earth's Mightiest Heroes.

Right from the start, the Avengers' roster was destined to be constantly in flux. Heroes would join and depart, depending on their politics or the circumstances of their own often-complex personal lives. Iron Man soon decided that he could no longer carry on his duties as a permanent member. However, he still contributed to the team's funding and housing. He also continued to supply them with innovative modes of transport, such as their famed, high-speed Quinjet airplanes, and recommended Clint Barton, the archer who had once opposed the Golden Avenger as the masked vigilante Hawkeye, for Avengers membership.

Over the years, Iron Man has returned to the Avengers' fold many times. He's been a constant influence on the team's direction, helping to found several different incarnations of the team, including the West Coast Avengers, the New Avengers and the Mighty Avengers. And even though Tony sometimes finds himself at odds with the group (on one occasion he was so frustrated with his teammates that he created his own super-powered splinter group called Force Works), Iron Man is always drawn back to the team he has invested so much of his money, energy, and heart into.

After the earth-shattering Super Hero Civil War, Tony Stark became head of the government peacekeeping agency SHIELD, and was thus in a position to shape the Avengers team to his liking.

TEAM UPS

These team-ups have played a big part in Iron Man's career, giving him a wide array of fellow heroes to call on when the need arises.

Ms. Marvel

Carol Danvers has had many names over the course of her long career. She has been known as Warbird, Binary, and Ms. Marvel. Carol lost her powers for a while when the mutant Rogue (then a member of the Brotherhood of Mutants) absorbed them; however, she gained new ones while fighting alongside the X-Men in space. She was Iron Man's first choice as field leader when he formed the Mighty Avengers, but has more in common with Tony than merely their crime-fighting past. Like Tony, the stress of her double life took its toll and she turned to alcohol to cope with her problems. Recognizing the signs from his own troubled past, Tony offered Carol his help, even revealing his dual identity to her. While it took Ms. Marvel time to acknowledge her addiction, she was able to conquer it, just as she had overcome many other hurdles in her life.

Reed Richards and the Fantastic Four

Tony Stark has found few men that equal or surpass his intellect, but Reed Richards is one of them. The founding force behind the super family of heroes known as the Fantastic Four, Reed (the Fantastic Four's super-malleable Mr. Fantastic) has formed a firm friendship with Tony, each respecting the other's scientific achievements. With many common interests, including a regular chess game, it's no surprise that the two friends have come to each other's aid on the battlefield as well. Alongside his wife, Sue Richards (the Invisible Woman), his brother-in-law Johnny Storm (the hotheaded Human Torch), and his old friend Ben Grimm (the irrepressible Thing), Mr. Fantastic has used his elastic powers to help Iron Man many times. On one occasion, Iron Man and the Fantastic Four squared off against a barrage of monsters on the streets of Tokyo, Japan, as well as a giant creature from another dimension. Tony and Reed were also both members of the top secret group known as the Illuminati and pivotal players on the government's side during the Civil War (see pp. 162–163) that ravaged the Super Hero community.

Spider-Man

Possessing a curious scientific mind like Stark's, Peter Parker has always looked up to Tony as a role model and a mentor. Even when fighting side-by-side as Spider-Man and Iron Man, or during their time on the same Super Hero team, the New Avengers, Spider-Man looks to Iron Man for guidance and advice.

Sharing many of the same mutual foes, such as the armored Beetle, the criminal mastermind Justin Hammer, and the poisonous Radioactive Man, Iron Man and Spider-Man have teamed up many times over the years. Side by side with the other New Avengers, they've faced down threats such as Hydra doppelgangers and armies of deadly Hand ninja. And as partners, they've tackled the likes of Radioactive Man, the Terrible Thinker, and Big Wheel. Peter Parker even served as Tony's right-hand man before the complex issues of the Super Hero Civil War tore their friendship apart.

Ka-Zar of the Savage Land

Over the years, Iron Man has paired with some unlikely partners. Perhaps none was more improbable than Lord Kevin Plunder, the jungle dwelling Ka-Zar. Iron Man met up with Ka-Zar when the hero left his home in the lost world named the Savage Land, situated somewhere in Antarctica, and journeyed to the Avenger's West Coast compound in California. Touring the grounds, contemplating life as a fully fledged Super Hero, Ka-Zar was taken by surprise when the Avengers' old enemy Fixer, in an attempt to steal Iron Man's armor, attacked the compound. Pitting his basic survival techniques against the high-tech arsenal of the Fixer, Ka-Zar captured the villain with a little help from Iron Man's ingenuity.

In more recent times, Ka-Zar and his wife, Shanna helped Iron Man fight the Skrull invasion when the Skrulls attempted to set up a base in the Savage Land.

The Champions

A short-lived team of unlikely allies, the Los Angeles-based Champions teamed with many heroes during their brief existence. Consisting of super spy Black Widow, spirit of vengeance Ghost Rider, former founding X-Men members Iceman and Angel, and the demigod Hercules, the Champions were a force to be reckoned with in their heyday.

On one particular adventure, the team crossed paths with Iron Man while the Golden Avenger was busy battling his enemy MODOK on the west coast of America. After contacting his two former Avenger colleagues, Black Widow and Hercules, Iron Man and the Champions set out to track down MODOK.

Iron Man finally discovered MODOK's hiding place and, with the Champions by his side, expelled excess energy directly at the robot villain, seemingly finishing him once and for all.

The Thunderbolts

Formerly the criminal Masters of Evil, the Thunderbolts appeared on the scene after the Avengers disappeared following their battle with the mysterious creature called Onslaught. Winning the public's support before revealing their former Super Villain identities, (members included Blizzard, Songbird, Jolt, Joystick, Charcoal, Moonstone, Beetle, Atlas, Speed Demon, and Radioactive Man) the Thunderbolts remained controversial figures in the minds of the Avengers upon that team's return from exile in a pocket dimension.

On one occasion, Iron Man masqueraded as the villain known as the Cobalt Man in order to infiltrate the Thunderbolts' ranks. Iron Man's deception was discovered by the Thunderbolt Moonstone, when she lost control of the vast energy she possessed. With the Avengers' help, Iron Man and the Thunderbolts took down the crazed villainess. During the Civil War, Iron Man utilized the Thunderbolts to help track down unregistered heroes.

Namor the Sub-Mariner

Ruling the underwater kingdom of Atlantis has done nothing for Namor the Sub-Mariner's modesty. With a hair-trigger temper and the brute strength to back it up, Namor has flip-flopped from hero to villain in the eyes of the public and their Super Hero protectors. Nevertheless, Namor possesses his own unique and unswerving moral code, which has led him to partnering with Iron Man from time to time and both have been members of the Avengers but were only briefly teammates.

On one occasion, Namor put himself at odds with the Golden Avenger after the sea king's reckless actions accidentally knocked a passenger plane out of the sky. Realizing that Namor's tantrum was caused by the activities of the corrupt Roxxon Oil company, Iron Man joined forces with the Atlantian and helped him destroy the company's criminal naval operation.

There have been times when Tony Stark has reluctantly stepped down and allowed other men and women to take up the Iron Man mantle.

HAPPY HOGAN
When the public began to suspect Tony's connection to Iron Man, his chauffeur Happy Hogan decided to save his boss's reputation by taking a turn in the Iron Man armor. By appearing in public, Happy put to rest any lingering suspicions that Tony Stark and Iron Man were one and the same.

EDDIE MARCH
Drawing inspiration from Iron Man's heroic exploits, prize-fighter Eddie March seemed the ideal choice to take over as Iron Man when Tony Stark decided to retire due to health complications. Unfortunately, March had a secret blood clot, and so Tony was soon forced to renew his role as the Golden Avenger.

BETHANY CABE
A trusted ally, though she never wore an Iron Man suit herself, Bethany Cabe first stepped into the role of Iron Man when Jim Rhodes recruited a team to pilot Tony's spare suits and battle the alien robot Ultimo. Bethany took to the equipment like a natural and played a crucial role in the ensuing battle.

MICHAEL O'BRIEN
Originally meeting Iron Man on the battlefield as the second Guardsman, Michael O'Brien later became a trusted friend of Tony Stark, and even wore the Iron Man armor to aid Tony in battle. Mistaken for the real Iron Man, O'Brien was captured by the Mandarin, forcing Iron Man to rescue him.

CARL WALKER
Formerly known as Clay Wilson, Carl Walker embarked on a criminal career as Force, until he became plagued by nightmares involving his misdeeds. With the help of his old enemy Iron Man, Walker left his criminal past behind him and even stood in as Iron Man when Tony needed his help against the notorious Fixer.

JIM RHODES
The only other person to take up the Iron Man role on a long-term basis, Jim Rhodes led the attack of Iron Men against Ultimo.

"Spare Parts Man"

When he discovered Iron Man's recovery armor on the ocean floor, the villainous Dr. Demonicus took the opportunity to take his revenge upon his hated foe. After meticulously scrutinizing the mechanics of the suit, Demonicus donned the armor and headed in search of the West Coast Avengers' hideout.

As luck would have it, his path soon crossed that of Tony Stark who, without an Iron Man suit for the time being, was clad in a makeshift uniform that he had assembled from spare costumes found around the West Coast Avengers' compound. Dubbed

"Spare Parts Man" by his old teammate Hawkeye, Tony was soon forced to put his rough and ready costume to work battling Demonicus aboard an Avengers' Quinjet. Managing to save his own life and subdue his twisted enemy, Tony was then in a position to retire "Spare Parts Man" for good.

IRON MEN ARMY

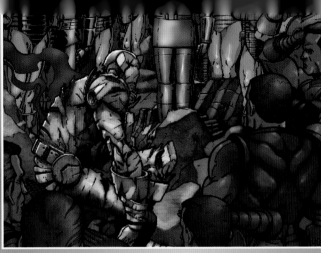

While briefly serving as the US government's Secretary of Defense, Tony was able to regulate the use of the technology that the government had appropriated from him over the years. However, owing to the political scheming of Under-Secretary Sonny Burch, dozens of malfunctioning Iron Men suits were developed without Tony's knowledge and they were about to be put into use. Luckily, Tony discovered the plot and when the Iron Men were being transported across the skies of Washington, Tony rescued the plane carrying them, just before it was about to crash.

WOLVERINE

When hunting down the super criminal known as Nitro, the villain responsible for the destruction of the town of Stamford, Connecticut, Wolverine called upon his New Avenger teammate Iron Man for help. Borrowing a suit of Tony's hydro armor, Wolverine was able to travel to the ocean floor to the ancient city of Atlantis, in order to see to it that Nitro was brought to justice.

• The only child of wealthy arms manufacturer Howard Stark and his wife Maria, Tony is raised in a mansion neighboring New York City's Central Park. His father's strict discipline and alcohol abuse turns Tony into a quiet, withdrawn child.

• To escape his family's troubles, Tony becomes fascinated with his erector set and builds a toy Iron Man.

• At age seven, Tony is sent away to boarding school—an attempt by his father to "toughen" him up.

• Finding it difficult to relate to other children, Tony escapes into the realms of science fiction and Thomas Mallory's tales of King Arthur and his Knights of the Round Table.

• A child prodigy, Tony enrolls at MIT at age 15, double majoring in physics and engineering and studying under many esteemed professors, including Ted Slaught.

• Tony begins dating Meredith McCall, his first serious relationship.

• Tony begins work for his father at Stark Industries. He doesn't take the job very seriously, preferring the life of a millionaire playboy.

• While driving to Long Island from a function in the city, Howard and Maria Stark lose control of their luxury sedan owing to a brake failure secretly engineered by a group of corrupt industry competitors who would go on to form Roxxon Oil. Howard and Maria are both killed in the wreck, leaving the apparently irresponsible Tony in charge of their entire estate.

• As his first act as head of Stark Industries, Tony buys the manufacturer of his parents' car and fixes the design flaw that caused their supposed accident.

• Tony promotes secretary Pepper Potts to be his executive assistant after the alert young woman corrects an oversight when typing up papers for a government contract, saving the company over a half million dollars.

• As Tony flounders as head of Stark Industries, Pepper takes on more and more of his responsibilities.

• Tony and his girlfriend, Joanna Nivena, become engaged.

• On a trip to Afghanistan as a consultant to the US military, Tony is caught in the explosion of one of his own company's land mines when terrorist forces attack his convoy. With shrapnel lodged in his chest next to his heart, Tony is taken captive by the rebels and told to build a weapon that they can use against the Americans. With the help of fellow inventor and prisoner Ho Yinsen, Tony instead builds a primitive Iron Man suit that keeps him alive and allows him to escape the insurgents' camp.

• Still clad as Iron Man, Tony meets pilot Jim Rhodes and the two help each other escape enemy territory, finally returning to a US base.

• Back in the US, Tony wears his life-saving Iron Man chest plate to survive, but makes it thinner and more compact. He also develops a way to store the suit of armor in his briefcase. He decides to continue as Iron Man to combat crime, but keeps his dual identity a secret, announcing that Iron Man is his bodyguard and a Stark Industries' employee.

TIMELINE

• Tony reveals his double life to his fiancée Joanna Nivena. The two part when Joanna realizes that Tony's calling as a Super Hero will interfere with a normal family home life.

• After wrestling escaped lions at a circus as Iron Man, Tony paints his armor gold, realizing that his gray armor frightens the public.

• When testing his "Stark Special" racecar, Tony crashes and is pulled from the wreckage by former boxer Happy Hogan. Tony hires Happy as his chauffeur, and the two become fast friends.

• The villain Jack Frost attacks Stark Industries, rebelling against his own employer.

• Iron Man joins Ant-Man, the Wasp, Thor, and the Hulk to form the Avengers to thwart the trickery of Thor's evil brother, Loki. The team's headquarters is the Manhattan mansion that was Tony's childhood home.

• Iron Man battles Professor Vanko, the Crimson Dynamo, convincing the villain to defect to the US and work for Stark Industries.

• Bruno Horgan attacks Stark Industries as the Melter after the military contracts weapons from Stark Industries instead of his own company.

• Tony constructs a new red and gold Iron Man suit out of lighter material to help him defeat the villainous Mr. Doll.

• Iron Man heads to China at the behest of the US government and first battles the Mandarin.

• After a failed robbery, the contortionist known as the Scarecrow flees to Cuba to escape Iron Man.

• The Avengers unearth Captain America and add him to their ranks.

• Tony has a fling with the Soviet spy known as the Black Widow before learning of her treachery and foiling her schemes.

• Iron Man streamlines his "horned" helmet into a rounded shape.

• Iron Man fights the Unicorn when the villain decides to pit his strength against the hero.

• Black Widow returns to plague Iron Man, this time with marksman Hawkeye in tow as her love-struck partner.

• After besting the villain known as the Saboteur who was out to ruin Stark Industries' government contracts, Tony finally devotes himself fully to his company, to the relief of the overworked Pepper Potts.

• Iron Man quits the Avengers, yet remains their main financial supporter. He also backs reformed villain Hawkeye for team membership.

• Iron Man bests the communist Titanium Man in a televised fight for national pride. During the epic battle, Happy Hogan reveals that he has deduced Iron Man's double identity.

• Tony Stark helps found the government super spy agency SHIELD and is instrumental in recruiting Nick Fury as its director.

• The Mandarin discovers the alien android Ultimo and unleashes the 25-foot-tall behemoth on Iron Man.

• Pepper Potts and Happy Hogan get married.

• Whiplash slugs it out with Iron Man for the first time, and fights the hero to a standstill.

• Tony begins a romance with Janice Cord.

• Iron Man faces a batch of new threats, including Madame Masque, Mordecai Midas, and the Controller.

• When Iron Man suffers a heart attack in battle, Dr. Jose Santini transplants a synthetic heart into Tony's chest, freeing the hero from dependency on his Iron Man chest plate.

• Boxer Eddie March steps in as Iron Man when Tony retires. When Eddie suffers a severe injury at the hands of a new Crimson Dynamo, Tony returns as Iron Man, fighting the Crimson Dynamo in a battle that costs Janice Cord her life.

• The political activist Firebrand first comes into conflict with Iron Man.

• The original Spymaster and his Espionage Elite attack Stark Industries, taking Tony Stark hostage.

• Tony creates the Guardsman armor for engineer Kevin O'Brien, but the armor causes O'Brien to go insane, and attack Tony's new girlfriend Marianne Rodgers. Iron Man accidentally kills O'Brien in a later skirmish.

• Iron Man fights alongside the Avengers in the Kree/Skrull War. He later forms the Illuminati alongside Mr. Fantastic, Namor, Professor X, Dr. Strange, and Black Bolt in order to prevent such conflicts recurring in future.

• Tony changes the name of his company to Stark International to better reflect his role in the global marketplace. He abandons his work in munitions in favor of the more beneficial innovations of electronics development.

• Jack Frost returns as the criminal Blizzard.

• Michael O'Brien, the brother of the original Guardsman, investigates his brother Kevin's death and eventually takes up his mantle after briefly posing as Iron Man.

• Jim Rhodes, Bethany Cabe, and Bambi Arbogast all come to work at Stark International.

• Justin Hammer wages war on Stark's business.

• With Iron Man framed for murder, Tony undergoes training by Captain America in martial arts and other fighting techniques.

• Although Tony manages to escape Hammer's clutches, the stress of the ongoing skirmish and the threat of a hostile company takeover drive Tony to drink.

• With the help of his budding romance with Bethany Cabe, Tony manages to kick his drinking habit and reclaim his life.

• Iron Man tries out his first armor variation, his space armor, while investigating an orbiting Roxxon satellite.

• Industrialist Edwin Cord orders the Raiders to attack Iron Man, and is jailed.

• Dr. Doom and Iron Man travel back to the time of King Arthur and the Knights of the Round Table.

• Iron Man uses his new stealth armor to invade a top-secret East German research complex resulting in an ongoing feud with the villainous Living Laser.

• Obadiah Stane begins a hostile takeover of Stark International, setting his sights on destroying Iron Man while simultaneously scheming to return Tony Stark to the bottle.

Tony lapses into alcoholism once more, becoming incapable of operating the Iron Man suit.

• Pilot Jim Rhodes takes over Tony Stark's duties as Iron Man while Tony roams the New York City streets, reduced to little more than a penniless vagrant.

• Obadiah Stane takes over Stark International, renaming it Stane International.

• Iron Man Jim Rhodes is transported to Battleworld with many other heroes to fight at the whim of the mysterious Beyonder. There his armor is augmented by fellow hero Mr. Fantastic.

• After befriending a homeless pregnant woman and saving her son's life, Tony becomes sober again.

• Tony and a few friends move to California and create a new company called Circuits Maximus.

• Iron Man battles the seismic-powered Vibro.

• As Iron Man, Jim Rhodes joins the West Coast Avengers.

• When his new company is destroyed by Stane, Tony Stark dons new silver armor and reclaims his title as Iron Man. Iron Man attacks Stane, who has designed his own Iron Monger battlesuit, and defeats him. Stane takes his own life.

• Tony sets up a new company called Stark Enterprises.

• Iron Man dons his underwater armor for the first time when searching for chemical weapons at the bottom of the ocean.

• The Ghost attacks a new subsidiary of Stark Enterprises, bringing him into conflict with Iron Man for the first time.

• Tony hires reformed villain Force and discovers his new employee's armor contains stolen Stark components. This prompts Iron Man to embark on a renegade mission, dubbed the Armor Wars, to destroy all of his technology that has been appropriated by other hands over the years.

• Tony's extreme actions in the Armor Wars lead to Iron Man being kicked out of the Avengers and Tony creating a new Iron Man suit.

• The emotionally disturbed Kathy Dare becomes obsessed with Tony Stark and shoots and paralyzes him. Tony employs an experimental microchip to regain the ability to walk.

• Iron Man faces manipulation and control from outside forces, along with the revenge of a more powerful Living Laser in the second Armor Wars.

• Tony travels to China in an attempt to find a cure for his worsening spinal condition and instead encounters the Mandarin and Fin Fang Foom in the Dragon Seed Saga.

• Iron Man joins with the Avengers to fight in Operation: Galactic Storm during an interstellar war between the Kree and the Shi'ar.

• Undergoing experimental treatment to cure his ailing condition, Tony fakes his own death, promoting Jim Rhodes to CEO of Stark Enterprises and once again into the position of Iron Man.

• Tony is successfully revived, prompting Rhodes, sick of being kept in the dark, to angrily quit his employ. Rhodes adopts the War Machine identity and embarks on his own crime fighting career.

• War Machine joins the West Coast Avengers.

• In a battle with Ultimo, Iron Men past and present join forces after Tony's remote controlled NTU Iron Man fails to stop the giant alien android. The group defeats the villain only after Tony arrives clad in a new advanced Iron Man armor.

• Iron Man employs his Hulk-Buster armor during a fight with an intelligent Hulk regarding the destruction of a factory that produces gamma ray bombs.

• The West Coast Avengers disband, allowing Tony to form his own team of heroes, Force Works.

• Tony Stark and Jim Rhodes put aside their personal differences during a battle with the Mandarin.

• Tony is corrupted by the forces of Immortus in the guise of Kang the Conqueror and goes on a killing spree in service of his new master. This prompts the other Avengers to travel back in time and seek the aid of a young Tony Stark.

• In a final moment of heroism, the older Tony Stark sacrifices his life to help defeat Kang and his allies. The young Tony decides to carry on his duties as Iron Man in the present.

• The young Tony Stark, along with many other heroes, seemingly dies in order to save the world from the rampaging powerhouse Onslaught. In reality, the heroes are transported to an alternate pocket dimension.

• Iron Man returns to his rightful dimension as an adult, wearing a new suit of Iron Man armor.

• With the merger of Stark Enterprises and Fujikawa Industries occurring in Tony's absence, Tony decides to start a new proactive subsidiary called Stark Solutions.

• Iron Man joins a new incarnation of the Avengers with a familiar classic roster after an epic battle with Morgan le Fay.

• Tony meets Rumiko Fujikawa when fighting a new version of Firebrand on a tropical island, and the two begin dating.

• When his reputation is destroyed by Tiberius Stone, Tony Stark gives his fortune to the Avengers and the Maria Stark Foundation and begins life anew as computer tech Hogan Potts.

• Iron Man dons a new liquid metal Iron Man suit with the help of Askew Labs.

• Tony reclaims his fortune and, with Rumiko's help, reclaims his original company as well. He also adopts a new suit of armor.

• Iron Man decides to go public with his dual identity to save the life of a dog about to be hit by a car.

• Tony dons magic Thor-Buster armor for the first time during a conflict with the thunder god on foreign soil.

• When he discovers that several of his designs are being employed by the US government without his permission, Tony decides to regulate their use by becoming the US Secretary of Defense.

• After a scandal caused by the machinations of his fellow Avenger, the mentally imbalanced Scarlet Witch, Tony resigns from his government position in disgrace.

• Rumiko Fujikawa is killed by Tony's former business rival Clarence Ward, who is wearing a stolen suit of Iron Man armor at the time of the assassination.

• The Avengers officially disband after their ranks are decimated by the magic abilities of the Scarlet Witch.

With the help of his old friend Maya Hansen, Tony applies experimental Extremis technology to his Iron Man armor, allowing him to link directly into the Iron Man suit and other machinery with his mind, and making him more powerful than ever.

After a breakout at the maximum holding facility known as the Raft, Iron Man joins with several other heroes to form the New Avengers.

• The Scarlet Witch alters reality completely so that mutants are the dominant species, forcing Iron Man and other heroes to topple her new regime and restore the world to normal.

• Iron Man becomes a mentor figure to Spider-Man and even builds the hero his own suit of armor dubbed the Iron Spider.

Civil War breaks out between two factions of heroes when congress passes the Superhuman Registration Act. Iron Man spearheads a team of government-sponsored, legally registered heroes while Captain America leads a clan of vigilantes who refuse to give up their right to privacy. Iron Man and his allies ultimately win the war, resulting in Captain America's death.

• Happy Hogan is killed fighting the Spymaster, leaving Pepper Potts a widow.

• Iron Man is promoted to Director of SHIELD and instigates the Fifty State Initiative, a program that installs a Super Hero team in every state. Iron Man oversees a team of new Mighty Avengers, while assigning Pepper Potts to oversee the California-based premier team of new blood called the Order.

Exiled in outer space by the Illuminati, the Hulk returns and declares war on Super Heroes. Iron Man battles him and helps the heroes triumph by employing satellite technology.

• Ezekiel Stane, son of Tony's former arch-foe Obadiah Stane, steals and upgrades Stark technology and wages war on Iron Man and his companies, severely injuring Pepper Potts.

Jim Rhodes is nearly killed while on a military base in Dubai, but is rebuilt by Tony into a half-human cyborg as a newly advanced version of War Machine.

Earth falls victim to a Secret Invasion led by the alien shape-shifters called the Skrulls. During the devastating war, all Stark technology is rendered inert by the aliens, including Tony's Extremis technology.

Former Green Goblin, Norman Osborn, kills the Skrulls' queen, causing an upswing in public opinion for the one-time villain. He soon replaces Stark at the head of the reformed SHIELD organization (now called HAMMER) and frames Tony for war crimes. Osborn even steals an old Iron Man suit of Stark's and claims it for himself, leading a new group of Dark Avengers as the Iron Patriot.

• A fugitive from the law, Tony closes the doors to the financially crippled Stark Industries and erases all the files of the Superhuman Registration Act, even from his own mind, causing him to slowly lose his intelligence and subsequently downgrade his armor.

Pepper Potts adopts the identity of Rescue and her own set of defensive armor powered by the repulsor technology Tony used to save her life after her injury at the hands of Zeke Stane.

• After a fierce battle with the Iron Patriot, Tony is placed in a coma, virtually brain dead. Meanwhile, his old allies rally around a mysterious disc that could possibly be the key to his recovery.

TIMELINE

THE
1960s

The decade that saw Iron Man's creation also ushered in his most loyal friends and many of his most fearsome adversaries.

Iron Man was just trying to find his place in the world. The result of the marriage of two popular comic book mediums, science fiction and Super Heroes, Iron Man debuted in the pages of Marvel Comics' *Tales of Suspense #39* in March 1963. From the start, Tony Stark was thrown into the never-ending battle for popularity and page count. First sharing his title with other short science-fiction stories, and later with Captain America, Iron Man finally proved popular enough to be granted a solo title after *Tales* ended with issue *#99*.

Before making the leap to his own comic, Iron Man co-starred in a stand-alone special issue entitled *Iron Man & the Sub-Mariner #1* in April 1968. Featuring a story continued from *Tales of Suspense #99* and continuing in *Iron Man #1* the following month, this special served as a way to launch the individual series of both characters, while perhaps combining the characters' respective fans. No matter the method, five years after his debut in *Tales of Suspense #39*, Iron Man was finally standing on solid ground in the pages of his own comic.

And it was a good thing, too, because Iron Man's ever-growing supporting cast needed all the room they could muster. Not only had *Tales* introduced Tony's lifelong friends Happy Hogan and Pepper Potts, but Iron Man had also battled classic rogues like the Mandarin, the Crimson Dynamo, and Whiplash. Iron Man's early years also saw the debut of future fan-favorite heroes, Black Widow and Hawkeye.

OVERLEAF *Tales of Suspense #50*: Not only were the Mandarin's alien rings quite deadly, he had forged his body into a weapon as well, as demonstrated in his very first appearance.

TALES OF #48 SUSPENSE

PUBLICATION DATE
December 1963

EDITOR-IN-CHIEF
Stan Lee

COVER ARTIST
Jack Kirby and Sol Brodsky

WRITER
Stan Lee

PENCILER
Steve Ditko

INKER
Dick Ayers

Letterer
Sam Rosen

"And now, though Mr. Doll won the first round in his battle with the old Iron Man… he's liable to find the new Iron Man a far more difficult foe to beat!"

IRON MAN

MAIN CHARACTERS: Iron Man; Mr. Doll
SUPPORTING CHARACTERS: Pepper Potts; Happy Hogan; Charleton Carter; a Stark Industries security guard; New York City police officers
LOCATIONS: Stark Industries, Long Island, New York; Charleton Carter's mansion

BACKGROUND

As Iron Man's popularity grew, so did the length of his stories. By the end of his debut year, Iron Man's comics had grown from 13 pages to 18-paged "feature length" tales. A few guest artists helped with the increased workload, including Steve Ditko, who stopped by for a three-issue visit. Ditko was famous for co-creating and drawing Peter Parker, the amazing Spider-Man, so it made sense that, just a year after the debut of Mr. Parker's impressive duds, he was asked to pencil the first Iron Man issue featuring Tony Stark's new look.

This wasn't Iron Man's first costume change. As early as his second appearance, in *Tales of Suspense #40*, Iron Man had realized that his armor needed to appear less threatening to the public. He coated his suit in gold paint, turning himself into a modern-day knight in shining armor. Later, the red and gold look that Steve Ditko ushered in with *Tales #48* slimmed down the previously bulky suit, creating perhaps the most iconic version of the Iron Man armor to date.

The Story...

When his first clash with the villainous Mr. Doll leaves him at death's door, Iron Man decides to upgrade his armor to better battle his mysterious new enemy.

Mr. Doll's first strike hit Tony Stark right where it counted: his wallet. When wealthy steel man Charleton Carter backed out of a mutually lucrative business deal at the last moment, Stark decided to drop by Carter's mansion in order to talk some sense into his business associate. But as he pulled into the old tycoon's lane, Tony noticed an odd figure cloaked in what seemed like a masquerade costume **(1)** approaching Carter's home. Changing into his golden Iron Man armor to investigate **(2)**, Tony observed the costumed man blackmailing Carter out of his fortune by manipulating a small clay doll. It seemed the uniquely garbed individual was calling himself Mr. Doll, and his oddly shaped toy was a modern day voodoo doll, able to force the helpless Charleton Carter into obeying his every command.

Iron Man had seen enough, even if he didn't quite understand what was going on. He charged in through Carter's window, and lifted Mr. Doll into the air **(3)**, unfortunately giving the villain time to alter his doll's likeness to that of Iron Man himself. By squeezing the clay figure in his hand **(4)**, Mr. Doll made Iron Man feel as if his very bones were being crushed inside his armor. And if that wasn't bad enough, the power in Iron Man's suit was nearly depleted. If he didn't recharge his chest plate soon, he would suffer a fatal heart attack. Tony had no choice. He had to escape.

Reeling in pain, Tony sped back to his Long Island factory and stumbled into his private laboratory. There he managed to plug his chest plate into a special outlet even as he collapsed onto the floor, unconscious. Waking later thanks only to the miraculous device, Tony realized that it was his heavy, cumbersome armor that was slowing him down. If he was going to defeat Mr. Doll, he'd need a complete overhaul. He'd have to redesign Iron Man.

Hours passed as Tony toiled alone in his private workshop **(5)**. Meanwhile, across town, Mr. Carter was signing away his entire fortune. Mr. Doll's plan had succeeded, and it was time for the villain to pick a new target. He slowly reshaped his voodoo doll. Holding the totem to the light, Doll smiled as he looked down at a familiar face. The face of Tony Stark.

Back in his lab, Tony was finally completing work on his new armor **(6, 7, 8)**. Not only was his new Iron Man suit sleeker and more powerful than his last model, but it was slimmer and more compact as well. In fact, the arms and legs of the suit conveniently retracted into the glove and boot housings when not in use, making for much easier storage.

While the police grew wise to Mr. Doll's plans and set up a guard at Tony's office, Iron Man slipped out a secret passageway in order to surprise Mr. Doll when the villain finally reared his head at Stark Industries. After briefly being controlled again by Doll's clay figurine, Iron Man escaped to a nearby chamber. Locked safely away from his adversary, the hero then recharged his armor and began to construct his own little surprise for his unwanted trespasser. Attacking Mr. Doll once more **(9)**, Iron Man aimed his newly created pocket-sized device **(10)** at the clay voodoo doll before Mr. Doll could take hold of his faculties. And slowly, the clay figure began to shift its shape until it began to resemble Mr. Doll himself. In a moment of pure surprise, Mr. Doll dropped his prized totem, and as the doll hit the ground, the villain had no choice but to follow suit, collapsing to the floor, unconscious and thoroughly defeated **(11)**.

"I've got a little gadget here which is going to change all your evil plans... "

CAPTAIN AMERICA

He's a living symbol of freedom, and America's sentinel of Liberty. Captain America is a man Tony Stark has always wanted as a friend, but all too often faced as an enemy.

Anticipating Tony's attack on the Vault prison, Steve tried to talk some sense into Stark.

ARMOR WARS

Everyone Captain America ever knew was either extremely old, or buried in the ground. So naturally, the Avengers became his closest friends. Both sharing strong moral values, Cap and Iron Man instantly hit it off, but their friendship would be called into question time and time again. One of the most testing times in their relationship occurred during Iron Man's so-called "Armor Wars." Tony broke laws and betrayed other heroes attempting to destroy all of his technology that had fallen into other people's hands. Captain America took issue with the extreme methods his friend was employing. After trying to persuade Stark to give up his crusade, Cap felt he had no choice but to stop his old friend when Iron Man broke into a government installation, the Vault prison.

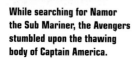

While searching for Namor the Sub Mariner, the Avengers stumbled upon the thawing body of Captain America.

MEETING THE AVENGERS

The phrase "man out of time" means more to Steve Rogers than most people realize. A shining example of what the common man could strive for during World War II, Rogers volunteered for a super-soldier program and became Captain America. An icon known the world over, Captain America was caught in an explosion and plunged into the ocean. While the world presumed their hero dead, Cap was actually frozen in a chunk of ice. When the Avengers stumbled upon his perfectly preserved body, they were as surprised as the public when the hero not only revived, but seemed to still be in top physical condition. Soon Cap joined the Avengers ranks, fighting for freedom in a new world.

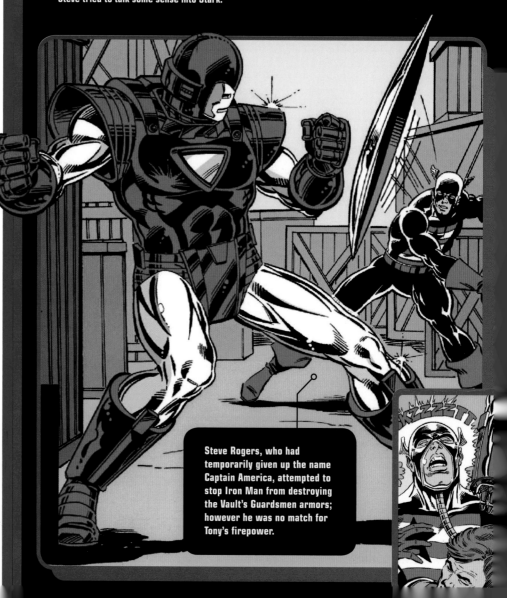

Steve Rogers, who had temporarily given up the name Captain America, attempted to stop Iron Man from destroying the Vault's Guardsmen armors; however he was no match for Tony's firepower.

A LOYAL FRIEND

Back when Tony Stark was suffering from his worst bout of alcoholism, he dropped out from society, lost in his world of booze and pain. Captain America went to visit Tony in his squalid surroundings, but Stark refused his help even after Rogers rescued him from a burning building.

Captain America was forced to rely on dirty tricks to defeat Iron Man.

CIVIL WAR

Iron Man and Captain America had violently disagreed on many issues over the years—the "Armor Wars" incident at the Vault, Tony dating the Wasp, the extermination of the alien Kree leader the Supreme Intelligence, to name just a few. But when the government passed the Superhuman Registration Act, Steve and Tony faced an insurmountable obstacle to their friendship when they realized that they were on diametrically opposed sides. It was a fight that neither wanted to lose, and neither could afford to win.

Iron Man never had the chance or the courage to tell Captain America why he had chosen to take a stand in favor of the Superhuman Registration Act.

DEATH OF A HERO

The Civil War was over and Iron Man's forces had been victorious. Left with no acceptable alternative, Captain America surrendered himself to the government. While walking up the steps of the courthouse to face his arraignment, Cap was shot—an assassination planned by his longtime enemy, the Red Skull. Captain America was dead, and Tony Stark never got the chance to say goodbye to his former friend and ally.

FIRST ENCOUNTER

Bruce Banner is one of the smartest men on the planet. Unfortunately, when he was doused with gamma radiation at a military testing site and transformed into the mammoth monstrosity called the Hulk, most of that fabled intellect didn't make the transition. Confused, angry, and just wanting to be alone, the Hulk escaped the military base into the surrounding desert. Terrified of their accidental creation, the military sent dozens of well-armed troops after the gray goliath, but to no avail. The Hulk smashed everything that came near him. But when he snatched Bruce Banner's girlfriend Betty Ross, the Hulk had gone too far. The army called in the big guns. They called in Iron Man.

The Hulk easily bested Tony in his original golden armor, leaving him broken and bleeding.

Iron Man needs special armor to deal with the threat posed by the Hulk—whether he's facing the gray, green or red incarnations of the gamma-spawned goliath.

IRON MAN VERSUS HULK

ENTER THE AVENGERS

All the Hulk wanted was to be alone. Instead he unwittingly helped found the mightiest Super Hero team of all time. Tricked by the Norse god of mischief, Loki, into battling Iron Man, Ant-Man, the Wasp, and Thor, the Hulk later joined with the heroes, who called themselves the Avengers. However, the Hulk quit the team during their next adventure, realizing that the other Avengers didn't fully trust him.

ARMOR ADAPTATIONS

Over the years, Iron Man and the Hulk have battled countless times, even as Tony Stark and Bruce Banner have developed a friendship based on mutual scientific respect. Despite his admiration for Banner, Tony has absolutely *no* respect for the Hulk. Realizing that his conventional armor can't hold up against the green goliath's brute strength, Tony has developed several Hulkbuster suits. With the Hulk, it's not a question of *if* there will be a next rampage, it's just a question of *when*.

GAMMA ARMOR

If there's one quality that Tony Stark is famous for, it's his determination to go above and beyond the call of duty. So when the US government asked him to create a radiation-proof suit, Tony devised a new Iron Man design that not only withstood the fallout from a normal nuclear device, but could withstand the radiation created by a gamma bomb, such as the one that birthed the incredible Hulk. Teaming with Bruce Banner, Stark then developed a new gamma-resistant suit that withstood gamma particles in the air and eventually eradicated them.

When testing gamma armor, Tony's judgment was impaired from lack of oxygen. Bruce was forced to switch to the Hulk in an attempt to stop his friend's dangerous behavior.

IRON BOOM HULKBUSTER!

HULKBUSTER!

When the Hulk stormed Stark Enterprises, Iron Man armed himself with a few new attachments for his modular armor. With his Hulkbuster gear in place, Iron Man battled the Green Goliath until he realized that the Hulk was actually in the right for once.

70-71

A captain of industry and the major weapons supplier to the US government, Tony Stark had painted a bright target on both his business and its heroic mascot, Iron Man.

UNICORN

Armed with a power horn that fired dangerous blasts and manipulated magnetic energies, the Unicorn set out from his native Russia to attack American weapons manufacturers. During his first raid on Stark Industries, he trounced Happy Hogan and kidnapped Pepper Potts. A recurring face in Iron Man's rogues' gallery, the Unicorn later joined a team of villains called the Stockpile.

BLACK WIDOW

When Natalia Romanova waltzed into Tony Stark's life, he was immediately struck by her exotic beauty. But when he faced her later as the Russian spy known as the Black Widow, his Iron Man persona wasn't quite as impressed. Not only did the Black Widow use her charms in an attempt to sabotage Stark Industries, she also seduced the archer Hawkeye into fighting Iron Man on her behalf.

As the years passed, Natalia saw the error of her ways and defected to the West. She soon became a hero and even a full-fledged Avenger, fighting alongside Tony on more than one occasion. The two becoming close friends and allies.

The Black Widow originally operated without a costume, but soon donned an outfit appropriate to her name. It allowed her to shoot projectiles from her wrist and scale flat surfaces.

Trained by some of the world's finest fighters, including the X-Man Wolverine, the Black Widow has been inoculated with a biological enhancement against the ravages of time.

TITANIUM MAN

Soviet fanatic Boris Bullski wasn't the only man to wear the Titanium Man armor, but he was certainly the most dedicated. Towering over his fellow officers at over 7 ft tall, Boris commissioned his heavy Titanium Man armor to impress his superiors. Since the first suit was so bulky, Boris' size and strength made him one of the only men capable of taking the armor into battle against the American foe, Iron Man. In time, a new, much lighter version of the Titanium Man suit was operated by the diminutive mastermind known as the Gremlin. However, Boris would later reclaim his rightful armor in an attempt to revive hardline communist ideology in a country that no longer embraced it.

The sheer power of the Titanium Man armor turned Boris Bullski into one of Iron Man's most formidable opponents.

CRIMSON DYNAMO

The pilots of the Crimson Dynamo armor have ranged from its inventor, Anton Vanko, to Russian teenager Gennady Gavrilov, who stumbled upon a prototype Dynamo helmet and found himself in control of one of the world's most dangerous weapons. Often viewed as an adversary in the US, the Dynamo is a hero to his own people, especially in the hands of its current operator, Dimitri Bukharin. Over the years, the Dynamo has served on various Super Hero teams, including the Soviet Super Soldiers and the current Winter Guard. Now an ally of Iron Man, the Dynamo recently gave his armor to Stark to help him flee from Norman Osborn and his corrupt HAMMER organization.

While wearing his stealth armor, Iron Man tackled the Crimson Dynamo on his home turf in Siberia.

"You forget... before I became the Titanium Man, I was known as Boris the Merciless!"

Titanium Man

DRAGON SEED

During a battle in an ancient valley in China, the Mandarin unwittingly helped unleash an army of dragons upon the world. By combining their powers, Iron Man and the Mandarin were able to defeat the alien creatures, but at the cost of the Mandarin's hands.

CULTURE CLASH

When Iron Man and the Mandarin first met, Iron Man was on a mission for the government. Sent to China on behalf of the peacekeeping agency SHIELD, Iron Man's assignment was to verify the existence of a warlord known as the Mandarin. Iron Man got much more than he bargained for, and was soon locked in a fierce battle with the man who would become his arch foe.

MANDARIN

Royal by birth and empowered by fate, the mysterious Mandarin stumbled upon a cave housing ten alien rings of vast energy—energy he manipulates in his tireless campaign for world conquest.

"There is nothing stronger than the will of the eternal flesh... even your beloved technology is not immune." The Mandarin

RINGS OF POWER

Originally used to power the vast spaceship belonging to a dragon-like alien race, the Mandarin's rings give him a range of incredible abilities. The ring on his left-hand little finger projects an ice blast; the ring on his third finger projects a mento-intensifier that enables him to control his victim's mind; the middle finger ring fires bolts of electricity; the index finger ring shoots fire; and the left thumb ring controls electromagnetic energy. On the Mandarin's right hand, the little finger ring creates a field of absolute darkness; the third finger's ring fires a disintegration beam; the middle finger ring controls a vortex beam that allows the Mandarin to levitate; the index finger ring shoots a beam of sonic force; and the thumb ring is able to change a substance's molecular structure.

ELUSIVE MASTERMIND

The Mandarin's costume and appearance have changed many times over the years since he first came into conflict with Iron Man. They have clashed spectacularly time and time again, but the ingenious villain, even if temporarily defeated, has never been captured for long.

When terrorist Karim Mahwash Najeeb sought out the Mandarin in order to form an alliance with him, the Mandarin refused to acknowledge him. Infuriated, Najeeb ordered his men to kill the aged villain, but it was Najeeb who was murdered.

EVOLUTIONARY PURGE

Freed from his cell and with his ancient rings returned to him, the Mandarin once again returned to his quest for power. After he arranged to have his rings surgically implanted into his spine, the now white-haired warlord created a new identity for himself as Tem Borjigin, CEO of Prometheus Gentech, Inc. In this new position of power, the Mandarin manipulated the brilliant scientist Maya Hansen, an old friend of Tony Stark's, into creating an airborne version of the Extremis virus. The Mandarin planned to unleash this plague in order to force millions of people up the evolutionary ladder, regardless of the cost of billions of innocent lives. When Maya unwittingly informed the government of the Mandarin's plans, Iron Man learned of his archenemy's scheme, and rushed to Borjigin's Nebraska operation.

Forced to face the Mandarin in an outdated model of his armor, Iron Man finally defeated him by savagely ripping the rings out of the Mandarin's spine. Mandarin then exposed himself to the deadly Extremis virus, only to escape later from inside the Extremis cocoon that had formed around his body.

TALES OF #62 SUSPENSE

TALES OF SUSPENSE
featuring
IRON MAN AND **CAPTAIN AMERICA**

MARVEL COMICS GROUP 12¢

62 FEB

APPROVED BY THE COMICS CODE AUTHORITY

"THE ORIGIN OF... THE MANDARIN!"

"BREAK-OUT IN CELL BLOCK TEN!"

ALL-NEW THRILLS WITH TWO OF AMERICA'S GREATEST AVENGERS!!!

"Yes, I walked proud! For I was the Mandarin! The blood of the Khans flowed in my veins! The world would one day be mine!"

THE MANDARIN

MAIN CHARACTERS: Iron Man (Tony Stark); Mandarin
SUPPORTING CHARACTERS: Mandarin's mother; father; aunt; and palace servants; Chinese government officials; villagers; military officers; Axxon-Karr; US military pilots
LOCATIONS: Mandarin's castle; Mandarin's family palace; an unnamed village; the Valley of Spirits; an unnamed military base (all in China)

PUBLICATION DATE
February 1965

EDITOR-IN-CHIEF
Stan Lee

COVER ARTIST
Jack Kirby and Vince Colletta

WRITER
Stan Lee

PENCILER
Don Heck

INKER
Dick Ayers

LETTERER
Sam Rosen

BACKGROUND

Tony Stark was in danger of losing the spotlight. When *Tales of Suspense* once again shifted formats with issue 59, the feature-length stories Iron Man was enjoying once again shrank to mere 13-page tales. It seemed that Captain America, the recently restored icon from the days of World War II, was starting to step on the Golden Avenger's toes by sharing his hard-earned title with him. But what fan could argue with two top-tier characters for the price of one?

And it was those self-same fans who would be instrumental in bringing about the landmark 62nd issue of *Tales*. With few villains making repeat appearances in Iron Man's early comics, there was little doubt that the mysterious Mandarin had claimed the role of Iron Man's arch enemy. As a result, fans were growing curious as to the origin of this exotic, enigmatic foe, and wrote in requesting information about the villain's origin. After a reported 500 fans demanded the character's back-story, Stan Lee and company finally gave in and the rest was history. For the Mandarin, at least.

The Story...

When captured by the Mandarin, Iron Man is told the tale of his arch foe's origin before escaping his bonds and preventing the start of what just might have been World War III.

Everyone thought Tony Stark was dead. And it was a fair assumption, considering that a powerful ray of unknown origin had struck his bedroom, reducing it to little more than rubble. The firefighters on the scene were convinced. If Stark was in his room at the time of the blast, he was gone, plain and simple. No human being could walk away from an attack like that. But then again, most human beings don't have an Iron Man suit...

While Tony's friends mourned and the media obsessed, Iron Man flew to China. He recognized the handiwork of the Mandarin and knew exactly where to find his old foe. After all, the location of the villain's castle was common knowledge and it was accessible to anyone foolish enough to step through its ancient doors. Foolish, because those unlucky individuals would have to deal with a variety of advanced weapon systems, including Koto, Mandarin's giant security robot.

Caught unaware by the mammoth automaton, Iron Man was knocked unconscious and dragged before the Mandarin. When he awoke, he found himself bound with titanium cords to a large wheel **(1)**. The Mandarin planned to spin the metal saucer at such high speeds that Iron Man would lose consciousness and die, despite the protection that his suit of armor gave him. However, the Mandarin couldn't help himself. He had his greatest enemy at his mercy, and he wanted the moment to last. So he decided to tell a story: the tale of his own mysterious past.

The Mandarin was born into a wealthy family that traced its lineage back to Genghis Khan himself. Orphaned at an early age, the Mandarin was raised by his aunt, who taught him the sciences, warfare, and the ways of royalty. Years passed, and as the Mandarin grew into a man, his family's wealth was depleted. Thrown out of his home by his country's government **(2)**, the Mandarin embarked on a focused quest to find his destiny, hardly even noticing the death of his only aunt. Soon the Mandarin's journey led him to a secret cave in the foreboding Valley of Spirits. There he not only discovered the remains of what appeared to be a dragon, but also an enormous alien spacecraft **(3)**. It seemed that the dragon was a survivor of interstellar travel, who had crash-landed on Earth only to be feared and hunted by its denizens. The alien had powered its awe-inspiring ship with ten ring-like devices **(4)** of almost unimaginable power. Mastering these ingenious rings, the Mandarin easily reclaimed his long-lost family fortune and stature.

"...the wheel... will never stop until Iron Man breathes no more."

With his story told and his boasting at a close, the Mandarin left Iron Man to his fate, starting the large wheel in its spin before his departure **(5)**. The villain had other business after all. He'd arranged for the Chinese government to fire a missile that would unwittingly strike Formosa, and trigger a chain of events that would result in a third world war. The missile was to be fired soon, and the Mandarin had to be on site to make sure everything went according to plan.

But there was one thing he hadn't accounted for. The Mandarin's story had given Iron Man enough time to charge his suit and break free of his bonds **(6)**. And just as the Chinese officials fired their rocket, Iron Man arrived at the scene, clamping himself onto the speeding projectile **(7)** and reversing its course back in the direction of the launch site.

Catching up to the fleeing Mandarin, Iron Man attacked his enemy, and the two engaged in a fierce battle **(8)**. Finally, the Mandarin cast a beam of pure darkness with one of his rings, blinding Iron Man momentarily. Using the time to his advantage, the Mandarin fled to the safety of his castle walls, forcing Iron Man to return to America, once again empty-handed **(9)**.

Her family's legacy of crime cost Whitney Frost her beauty and her sanity. But it was Tony Stark who stole away her heart.

WHITNEY FROST

She was a typical party girl. Born into money, Whitney Frost grew up spoiled, both by her adoptive father, Byron Frost, and later by her fiancé, lawyer Roger Vane. But when Byron died, Whitney discovered that she was actually the daughter of renowned gang boss and Avenger foe Count Luchino Nefaria. When Nefaria introduced himself in order to coerce his daughter into a life of crime, Whitney rushed to Vane's side for support, but found he was more concerned with his own image than the wellbeing of his fiancée.

When Vane chose to abandon Whitney, she reluctantly decided to follow in her father's footsteps.

Whitney plunged into a life of crime as gang boss Big M, to please her father, Count Nefaria.

Whitney Frost could never outrun the social stigma of her parentage.

BECOMING MASQUE

Whitney's main problem was that she always followed her heart. As the mysterious criminal leader Big M, Masque began to run an illegal seagoing gambling operation, and took on longtime Iron Man foe Whiplash as hired help. She then set her sights a bit higher, attempting to steal Tony Stark's weapons technology, and began to date Jasper Sitwell, a SHIELD agent assigned to Stark Industries. Hoping to acquire national security secrets, Frost instead developed romantic feelings for Sitwell. Her emotions got in the way of business, and soon Frost was forced to flee Stark Industries, crashing her escape craft in the process. Although she was pulled from the wreckage by crime boss Mordecai Midas's men, Whitney's face bore horrific scars, the terrible price for her actions. How could she look the world in the face again?

MIND SWAP

After her father seemingly perished during a skirmish with Iron Man, Whitney became a recluse, and hid away from society. She even developed bio-duplicate clones of herself to continue her criminal activities. One of her corrupt doubles teamed with Stark's adversary Obadiah Stane. Using the advanced technology of Dr. Theron Atlanta, Masque's clone switched minds with Tony's former lover Bethany Cabe. As Cabe, the Masque clone set out to assassinate Stark, but was stopped by the real Bethany, who was now trapped in Masque's disfigured form. Tony eventually switched the two women back into their proper bodies, but didn't realize that the clone wasn't Masque herself. Whitney would go on to use more bio-duplicates of herself in the future, including a rogue version (called simply Masque) that rejected her evil programming and aided Tony Stark and the Avengers.

Bethany struggled valiantly against the mind swap, but the technology won.

MASQUE & TONY

Mordecai Midas was obsessed with gold. So it made sense that when Frost began to work for him, she covered her disfigurement with a golden mask. Now calling herself Madame Masque, Frost set her sights on unfinished business, and Tony Stark in particular. However, Whitney's gentle heart overshadowed her ill intent once again. She became infatuated with Tony, after he showed her kindness and encouraged her to look beyond her facial scars. No longer loyal to Midas, Madame Masque helped Iron Man defeat her former boss. Later, Whitney and Tony even embarked on a full-fledged romance. Their love affair came to a dramatic end when she betrayed Tony by helping her father in a scheme to pilfer Stark technology.

Tony and Whitney became lovers, despite her scars. Tony even revealed his secret life to her.

A risk-taker all his life, Tony Stark has always been attracted to troubled women like Madame Masque.

DARK REIGN

Madame Masque reemerged in the public eye when she began a romantic relationship with the Hood, a crime boss intent on uniting the Super Villain community into a vast underground network. When the Hood joined forces with Norman Osborn, formerly the villain Green Goblin and the current head of the government organization HAMMER, Madame Masque began to work directly with Osborn. With such close ties to Iron Man, Masque was Osborn's first choice to kill the hero when Stark opposed HAMMER's new regime. Although the bounty of a billion euros hugely appealed to Masque, her grudge with Tony was personal. She successfully captured Stark and Pepper Potts, but Frost allowed her feelings to get the better of her. Still madly in love with Tony, Masque lashed out and caused an explosion that gave Tony and Pepper an opportunity to escape.

S.H.I.E.L.D

As one of its founders, Iron Man has a vested interest in the affairs of the Strategic Hazard Intervention Espionage Logistics Directorate.

The mammoth SHIELD helicarrier has a commanding presence, even to Iron Man, one of the vehicle's original designers.

EARLY YEARS

SHIELD, the world's leading peacekeeping organization, was originally an acronym for Supreme Headquarters International Espionage Law-Enforcement Division. As the government's largest weapons contractor back in those early days, Tony Stark had a hand in SHIELD's formation from the very beginning. He helped design their main headquarters' helicarrier, Life Model Decoy androids, and flying cars. Stark was even assigned a direct SHIELD liaison, Jasper Sitwell.

Although unwanted at first, Sitwell soon proved his worth in the fray with Iron Man.

NICK FURY

The greatest director in SHIELD history, Nick Fury used his military background and street smarts to lead many successful missions against megalomaniacs like the Yellow Claw and Baron von Strucker. He was ousted, however, when a black-ops mission led to an attack on Manhattan.

OVERBOARD

The world was changing, and so was Tony Stark. No longer wishing to manufacture weapons for the US government or anyone else, Tony switched his company's focus towards the field of electronics. So when the villain Spymaster attacked Stark, using technology Tony had developed for SHIELD years earlier, Stark was naturally suspicious. Paying a visit to the helicarrier, Stark was ambushed and thrown off by a rogue SHIELD faction. The attempt on Tony's life was just part of a plan to gain a controlling interest in Stark International and unlimited access to Tony's arsenal of advanced weaponry.

Luckily, Tony was able to change in midair and fly safely back to the helicarrier as Iron Man.

SHIELD radical Buck Richlen attempted to defeat Iron Man by threatening Nick Fury's life. In the end, all he achieved for his pains was an extended stay in prison.

ARMOR WARS

When Tony Stark was on a mission to destroy all of his old technology that had worked its way into other people's hands (see pp. 110–1), the Mandroid armors he had created for SHIELD were high on his list. So when Nick Fury asked Stark for help trapping his "bodyguard" Iron Man, who appeared to have gone rogue, Tony was happy to comply. Knowing SHIELD's plans to stop Iron Man in advance, Tony was then able to draw the Mandroids out and fry their circuits before they knew what hit them.

The last Mandroid ejected before Iron Man could attack.

Although they've been at odds over the years, Nick Fury and Iron Man have nothing but the utmost respect for one another.

THE
1970s

It was an era that established Iron Man as an icon, and invested the character of Tony Stark with a depth rarely seen in comic books.

The decade began with Iron Man giving up his super heroic identity, and ended with him nearly giving up on life itself. With the relative security of a successful monthly title, the Marvel staff, namely writer Archie Goodwin and artist George Tuska, decided to throw their audience a curveball and have Iron Man retire from his life of fighting crime. Worried about his health, Tony passed on his mantle to boxer Eddie March. However, Eddie would carry on Tony's legacy for only a few issues before his own medical complications brought the rightful Iron Man back to his super heroic life.

And for Earth's sake it was probably just as well that Tony had returned. Because the Avengers were soon entangled in the alien conflict that famously became known as the Kree/Skrull War. In a story of epic proportions that paved the way for the giant crossover events of years to come, Iron Man defended the planet with the help of the Avengers and the imagination of their teenage sidekick, Rick Jones.

While the 1970s saw Iron Man's title hit its landmark 100th issue, and the debut of Tony's close friend and pilot Jim Rhodes some 18 issues later, perhaps the most historic contribution to the Iron Man story came from writer David Michelinie and artist Bob Layton in 1979. A partnership that ushered in what is still regarded by many fans as Iron Man's heyday, Michelinie and Layton introduced Tony to the most deadly foe to ever plague his existence: alcohol. In one fell swoop, Iron Man went from being a cookie-cutter playboy hero, to a tortured man with flaws and personal demons.

OVERLEAF *Invincible Iron Man* *#33*: The first appearance of a string of villains to call themselves Spymaster, this issue saw the villain unleash a scheme to kidnap Tony Stark.

Armor Malfunction

For Tony Stark, nothing seemed to be working smoothly. Not only were his former allies at the government agency SHIELD trying to stage a hostile takeover of Stark International, but his Iron Man suit was malfunctioning: activating his jet boosters at an inopportune moment and, on another occasion, failing to seal airtight while underwater.

Unable to deduce the reasons for his suit's recent glitches, Tony decided to forget his troubles by heading off to Atlantic City with his new girlfriend Bethany Cabe and a few bottles of champagne. But even away from his duties at Stark International, trouble still plagued Tony, in the form of Iron Man's old foes Blizzard, Whiplash, and the Melter.

DEMON IN A BOTTLE

The stress of the boardroom and the battlefield were mounting, but Tony Stark's real troubles were only just beginning.

Tony Stark: Murderer!

Unable to unwind, even on vacation, Tony returned to Stark International after besting the villains with a little help from Bethany. Finding himself unable to concentrate on design work—which he usually found relaxing—Tony poured himself a drink. He then headed off to meet Ambassador Kotznin as Iron Man in a televised ceremony. But when he greeted the dignitary on stage, Iron Man's repulsor beam suddenly went off, instantly killing the official.

The Hunt Begins

With his Iron Man suit commandeered by police, Tony returned to work, and to the bottle, drinking more now than ever. But despite it all, Tony refused to acknowledge defeat. Instead, he visited Avengers Mansion and began a rigorous training program with Captain America, in order to learn unarmed fighting techniques. He then set out with his best friend, pilot Jim Rhodes, to track down a man Whiplash had mentioned during his attack at the casino. A man known only as Hammer (right).

Fall of the Hammer

Landing in Monaco, Stark and Rhodey stumbled upon a band of Hammer's mercenaries out for blood. Taken captive despite Captain America's training, Tony found himself a prisoner on board Justin Hammer's floating island headquarters. The unscrupulous millionaire industrialist just happened to be a major business competitor of Tony Stark's. Hammer had been manipulating Tony's life, aiming to push his rival over the edge. He had even gone so far as to hack into Iron Man's controls and kill Ambassador Kotznin. Escaping from his cell, Tony changed into a spare Iron Man suit and, with the help of Bethany and Rhodey, managed to sink Hammer's island for good.

"Can't you see? You're becoming your own worst enemy! And you're trying to kill that enemy with a bottle..."
Bethany Cabe

Rehabilitation

With the resignation of his longtime butler Jarvis eating away at him, Tony began to drink more and more, even endangering innocent lives while piloting his Iron Man suit intoxicated. Thankfully for Tony, he had his own protector in the form of Bethany Cabe. Not wanting to see her current love end up like her late husband, Bethany stayed with Tony to help him battle his addiction. And Tony Stark proved worthy of her investment as he not only kicked his drinking habit and convinced Jarvis to return to his employ, but he also gained a new lease of life, determined to face it one day at a time.

IRON MAN #128

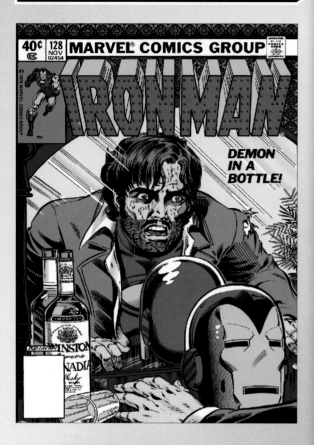

40¢ 128 NOV 02454
MARVEL COMICS GROUP
IRON MAN
DEMON IN A BOTTLE!

PUBLICATION DATE
November 1979

EDITOR-IN-CHIEF
Jim Shooter

COVER ARTIST
Bob Layton

WRITER/PLOTTER
David Michelinie

PENCILER
John Romita Jr.

FINISHED ART/PLOTTER
Bob Layton

COLORIST
Bob Sharen

LETTERER
John Costanza

"I feel like I've just taken life's best shot, and I'm still standing. And somehow, my other problems don't seem so tough anymore."
TONY STARK

MAIN CHARACTERS: Iron Man (Tony Stark); Bethany Cabe; Edwin Jarvis
SUPPORTING CHARACTERS: Alexander Van Tilberg; Mrs. Whiggins; Mr. Benchley
LOCATIONS: Stark International; a railroad crash site (both Long Island, New York); a social gala; Alexander Van Tilberg's home and office; Avengers Mansion; Rockefeller Plaza (all New York City)

BACKGROUND

David Michelinie and Bob Layton had just put Tony Stark through the proverbial wringer, and the fans loved them for it. Alongside artist John Romita Jr., the plotting team of Michelinie and Layton had introduced a string of characters and a creative direction that remains one of the high points of Iron Man's lengthy career. With new supporting characters such as pilot Jim Rhodes and complex love interest Bethany Cabe helping to flesh out Stark's social circle, and the machinations of crime boss Justin Hammer, Iron Man's world had never been richer. In a few months, Tony Stark had battled the Sub-Mariner, been framed for murder, undergone training by Captain America, and fought a virtual who's who of second and third tier rogues.

But Michelinie and Layton were just getting started. Looming behind the scenes was Tony's increasing reliance on alcohol. He was reaching a crossroads, and his inner turmoil would lead to one of the most eye-opening and topical comic books of its day.

The Story...

As Tony Stark's alcoholism begins to interfere with his duties as Iron Man, the hero is forced to confront his addiction with the help of his loving girlfriend, Bethany Cabe.

Tony Stark's life had reached a new low. One of his oldest allies, the government agency known as SHIELD, was attempting a hostile takeover of Stark International. Only a few measly shares kept Stark's lifework from slipping through his fingers and into the hands of the government. To make matters worse, in his other identity as Iron Man, Tony had been framed for murder, forced to kill an innocent diplomat with his own iron hands when remotely controlled by corrupt businessman Justin Hammer. With the stress of his troubles building up to new levels, and a man's life on his conscience, Tony had begun to rely on alcohol to help relieve the extreme tensions in his life **(1)**. And this new dependency in turn caused the resignation of his longtime servant Edwin Jarvis, driving Tony even further into the bottle. Tony Stark's life needed a drastic change, but unfortunately for him, Tony hadn't realized this yet.

Blaming all his troubles on his civilian life, the fairly intoxicated Stark decided to don his armor and give his Iron Man persona a chance to shine. But that wouldn't be quite the case. Instead, he quite literally flew through his office window **(2)** before flying a slightly erratic path to the tracks of a nearby wreck on the Long Island Railroad **(3)**. There, in an attempt to help the rescue workers, Iron Man's carelessness accidentally resulted in a gas tanker springing a leak **(4)**, forcing a massive evacuation. Even as Iron Man, Tony Stark was a failure **(5)**.

Tony returned home to his plush penthouse, and to his familiar glass-topped bar. But as he poured himself a drink, Tony Stark felt a hand on his arm **(6)**, the hand of Bethany Cabe, Tony's new girlfriend. She had seen the signs, and knew Tony needed help, even if *he* didn't realize it. Bethany had seen it all before: her late husband, Alexander Van Tilberg, had let the pressures of his job as a foreign ambassador turn him into an addict. He relied on pills to keep him awake, put him to sleep, or just help him escape. One fateful night, those same pills had seemingly caused him to lose control of his car and drive it off a bridge. So Bethany told Tony the story of her husband, and Tony Stark finally admitted that he truly needed help.

For the next few days and nights, Bethany stayed by Tony's side. Through his emotional outbursts, fits of rage and frustration, Bethany stuck with him, until Tony felt he was ready to regain control of his life. And his first step toward that goal, was persuading his faithful butler, Jarvis, to return to his service.

After a bit of convincing, Jarvis agreed to stay on at Avengers Mansion, but there was one complication. Jarvis had recently experienced some financial problems and had sold his two shares in Stark International to Mr. Benchley, a loan shark out to make a quick buck. Taking action as Iron Man, Tony flew to Benchley's Rockefeller Plaza office **(7)** and attempted to buy back Jarvis's shares, only to discover that SHIELD had beat him to the punch, and was now the majority shareholder of Tony's company.

Defeated once more, Tony returned home and once again, went straight to his bar **(8)**. But as he was about to pour a glass of whiskey, he stopped himself. He realized that his relationship with Bethany and a life without alcohol were what he truly desired. He put the cap back on the bottle **(9)**. And set out once again to win his life back **(10)**.

"I'm going to keep on fighting, to get Stark International... back in my hands."

The Secretive Schemer

It was just business to Justin Hammer. The owner of Hammer Industries, the company behind dozens of smaller subsidiaries and front operations, Hammer was wealthy beyond most people's dreams, but he wanted more. Operating from a secret floating villa in the Mediterranean, Hammer targeted Stark Industries. He believed that Stark was taking business from his various companies, so he hatched an elaborate plan to ensure that Stark Industries' reputation was ruined.

Hiring technician Phillip Barnett to hack into Iron Man's system, Hammer successfully framed the hero for the murder of the ambassador to the nation of Carnelia. The police impounded Iron Man's armor, Tony Stark began to drink heavily, and Hammer hijacked Stark's pending deal with the Carnelian government. When Tony began to investigate Hammer's holdings, the corrupt businessman had him kidnapped and brought to his mobile island stronghold.

Hammer had no qualms about revealing his plans to Tony Stark. He was more interested in the mysterious contents of Stark's briefcase.

After Justin Hammer kidnapped Tony, he prepared living quarters for him. But what Hammer hadn't aniticpated was that his prisoner had been trained in unarmed combat by Captain America.

Tony Stark had never heard of the business mogul, but Justin Hammer would be a name he would never forget.

JUSTIN HAMMER

Beating the Super-Army

Tony Stark managed to escape his plush cell and retrieve his trademark briefcase. Changing into his spare Iron Man armor in the nick of time, Tony was attacked by dozens of costumed criminals. One of Hammer's most lucrative businesses was to supply villains with advanced technology in exchange for a cut of the spoils from their criminal endeavors. Despite facing a small army of these super-soldiers, Stark managed to sink Hammer's island base and escape with Phillip Barnett, who could prove Iron Man's innocence.

Diagnosed with a terminal illness, Hammer was forced to live out his final years on a space station. The null-gravity environment slowed down his disease.

Breaking the Silence

Despite Tony's best efforts, Justin Hammer did manage to get his hand on Stark International. After Tony's company had fallen under the contro of Obadiah Stane and Tony had mov on to form a new company, Stane killed himself during a battle with Iron Man. Instead of reacquiring Stane International, Tony had distanced him from his former corporation, giving Hammer the opportunity to swoop. Hammer then used Stane's holdings to frame Tony for industrial negligenc tricking the armored avengers know the Masters of Silence into attemptin to assassinate Stark. Turning the tab on his old enemy, Stark convinced the Masters of Silence that Hammer was guilty and, leading his new allies into battle in his War Machine armor stormed his adversary's stronghold.

With the Masters of Silence looming over him, Hammer agreed to sell Stane International back to Stark for the sum of one dollar.

Bad Blood

Justin Hammer was dying, and he planned to take Tony Stark with him. Utilizing the weightless environment of his space satellite home to prolong his life, Hammer decided to lash out at Tony from a distance. Hiring the second Spymaster to aid him in his scheme, Hammer had Stark injected with rogue cells that would later alter his personality and cause him to experience fits of cruel rage. Tony was saved by his old friend Jim Rhodes and, as Iron Man, invaded Hammer's space station. But Hammer was one step ahead of him; he captured Stark with the help of technology he had cunningly purchased earlier from Tony when his mind had been disturbed.

Hammer took a break fr reveling in his momenta victory over Iron Man i to blow up the escape c his lackey, Phillip Barne

The subsequent explosio combined with Iron Man' escape, knocked Hammer his swimming pool into s seemingly freezing the vi for all eternity.

DOCTOR DOOM

A scientific genius who uses his incredible intelligence for personal gain and conquest, Victor von Doom serves as a corrupt version of Iron Man, complete with a suit of armor that rivals even Tony Stark's technology.

Venom Bomb

When a fluke of technology unleashed a plague of alien symbiote organisms on New York City, Iron Man traced the creatures' origins back to Latveria. He realized that this infestation of shape-shifting monsters was the result of a "Venom bomb" devised by Dr. Doom himself. Leading his team of Mighty Avengers to Doom's castle, Iron Man and Dr. Doom were once again accidentally transported through time during the chaos of the battle. Returning to the present, Iron Man managed the near impossible: with the help of a powerful ally, the Sentry, he finally arrested Dr. Doom.

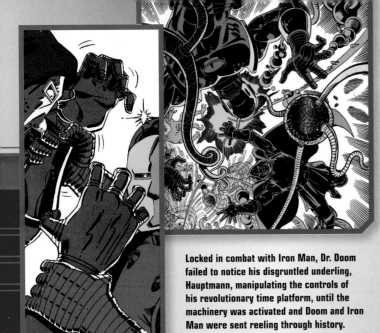

Doomquest

It was supposed to be just your average everyday clash with a Super Villain. But when Iron Man flew to Dr. Doom's home in Latveria in order to reclaim some stolen Stark International equipment, the two found themselves transported back in time to the land of ancient Britain. Arriving in Camelot during the time of King Arthur and his Knights of the Round Table, Dr. Doom immediately sought out the evil sorceress Morgan le Fay, hoping to learn her mystic secrets. Brokering a deal with the scheming witch, Doom led an army of the undead against Arthur and Iron Man, only to be defeated when Iron Man took the fight to Morgan's home and bested the sorceress, forcing her to retreat to a different dimension.

Locked in combat with Iron Man, Dr. Doom failed to notice his disgruntled underling, Hauptmann, manipulating the controls of his revolutionary time platform, until the machinery was activated and Doom and Iron Man were sent reeling through history.

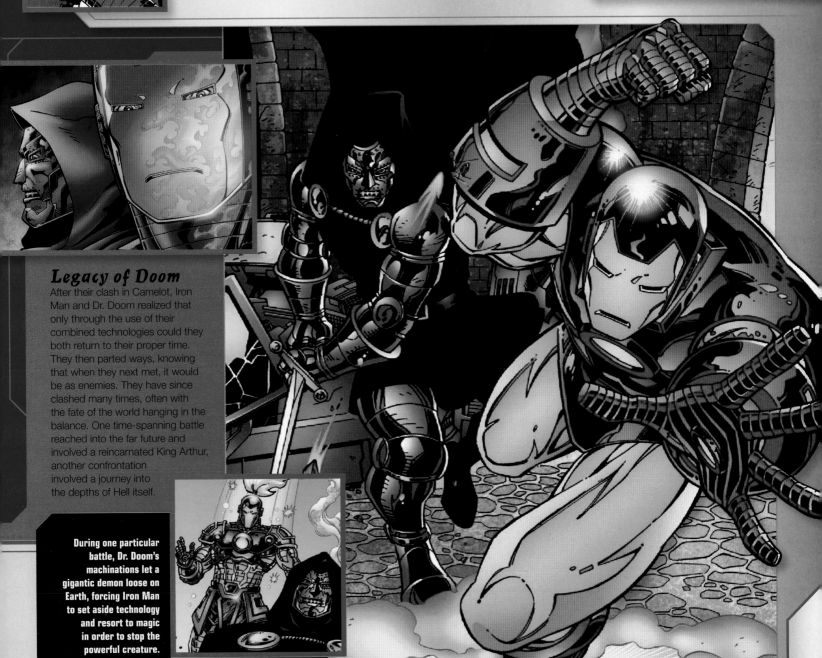

Legacy of Doom

After their clash in Camelot, Iron Man and Dr. Doom realized that only through the use of their combined technologies could they both return to their proper time. They then parted ways, knowing that when they next met, it would be as enemies. They have since clashed many times, often with the fate of the world hanging in the balance. One time-spanning battle reached into the far future and involved a reincarnated King Arthur, another confrontation involved a journey into the depths of Hell itself.

During one particular battle, Dr. Doom's machinations let a gigantic demon loose on Earth, forcing Iron Man to set aside technology and resort to magic in order to stop the powerful creature.

THE 1980s

The face of comics was changing, but Iron Man, no stranger to evolution, was one step ahead of the pack.

The 1980s began in familiar territory, but they would end in uncharted waters. Little by little, comics were beginning to grow up. Mature themes were creeping into the daily struggles of Super Heroes and their respective villains. Conventions such as thought balloons and heavily-narrated caption boxes were slowly disappearing, and threat levels were being raised. However *Iron Man*, a comic book that had already dealt with the issue of alcoholism and the ethics of weapons manufacturing, continued to push the boundaries by taking an even harder look at subjects it had only touched upon earlier.

Writer Dennis O'Neil threw Tony back into alcohol addiction and this time offered him no easy outs. In a radical move for the time, O'Neil actually replaced the Golden Avenger on a permanent basis. Jim Rhodes became the new Iron Man, while Tony wasted his life away at the bottom of a bottle. Fans were hooked, and while they argued on letters pages and at comic book conventions about who deserved to wear the mantle of Iron Man, other industry professionals took note. In the following decade, similar "replacement" storylines would be attempted with almost every major comic-book character, including Superman, Batman, Spider-Man, and Wonder Woman.

By the end of the 1980s, the birth of the comic book store and the limited mini series changed the face of the comic industry, allowing for finer print quality and direct distribution. Comics were heading towards a burst of popularity, and Iron Man was preparing to branch out.

OVERLEAF *Iron Man #200*: Even Iron Man's friends in the West Coast Avengers were impressed by his silver centurion suit, just one of many different armors Tony wore in the 1980s.

BEGINNING-- A NEW ERA!

A DEADLY GAME

Obadiah Stane was an eccentric millionaire who viewed the world of business as if it were an elaborate chess match—a match he was determined to win. Stane had set his sights on destroying Stark International. Using his gang of super-powered henchmen, known as the Chessmen, to draw Iron Man out to his munitions base in Utah, Stane forced the hero to run a gauntlet of deadly technological traps. He then met Iron Man face to face. Stane claimed that he had been creating an alliance of the world's elite "movers and shakers" in order to bring order to some of the more chaotic parts of the world. Stark International had opposed his unscrupulous business dealings at every turn. As a result, Stane had been forced into action, sabotaging Stark's plants and orchestrating attacks on Iron Man. Now able to put a face to his pain, but with no hard proof of Stane's illegal activities, Tony departed the villain's factory. All the time he was secretly yearning for the escape from reality that life as an alcoholic had once given him.

With his best friend Jim Rhodes missing and his company losing valuable contracts to Obadiah Stane's European outfits, Tony Stark was finding it hard to resist a growing desire to turn to drink once again.

ALCOHOL RELAPSE

Years ago, Tony Stark had fought his way out from the bottom of a bottle. Now, thanks to the cruel machinations of Obadiah Stane, he found himself right back where he started...

AN EMPTY SHELL...

OFF THE WAGON

The mighty had fallen yet again. Obadiah Stane's devious chess game had taken its toll on Tony's state of mind, and he'd ended up just where the scheming villain had wanted him to be: with a drink in his shaking hand. Tony's first bender led to a pointless and violent conflict with the misunderstood hero Machine Man. Tony couldn't conquer his demons and instead of addressing his company's current financial plight, he hid himself away in his Manhattan penthouse with a few bottles of his favorite poison for company.

Stane didn't just want to defeat his business rival. No, Stane's endgame was nothing less than the complete humiliation of Tony Stark.

A MOMENT OF WEAKNESS

Pushed beyond endurance, Tony traveled to Switzerland in an attempt to organize more opposition to Stane's financial scheming. He found himself facing a boardroom of brainwashed yes men, and another violent attack by Stane's Chessmen. With nowhere left to turn, Tony hit the bottle once more.

"WHO DID THIS TO ME? WHO PUT THIS... TEMPTATION HERE?"

Indries Moomji was the straw that broke the camel's back. Secretly employed by Stane, Indries won Tony's affections, and then broke his heart when he was at his lowest point.

THE DESCENT

Tony Stark was at the end of his tether, but Obadiah Stane wasn't going to let up now. Brokenhearted and defeated, for Tony one night of drinking bled into the next. Even the safe return home of his friend Jim Rhodes did little to lift Tony out of his self-imposed funk. Tony's drinking was becoming so severe that he began to have trouble piloting the Iron Man suit. When circumstances forced Rhodey to wear the armor into battle on one occasion, Tony barely noticed that another man was taking over the role he'd previously protected with his life. Tony Stark was just a shadow of the man he used to be, and the real problem was, he didn't seem to care.

As Jim Rhodes took over the Iron Man identity on a more regular basis, Tony began to surround himself with enablers, other rich socialites who saw nothing unusual in choosing to escape the perceived pressures of their pampered lives with drugs or alcohol. But soon Tony's drinking became too much even by his new peers' standards, and the former idol of millions was reduced to little more than a drunken beggar wandering the streets of Manhattan. Tony Stark had truly hit rock bottom, and only he could claw himself out of the hole he had dug for himself.

IRON MAN #182

PUBLICATION DATE
May 1984

EDITOR-IN-CHIEF
Jim Shooter

COVER ARTIST
Luke McDonnell and Steve Mitchell

WRITER
Denny O'Neil

PENCILER
Luke McDonnell

INKER
Steve Mitchell

COLORIST
Bob Sharen

> "What *am* I celebrating? A very, very good question. If I had to give an answer, I'd say... I'd say I'm celebrating the end. The living end. The end of living."
>
> TONY STARK

MAIN CHARACTERS: Tony Stark; Gretl Anders; Timothy Anders; Iron Man (Jim Rhodes)
SUPPORTING CHARACTERS: New York City police; Thor; Captain America; Hawkeye; Captain Marvel; Morely Erwin
LOCATIONS: A pawnshop, St. Vincent's Hospital; a graveyard, Central Park; Morely Erwins' apartment (all New York City)

BACKGROUND

By the mid-1980s, Dennis O'Neil was a prominent figure in the comic writing world. He had helped bring DC Comics' Batman back to his dark roots in the 1970s, and had achieved great acclaim for his mature storytelling and subject matter in a medium still primarily targeted towards youth.

When O'Neil took over writing *Iron Man* for a lengthy run of nearly 50 issues, it came as no surprise to readers that he threw Tony Stark's world on its end. Through the machinations of a new villain, Obadiah Stane, O'Neil reduced Stark once again to a desperate alcoholic, showcasing the gritty reality behind his disease. And this time there would be no easy out for Tony Stark...

After O'Neil's groundbreaking story, which culminated in issue #182, Stark would find it impossible to shelve his lingering addiction, and would live out his life haunted by his past weaknesses and failures.

The Story...

Reduced to little more than a homeless derelict, Tony Stark trudges through the streets of New York City in a snowstorm, forced to either succumb to his inner demons or rise above them.

It was one of the worst blizzards New York City had ever seen, and Tony Stark was caught right in the middle of it. With only a thin coat and a swig of alcohol in his belly to keep him warm, Tony's life had been reduced to a pathetic mantra: find Gretl. She was his drinking partner and his only friend since he had begun to live on the streets. Plus she was nine months pregnant and probably caught in the same storm he was. He had to find her. But as he drained the last drop from his bottle **(1)**, Tony realized that he also had to find another drink.

Wandering into a rather unwelcoming pawnshop, Tony traded his coat for a mere ten dollars **(2)**. He went back out into the snow, walking past a cheap hotel in favor of ducking into the nearest liquor store **(3)**. There he spent his last few dollars and headed out into the cold, content to lean up against a nearby building and die. And that's when Gretl found him. And she was ready to have her baby.

Tony's first thought was to get his friend to a hospital. But it was too far away, and the storm was too fierce. Instead the two ducked into a nearby doorway, and huddled together for warmth **(4)**. As Tony continued to drink, Gretl began to go into labor, finally giving birth to a baby boy **(5)**. But the pain and the cold proved too much for the frail woman. As Tony warmed her child inside his suit jacket, Gretl died in his arms.

Tony probably would have died too if the police hadn't wandered by the next morning, finding him still huddled in the doorway, holding the still-breathing child **(6)**. Both Tony and the infant were taken to nearby St. Vincent's hospital. Gretl was buried, just another forgotten casualty of the New York City streets.

A few hours later in Central Park, a strange structure seemingly appeared out of nowhere. Suddenly, from inside it, a parade of costumed heroes emptied out onto the earth below **(7)**, happy to be touching familiar soil once more. From Captain America to Hawkeye to Iron Man himself, the heroes departed the strange vessel and went their separate ways, their adventure on the planet known as Battleworld finally at a close. As Iron Man, in the person of Jim Rhodes, was still fairly new to the Super Hero game, he had brought back a souvenir: a newly augmented suit of advanced armor. Testing his new suit's firepower on a nearby hill **(8)**, Rhodey realized that the armor was much too powerful, and decided to pay a visit to his technical advisor, Morley Erwin.

After learning from Erwin that Tony Stark was hospitalized earlier that day, Rhodey flew to St. Vincent's to pay his old friend a visit. As the new Iron Man loomed over the injured body of his predecessor **(9)**, Tony awoke, telling Rhodey that he had come to an epiphany, and he was finally ready to straighten out his situation. Seeing firsthand how precious life truly was, Tony was determined to end his nightmare. He was ready to start his life over, even if he wasn't quite prepared to don the Iron Man armor again.

A day passed, and then a week. Tony Stark was released from the hospital. He walked down the city streets with a new outlook on life, at a crossroads that could take him virtually anywhere he wished to go **(10)**.

> "I'd say I'm celebrating the end. The living end. The end of living."

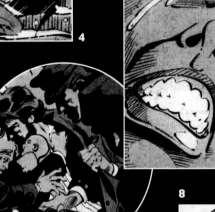

Tony Stark needed help. And Jim Rhodes always came through in a crisis, no matter what. Even if it meant becoming the next Iron Man...

PASSING THE TORCH

Obadiah Stane had finally won. After launching a meticulously calculated assault on Tony Stark, Obadiah had reduced his business rival to an incoherent drunk. To make matters worse, a minor-league villain named Magma hatched a revenge plot against Iron Man by attacking Stark Industries. After learning that his longtime friend and employer led a double life as Iron Man, James Rhodes looked on as Tony began drinking heavily instead of combating the intruding villain. With innocent lives in danger and Stark intoxicated and unconscious, Rhodey had no choice but to strip Tony of his Iron Man suit, and don the armor himself.

"I CAN'T HANDLE IT ANYMORE! YOU BE IRON MAN!"

Tony Stark

With the help of Stark International scientist Morley Erwin, Rhodey figured out how to pilot the Iron Man armor.

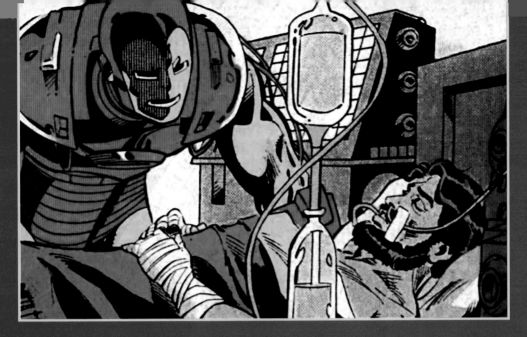

STAYING IN CHARACTER

Jim Rhodes was starting to get the hang of being Iron Man. While Stark ignored all his friends' advice and continued down his personal road to alcoholic ruin, Rhodey was battling the likes of Thunderball, Firebrand, and the Mandarin in his best attempt to fill in for his friend. When Tony finally realized the error of his ways and got back on the wagon, he decided to let Rhodey keep the armor. Tony decided he had to concentrate on his recovery before he added any more pressures to his already stress-filled life.

"HE WANTS TO BE IRON MAN AGAIN. I WILL NOT LET HIM!"
James Rhodes

RHODEY'S HEADACHES

Although Jim Rhodes had grown to enjoy being Iron Man, he didn't realize that the armor didn't feel the same way about him. Tuned to Tony Stark's specific brainwaves, the Iron Man helmet started to give Rhodey headaches. Soon, Rhodey began to experience sudden mood swings and fits of rage. When Tony, along with Morley Erwin and his sister Clytemnestra, moved to California to start up a new electronics company called Circuits

Maximus, Rhodey accompanied them, nursing both a sore head and a chip on his shoulder. That chip would grow bigger when Rhodey discovered that Tony was working on a brand new set of Iron Man armor.

IRON MAN VERSUS IRON MAN

After weeks of watching his friend's personality change for the worse, Tony realized he could not stand idly by and wait for Rhodey to snap. He constructed a suit of recovery armor. When an enraged Rhodey went into battle with the villain Vibro, Tony was forced to don this new gray armor and confront his best friend. Later, Rhodey discovered that the Iron Man helmet was the root of his problems, and Tony altered its frequency. Rhodey resumed Iron Man duties until Tony was finally ready to reclaim his mantle.

SECRET WARS

Drawn across the universe to a barren planet, Iron Man found himself locked in gladiatorial-like combat with a gallery of deadly foes.

While examining a strange structure that had magically appeared in Central Park's famous Sheep Meadow, Iron Man Jim Rhodes was suddenly transported to Battleworld, a far away globe in a distant galaxy. There, he and a handful of Earth's greatest heroes, including Spider-Man, the Fantastic Four, and a select band of X-Men and Avengers, were met by villains like Dr. Doom, the Wrecking Crew, Ultron, Kang, and Galactus. After witnessing a display of enormous power by a supreme being calling himself the Beyonder, Iron Man and the others were instructed by the entity to slay their enemies in exchange for fulfillment of their every desire.

IRON MAN'S STARRING ROLE

Locked in battle with the naturally greedy villains and a multitude of alien creations, Iron Man proved his worth to his super-heroic allies by shattering a huge metal projectile hurled at his impromptu teammates. Later, he also shined when he helped the heroes burrow out from under miles of earth. Later, Jim Rhodes was treated to a power upgrade when his armor was damaged and Mr. Fantastic used spare alien parts to improve upon its design.

Iron Man and the other heroes eventually found a way to teleport from the alien world and get back home. However, Iron Man failed in his attempts to win the affections of fellow hero, Captain Marvel.

ORIGIN STORY

Obadiah Stane was obsessed with winning. His father had unwittingly seen to that. A failure and a drunk, Obadiah's father, Zebediah, had won a large sum of money gambling. Convinced that his bad luck had finally changed for the better, Zebediah decided to play a game of Russian roulette in front of his young son to prove his point. He spun the chamber and put the gun to his head—with tragic results. Obadiah later swore never to become like his father.

Shy and bookish, Obadiah was terrified by his father's rash actions.

Zebediah held the gun to his head, ignoring the protests of his son.

Obadiah was so traumatized, he subsequently lost all his hair.

OBADIAH STANE

Obadiah Stane was a man of power, first and foremost. Possessing one of the most devious minds Iron Man had ever faced, Stane left a legacy of pain and suffering in his wake.

OBADIAH'S PLOT

Stane had taken everything that mattered from Tony Stark. Previously an ever-present thorn in the side of Stane's corporate dealings, Tony had been reduced to a homeless alcoholic, a tragic victim of Stane's brilliant scheming. By slowly buying up Tony's debts and filing civil suits against Stark International, Stane had unleashed a hostile takeover of the company. Now the majority shareholder, Obadiah rechristened the company Stane International, and began to pursue weapons contracts, rather than continue Tony's research in the field of electronics. Tony Stark was in check, and he was fast running out of moves.

*"ANTHONY STARK...
I WANTED YOU TO SHARE
THIS MOMENT WITH ME.
WILL YOU JOIN ME IN
A TOAST?"*

OBADIAH STANE

THE CHESSMEN

Though a vengeful, passionate man, Obadiah was fond of using the game of chess as a metaphor for his business dealings. He also liked to indulge in eccentric role-playing games. Wishing to hire a gang of henchman to sabotage Stark Industries and battle Iron Man, he unearthed a group of Super Villains and tricked them out as if they were live chess pieces. From the armored Knight who rode a metallic, hovering steed and fired energy blasts from his lance, to a flying Bishop armed with a battle staff, to lowly messenger Pawns, Stane's Chessman were a powerful force, who further drained Tony Stark's physical and mental resources.

ENTER THE IRON MONGER

Although he preferred to manipulate events from behind the scenes, Obadiah was well aware that certain circumstances called for direct action. When Iron Man, clad in his newly designed Silver Centurion armor, charged the corporate headquarters of Stane International in retaliation for Stane's attack on Circuits Maximus, Stane donned a battlesuit built from notes stolen during his hostile takeover of Stark's holdings. As the Iron Monger, Stane engaged Iron Man in a duel to the death.

Defeated by Iron Man and realizing that Tony was truly his superior, Obadiah Stane chose to kill himself rather than face the consequences of his actions.

NNER TAKES ALL

ite everything Stane had thrown
n, Tony Stark had survived.
diah had taken Stark's every
y, broken his company, spirit, and
eart. He had even engineered
s descent into alcoholism. And
tark had managed to overcome
ane's plots. He had beaten his
demons and begun to claw his
ack up the corporate ladder,
g his latest brainchild, Circuits
mus, into a successful business.
Obadiah Stane always played
n, and he resolved never to
restimate his opponent again.

Original Team

The first roster of the West Coast Avengers included the ionic Wonder Man, former SHIELD agent Mockingbird, her husband the archer Hawkeye, the feline Tigra, and Iron Man Jim Rhodes (the team initially thought that Rhodey was Tony Stark, his predecessor as Iron Man).

WONDER MAN

MOCKINGBIRD

HAWKEYE

TIGRA

IRON MAN

WEST COAST AVENGERS

The Avengers were Earth's mightiest heroes, but even they couldn't be everywhere at once. In a world where threats could strike from any direction, the West Coast Avengers assembled to guard America's other coast.

West Coast Worries

When Hawkeye was chosen to lead a new west coast branch of the Avengers, he moved to California with his wife Mockingbird and set up shop in an impressive compound, equipped with every luxury an Avenger could desire. Recruiting Wonder Man, Tigra, and Iron Man, Hawkeye and his new team began training, learning to work together like a well-oiled machine.

Almost immediately, that machine was put to the test. The old Avengers foe Graviton was returned to Earth from his prison void, revenge his only thought. With a little help from the secretive hero known as the Shroud, Iron Man and his new teammates infiltrated Graviton's base and, thanks to strategy and cunning, took the powerful villain down.

However, villains weren't the only concern on Jim Rhodes' mind. He was more worried about how his new teammates would react when they discovered that he wasn't Tony Stark, the original pilot of the Iron Man armor. Mustering his courage, Rhodey finally revealed his identity to his team. Having already proved his mettle on their previous missions and during Iron Man's time in the Secret Wars, Rhodey was soon accepted by the team—even by the habitually skeptical Hawkeye.

Rhodey originally joined the West Coast Avengers when Tony Stark moved to California in order to set up a new electronics company, Circuits Maximus. After Jim stepped down as Iron Man, Tony eagerly reclaimed his place alongside his old friends in his new silver centurion armor.

Iron Man's Return

During the so-called "Armor Wars" (see pp. 110–1) when Tony Stark waged war on anyone who had gained access to his stolen Iron Man technology, the Avengers were forced to dismiss Tony from their ranks due to his illegal actions. But after faking Iron Man's death, and informing the public that he'd hired a new Iron Man, Tony returned to the team in new armor, hoping for acceptance. With a different roster in place, including the Wasp, Hank Pym, USAgent, the Vision, and the Scarlet Witch, the team doubted Iron Man's motives and asked him to reveal his identity. Stark refused, preferring to earn the team's respect on the battlefield instead.

Reunited with his teammates, Iron Man had little time to relax before having to battle the evil Master Pandemonium.

"We know you used to be TONY STARK, Iron Man. And we know Stark isn't dead. So tell us now… ARE YOU STARK?"

Hank Pym

Future Foes

Although their line-up changed many times, the West Coast Avengers remained dedicated to their mission. Fighting the likes of the mutant Magneto, the time-defying Immortus and the mad scientist Dr. Demonicus, the Avengers soldiered on, even after Tony Stark quit their ranks. But they wouldn't be without an armored Avenger for long. Jim Rhodes rejoined the team he helped found. Only now, Rhodey was his own man, out of Stark's shadow and clad in new armor as War Machine.

Steeling for Battle

Tony was angry with himself. He should have seen this coming. Someone had stolen his secrets; technology so important, he didn't even patent it, for fear of imitation. When Tony chanced upon his prized Iron Man circuitry built into the confiscated armor of his old enemy Force, he felt responsible for all the pain and destruction Force had inflicted on the world. Knowing that people were using his stolen technology for their own selfish needs, Tony decided there was only one course of action he could take. He would have to retrieve or destroy all his stolen technology. And so Tony Stark went to war.

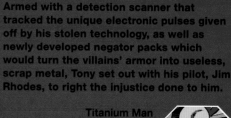

ARMOR WARS

It was Justin Hammer's most ingenious scheme. His employee Spymaster had planted a bug in Stark International years ago, stealing Tony's secrets and selling them to improve Hammer's army of criminals. But now Iron Man had had enough.

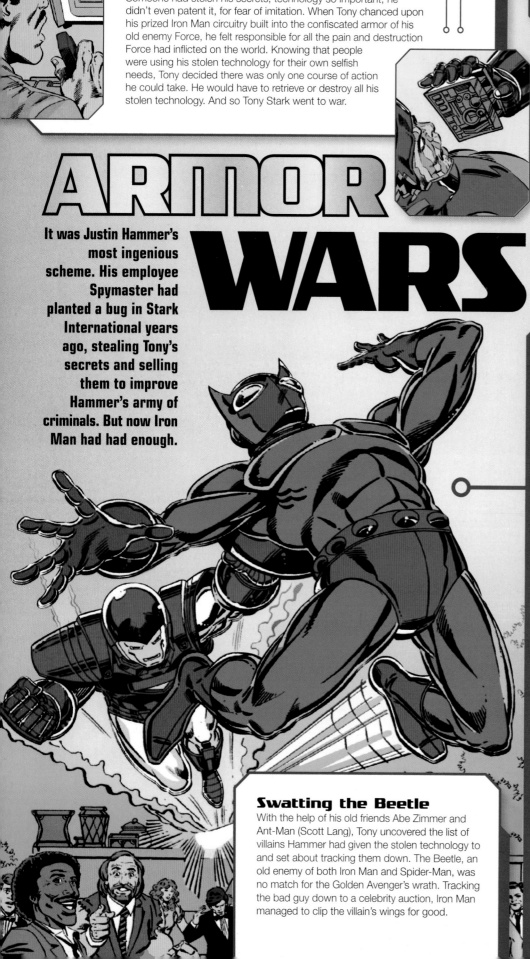

Armed with a detection scanner that tracked the unique electronic pulses given off by his stolen technology, as well as newly developed negator packs which would turn the villains' armor into useless, scrap metal, Tony set out with his pilot, Jim Rhodes, to right the injustice done to him.

Titanium Man
One of his most challenging obstacles was the mutant known as the Gremlin, the latest pilot of the Titanium Man armor.

Stilt Man
Iron Man's first target, Stilt Man was busy attempting a break in seven stories high when Tony brought the villain down to Earth.

The Mauler
When Tony tracked the Mauler down at a soldier of fortune convention, the villain gave up his gear without a fight.

Stingray
With one name missing from the list, Tony mistakenly accused the hero Stingray, only to realise his error after a fight.

Raiders
In a midair battle with the Raiders, Iron Man saved a plane filled with electronics while taking out the trio of high tech thieves.

Beetle
After saving celebrities from a rockslide caused by the Beetle, Iron Man slapped a negator pack on his back.

Mandroids
Unable to trust SHIELD with his technology, Iron Man tricked Nick Fury so he could take the machines out of commission.

Controller
Using a salon as a front to create an army of mind-controlled minions, the Controller found he was no match for Iron Man.

Crimson Dynamo
Using his stealth armor, Iron Man was able to get the jump on the Crimson Dynamo and negate his suit's abilities.

Guardsmen
Produced by Obadiah Stane and sold to the Vault as guards, they were stopped by Iron Man fusing their circuits.

Firepower
The last beneficiary of the stolen technology, Firepower was a secret project commissoned by the US government.

Swatting the Beetle

With the help of his old friends Abe Zimmer and Ant-Man (Scott Lang), Tony uncovered the list of villains Hammer had given the stolen technology to and set about tracking them down. The Beetle, an old enemy of both Iron Man and Spider-Man, was no match for the Golden Avenger's wrath. Tracking the bad guy down to a celebrity auction, Iron Man managed to clip the villain's wings for good.

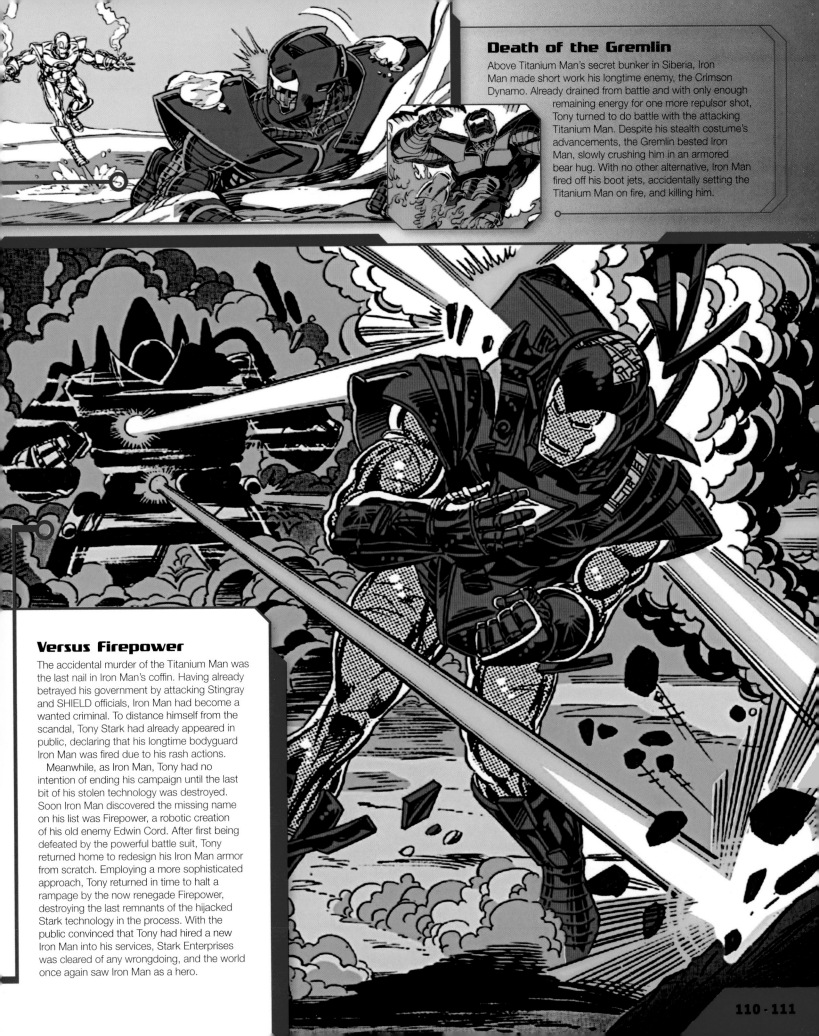

Death of the Gremlin

Above Titanium Man's secret bunker in Siberia, Iron Man made short work his longtime enemy, the Crimson Dynamo. Already drained from battle and with only enough remaining energy for one more repulsor shot, Tony turned to do battle with the attacking Titanium Man. Despite his stealth costume's advancements, the Gremlin bested Iron Man, slowly crushing him in an armored bear hug. With no other alternative, Iron Man fired off his boot jets, accidentally setting the Titanium Man on fire, and killing him.

Versus Firepower

The accidental murder of the Titanium Man was the last nail in Iron Man's coffin. Having already betrayed his government by attacking Stingray and SHIELD officials, Iron Man had become a wanted criminal. To distance himself from the scandal, Tony Stark had already appeared in public, declaring that his longtime bodyguard Iron Man was fired due to his rash actions.

Meanwhile, as Iron Man, Tony had no intention of ending his campaign until the last bit of his stolen technology was destroyed. Soon Iron Man discovered the missing name on his list was Firepower, a robotic creation of his old enemy Edwin Cord. After first being defeated by the powerful battle suit, Tony returned home to redesign his Iron Man armor from scratch. Employing a more sophisticated approach, Tony returned in time to halt a rampage by the now renegade Firepower, destroying the last remnants of the hijacked Stark technology in the process. With the public convinced that Tony had hired a new Iron Man into his services, Stark Enterprises was cleared of any wrongdoing, and the world once again saw Iron Man as a hero.

IRON MAN #232

MARVEL
75¢ US
95¢ CAN
232
JUL
02454

"How long have I been hunting it? All night? Forever? Doesn't matter. Nothing matters. I've got to keep on. Do whatever I have to. Got to find it. So I can kill it..."

IRON MAN

MAIN CHARACTERS: Iron Man (Tony Stark); Iron Man (Jim Rhodes)
SUPPORTING CHARACTERS: Various corpses
LOCATIONS: A dream world inside Tony Stark's mind; Tony Stark's coastal mansion, California

PUBLICATION DATE
July 1988

EDITOR-IN-CHIEF
Tom DeFalco

COVER ARTIST
Barry Windsor-Smith

WRITER/PLOTTER
David Michelinie

PENCILER/PLOTTER
Barry Windsor-Smith

INKER/COLORIST
Barry Windsor-Smith

LETTERER
Bill Oakley

BACKGROUND

Barry Windsor-Smith was about to make history. Already well known for his groundbreaking artwork and storytelling skills on Marvel's *Conan the Barbarian* series in the 1970s, he had returned to Marvel in the 1980s, ready to breathe new life into a few of their Super Hero properties. He would soon reach comics superstardom by writing and drawing the landmark origin story of the X-Men's Wolverine in a series entitled *Weapon X*.

But before Windsor-Smith turned the life of Wolverine upside down, he dabbled in Iron Man's world. First coming into contact with the Golden Avenger in the second Machine Man limited series, he went on to plot, pencil, and color a surreal Iron Man adventure with the help of the current Iron Man team, writer David Michelinie and inker Bob Layton. An epilogue to the memorable *Armor Wars* storyline, readers were given a rare glimpse into the nightmares that haunt Tony Stark's psyche, while simultaneously shown the imagery of a breathtaking artist in his prime.

The Story...

Trapped in a vicious nightmare, Iron Man must come to terms with his inner demons and the many mistakes of his past.

It was a labyrinth of wires, computer consoles, and shadows. Stalking through the mysterious landscape, was Iron Man, clad in his now outdated silver centurion armor **(1)**. He didn't know how long he had been on the hunt, he just knew that he had to continue. There was something out there in the darkness, and Iron Man was going to find it and kill it.

Suddenly an strange hum sounded in the distance. Iron Man lashed out towards it, firing his repulsors into the blackness **(2)**. But nothing happened, and the hum slowly turned into laughter.

Just then, Iron Man began to realize where he was. He was in his prey's lair. He felt overcome with fear, but it was too late. The creature was standing right in front of him. Iron Man again began to fire his blasters at full power, but the creature just absorbed it all, growing stronger and larger. The beast was an enigma. It was a gigantic robot husk, an elaborate tapestry of tubes and dials **(3)**. But its face, Tony Stark recognized all too easily. Because the creature was wearing the faceplate of an Iron Man.

As their battle raged, Iron Man fiercely attacked the robotic horror with his bare hands, managing to tear its head right off its shoulders. And just like that, it was over.

Tony could lie down for just a minute and catch his breath. But the ground below him had changed. He now found himself lying upon miles and miles of rotting corpses **(4)**.

Through the horrific landscape, a solitary figure trudged. It was Jim Rhodes, wearing his old Iron Man armor once more **(5)**. When Tony asked his friend where they were, Rhodey simply said that they were in a place Stark himself had made. The carnage was all Tony's fault and Rhodey was merely the custodian. With that, the landscape began to shift once more. Suddenly, Tony was standing in a bar, with Rhodey manning the counter. As Tony reluctantly ordered a vodka tonic, resigned to escaping his troubles at Rhodey's suggestion, thick cords began to appear around Tony's body. Restrained and helpless, Tony looked up once more at the creature he had been hunting. And this time, the horror was wearing his own face **(6)**.

But Tony wouldn't give up without a fight. Channeling all his energy into one burst of his rocket boots, Stark freed himself, falling to the ground below him. But the beast was barely phased, and it was coming for him. Tony tried to run **(7)**, but the hands of his victims shot up from the metal cords below his feet. They grabbed at Tony, impeding his escape. Tony needed to think of another way to get free.

Realizing that his attacks on the creature only made it stronger, Tony set his repulsors to absorb energy, rather than release it. And with all the strength he could still muster, Tony charged the beast, sucking its raw energy into his armor. But Tony couldn't take much more and his frame exploded **(8)**, unable to contain all of the beast's powerful essence. And that's when Tony Stark woke up **(9)**.

Tony was safe and secure in his plush coastal mansion. It had all been a vivid nightmare, a way for his subconscious to tell him what he already knew deep down. Yes, the Armor Wars were over. Tony had succeeded in eliminating all the known cases of stolen and pirated Stark technology. But the guilt still remained, and Tony felt haunted by all the innocents killed or injured due to his misused innovations **(10)**. He could no longer keep fighting the guilt, or denying it. His mind was telling him to accept it as part of who he was now. And as Tony Stark looked out his bedroom window at the beautiful ocean beyond, he knew he would have to do just that. And continue the rest of his life as best he could.

"The worst bloody nightmare I've had in my life!"

ARMOR WARS II

Tony Stark was about to become a living puppet, with a criminal mastermind pulling the strings and controlling his every move.

When testing out his helmet's new encephalo-circuits, Tony was able to pilot a spare Iron Man suit into battle with him by remote control, besting a giant robot operated by Jim Rhodes.

DEWITT'S PLAN

Kearson DeWitt had hated Tony Stark for years. Considering Tony his main competitor in the world of high finance, Dewitt had aligned himself with the financial backing of Desmond and Phoebe Marrs, old foes of the sea king, Namor. Together, they sabotaged a surgical operation that Tony Stark underwent to cure his paralyzed condition after he had been shot by a crazed ex-girlfriend. Adding their own circuitry to the microchip embedded in Tony Stark's spine, DeWitt gained total control of Tony's nervous system, able to manipulate his every move like a remote-controlled toy.

> "Your time has come, Iron Man. As you killed me, so now I claim your life!"
>
> Titanium Man

OUT OF THE PAST

The Titanium Man was back. Or was he? Alerted by a disturbance at his nuclear research facility, Tony wasted no time changing into his Iron Man armor and heading to the scene. As he inspected his plant, Iron Man was buried under tons of rubble. He was then confronted by an opponent who seemed to be the ghost of his old enemy from the days of the Cold War—the Titanium Man. Iron Man was forced to flee, but still managed to avert a nuclear meltdown at his factory.

MANDARIN

While Tony Stark battled threats close to home, the Mandarin was busy with his own agenda: to "rekindle the flame" of old, pre-Communist China, with himself as supreme ruler. Discovering that one of his rings of power had been replaced by a forgery, the Mandarin sought out the thief Chen Hsu, a powerful old wizard. Regaining his ring, and with it memories thought lost, the Mandarin realized his true mission. With Chen Hsu in tow, the warlord set out for the

"Well, flesh? You have waked me from my dreamless sleep. Why?"

Fin Fang Foom

secret Chinese location of the Valley of the Sleeping Dragon. Daring to venture alone into a dark cavern, the Mandarin finally discovered what he had been searching for. In front of him lay a slumbering dragon of legend named Fin Fang Foom. With the help of an ancient leaf, the Mandarin woke the sleeping giant, unleashing the angered beast's wrath on a battalion of Chinese military. Then, with the help of Chen Hsu, the Mandarin put the dragon back to sleep, knowing the powerful creature was his to control.

REMOTE-CONTROL SAVIOR

Tony Stark woke up in San Francisco. Which was a bit odd, as his last memory was being home in LA. After flying back to Stark Enterprises, a thoroughly confused Iron Man was once again attacked by the ghost of the Titanium Man. As the two battled, "Titanium Man" revealed his true identity: Stark's light-manipulating foe the Living Laser. At that moment DeWitt's people shut down Tony's functions, forcing the hero to use his remote controlled Iron Man suit to retrieve his paralyzed body from the scene.

DEWITT'S DOWNFALL

With DeWitt's people attempting to control Tony Stark's every move, he had no choice but to don his encephalo-controlled armor, piloting the suit with his mind. Despite the severe damage done to his body by overriding its commands and sealing it in the armor, Iron Man still fought a returning Living Laser, defeating him with the help of his old friend Wonder Man. With one villain down, Tony set his sights on DeWitt, the grand puppet master himself.

Tracking the microchip in his spine back to its creators, Iron Man quickly flew to the Marrs Corporation...

...There he encountered DeWitt encased in his own suit of armor. Fighting the pain of overriding his body's remote commands, and with a little help from Rhodey, Iron Man defeated DeWitt—and discovered that he didn't even recognize his enemy.

THE
1990s

The decade of foil-embossed covers, large event story arcs, and edgy anti-heroes hit Iron Man's world, with mixed results.

It was a time for blockbusters and chart-toppers. Reinventing the wheel seemed to have become the standard, even if some wheels were performing just fine. The comics specialty market had opened up the doors for variant covers, crossovers, and tie-in trading cards, the likes of which the industry had never seen. The editors of *Iron Man* not only embraced the changes, indulging in the occasional polybag wrapper or gold foil title, but they also utilized these trends to help launch a companion comic, *War Machine*.

With years of grooming as Iron Man's replacement and a fan base all his own, Jim Rhodes split off into his own title, with an edgier, more violent outlook on life. War Machine became the darker counterpart to Iron Man, and a reflection of other top-selling anti-hero comics such as *Punisher*, *Lobo,* and *Wolverine*.

As crossover events like the grand scale *Infinity Gauntlet* and the Avenger's *Crossing* epic dealt with cataclysmic threats, Iron Man was killed and replaced by a younger version of himself. But before this new Iron Man could even sink in with the readers, the *Onslaught* crossover rocked the Marvel Universe and the *Iron Man* title was cancelled. The series was immediately restarted, however, featuring yet another new take on Iron Man, with a new origin and history.

It wasn't until near the end of the decade that Iron Man was restored to his former glory in yet another Earth-shattering event called *Heroes Return*. With the debut of his third ongoing series, Iron Man was returned to his roots, much to the relief of a perplexed readership.

OVERLEAF *Iron Man #300*: War Machine led an Iron Legion of former Iron Men against the alien Ultimo in the landmark 300th issue of Iron Man's title.

DRAGON SEED SAGA

Tony Stark traveled to China in search of a cure for his inoperable condition only to be confronted by the Mandarin and an army of alien dragons.

Critical Condition

After a gunshot wound left Tony Stark crippled, he had undergone experimental surgery to have a microchip grafted onto his spine. However, when an unknown business rival named Kearson DeWitt used technology hidden within the chip to control Tony's nervous system, his body was damaged beyond repair.

Employing the world's leading neuro-biologist, Dr. Su Yin, Tony found himself at the doctor's mercy in more than one area.

The Deal

In exchange for treatment from Dr. Yin for his body's seemingly inoperable condition, Tony was forced to offer his "bodyguard's" services to the Chinese government. The Mandarin was demanding the country's submission, and only Iron Man could stop him.

Chen Hsu's Secret

While Jim Rhodes became Iron Man once again to fight in the place of his debilitated boss, the Mandarin used his dragon, Fin Fang Foom, to fight his battle for him. Meanwhile, the Mandarin's mentor Chen Hsu, was busy furthering his own plans. Chen had an astonishing secret. He wasn't a human being at all but actually an alien dragon in disguise.

The Gathering

Despite the valiant effort of the Iron Men, they still proved no match for the combined might of the Mandarin and Fin Fang Foom. But just as Tony seemingly fled, the Mandarin was greeted by several new guests: Hsu Chen's dragon army.

The Sleeping Dragons

As Chen Hsu gathered the fellow members of his race from all corners of the globe, Rhodey finally lost his violent battle with Fin Fang Foom. But it wasn't long before Tony Stark would join the fray. Tony, utilizing the encephalo-link that allowed him to pilot an Iron Man suit by remote control, summoned a suit from America and used it to attack the Mandarin.

Ancient History

Chen Hsu belonged to an ancient alien race from the planet Kakaranathara. Bored of their idyllic lives, he and a select group had traveled to Earth in a spaceship powered by ten powerful rings, only to crash land. Learning to morph their dragon-like appearances into that of humans, the aliens walked freely among Earth's population, amassing strength and power until they were ready for their eventual gathering — where they would regain their rings and dominate the Earth.

Uneasy Alliance

The Mandarin wouldn't go down without a fight. Refusing to give his rings back to their original alien owners, the Mandarin battled the dragons with the help of Rhodey. Tony soon arrived, in full Iron Man armor, and channeled all of his power into the Mandarin's rings. The resulting explosion annihilated the dragons, and destroyed the Mandarin's hands.

It wasn't the first war the Avengers had been caught up in, but it was one of the most devastating. And a judgement made at the war's conclusion would divide the team for years to come.

THE RIPPLES OF WAR

Beyond the stars, in a far-flung galaxy, there existed an empire belonging to an alien race called the Kree. The race was ruled by a living computer that was a culmination of the minds of the greatest thinkers in Kree history. Named the Supreme Intelligence, the computer eventually developed a personality of its own, as well as a lust for power. With the Supreme Intelligence in command of their every action, the Kree knew few moments of peace, and spent much of their time in combat with longtime enemies such as the shape-shifting alien race named the Skrulls.

However, it wouldn't be the Kree that dragged the Avengers into Operation: Galactic Storm. It would be their opponents, another alien empire, the Shi'ar. When the Shi'ar captured Rick Jones, an old ally of Captain America and the Avengers, they only wished to discover the location of a Kree outpost on earth. Instead, they were greeted by Captain America and an assembled team of West Coast Avengers, eager to protect their old friend. To make matters worse, during their battles with the Kree, the Shi'ar were traveling via a wormhole that was perilously close to Earth. When the rift in space was utilized, the sun was severely affected and if this activity didn't stop soon, the traumatized star was going to explode.

OPERATION:
GALACTIC STORM

THE KREE TEAM

The Avengers couldn't just stand by and watch their sun, and all life on Earth, be destroyed by the Shi'ars' negligence. They divided their forces and sent peace envoys to both sides of the intergalactic conflict, while also keeping several Avengers on Earth. Iron Man, was among those chosen to visit the Kree, along with Captain America, USAgent, Crystal, Hercules, the Black Knight, and Sersi.

SERSI

THE BLACK KNIGHT

HERCULES

CRYSTAL

IRON MAN

USAGENT

HOSTILE NEGOTIATIONS

Unhappy at being assigned to stay behind on Earth, Hawkeye took Giant-Man's growth formula and used his powers to replace USAgent on the trip to the Kree Empire. But while the Shi'ar envoy managed to talk some sense into that empire's leader, Iron Man's team soon found themselves prisoners of the Kree state. They only escaped by impersonating Kree security guards.

For his trip to the Kree Empire, Iron Man piloted the Mark 2 redesign of his space armor.

THE SKRULL'S PLOT

The Avengers discovered that a Shi'ar Nega Bomb had been strategically positioned to destroy the entire Kree race—a plot cooked up by the Kree's own Supreme Intelligence with help from the Skrulls. The Avengers battled the Skrulls for control of the device but, despite their best efforts, the bomb was detonated.

SPLIT DECISION

The Nega-Bomb decimated the Kree Empire, just as the Supreme Intelligence had planned from the very beginning. He had manipulated events to kill billions of his own people, so that the survivors evolved into a more superior race. Face-to-face with this remorseless mass murderer, Iron Man and his allies wanted to destroy the Intelligence, while Captain America and his side maintained they didn't have that right.

A PEACEFUL DELEGATION

As the only founding member of the Avengers present, Iron Man pulled rank on his old friend Captain America, and led a band of heroes to destroy the Supreme Intelligence. The Avengers then returned to Earth, secure in the knowledge that the Shi'ar were resolved to keep the peace.

"The Supreme Intelligence is a machine... a soulless piece of hardware... that we will destroy so that nothing like this will ever happen again." Iron Man

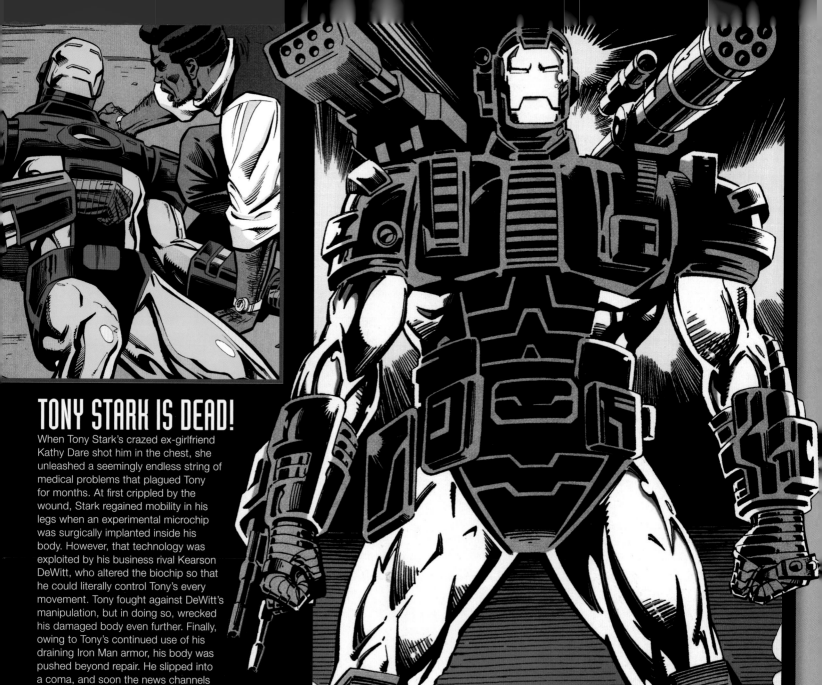

TONY STARK IS DEAD!

When Tony Stark's crazed ex-girlfriend Kathy Dare shot him in the chest, she unleashed a seemingly endless string of medical problems that plagued Tony for months. At first crippled by the wound, Stark regained mobility in his legs when an experimental microchip was surgically implanted inside his body. However, that technology was exploited by his business rival Kearson DeWitt, who altered the biochip so that he could literally control Tony's every movement. Tony fought against DeWitt's manipulation, but in doing so, wrecked his damaged body even further. Finally, owing to Tony's continued use of his draining Iron Man armor, his body was pushed beyond repair. He slipped into a coma, and soon the news channels announced that Tony Stark was dead.

On his deathbed, Tony Stark willed his company and his identity as Iron Man to his best friend, Jim Rhodes.

THE COMING OF
WAR MACHINE

Having recorded a CD-Rom before his death, Tony asked Rhodey to carry on for him as Iron Man and as Stark Enterprises CEO.

BACK IN UNIFORM

What James Rhodes didn't know was that Tony hadn't died at all. In reality he was cryogenically frozen, so that Abe Zimmer and a handful of other experts could use an experimental procedure on him in a last-ditch effort to save his life and cure his ailing condition.

As Stark underwent this treatment, Rhodey mourned him and defended Stark Enterprises from an attack by Spymaster, Blacklash, the Beetle, and the Blizzard. Even in a deep coma, Tony was still plagued by his inner demons, and the traumatic memories of his troubled childhood.

Even though he had originally piloted it himself, Tony developed his War Machine Iron Man armor specifically with Jim Rhodes' fighting style in mind.

While frozen, Tony was injected with a virus that gave his body an artificial nervous system.

THE END OF AN ERA

Once again, Rhodey was getting the hang of being the replacement Iron Man. He held his own in battles with Firepower, the powerhouse known as Atom Smasher, and even the Living Laser. He also won over the staff in his new role as Stark Enterprises CEO and began dating Tony's ex-girlfriend Rae LaCoste. When Tony awoke from his coma, and Rhodey discovered his friend's boldface lie, Jim furiously ended his association with both Stark and his heroic legacy. Rhodey quit as CEO and as Iron Man, but kept his armor, changing his moniker to the more appropriate War Machine. Tony was left alone and temporarily paralyzed, so he did what he always did. He continued to fight, by developing a new telepresence remote-controlled Iron Man armor.

War Machine fought alongside Stark's new remote-controlled armor to defend Stark Enterprises from saboteurs, but the two soon parted ways, and Jim embarked on his bold new life.

He severed his ties with Tony Stark and all the trouble that came with him. After all, War Machine was perfectly capable of getting into trouble all by himself.

GOING SOLO

SOLDIERING ON

James Rhodes was finally his own man. His feud with Tony Stark had sent him out into the world alone, whether he was ready for it or not. Luckily, he'd packed for the occasion, with his heavily armored War Machine technology. Jim Rhodes was a soldier at heart, and it was time for him to wage his private war.

With his girlfriend Rae LaCoste at his side, Rhodes began working for the Human Rights organization, Worldwatch Incorporated. His affiliation with Worldwatch led to adventures all over the world, facing a myriad of obstacles along the way. As War Machine, Rhodey faced the likes of X-Force's Cable, the cyborg Deathlok, the psychotic Deathtoll, and even the Mandarin. After fighting alongside Iron Man's team Force Works, and Iron Man himself, Rhodey was finally able to mend his rift with Tony. Nevertheless, War Machine decided to continue on his own path, one that led to him briefly using an alien suit of armor (known as Warwear) and later to his employment in the giant Sentinel ONE program.

Seriously wounded during an attack on a military base in Dubai, Rhodey was rebuilt by Tony Stark into a half-human cyborg. As an emergency backup, Tony equipped Rhodey with non-Stark technology and gave him a satellite base.

Tony cloned a new body for Rhodey, but it was later seized by Norman Osborn.

Rhodey's new armor could attract and incorporate other devices, making War Machine truly worthy of his name.

A Mean Machine

When Tony was promoted to head of the government agency SHIELD, he asked Rhodes to work as the commander of his new 50 State Initiative's Camp Hammond base. Happy to be training the next generation of Super Heroes, Rhodey oversaw the camp until events during the Secret Invasion (see pp. 180–1) saw Tony ousted from his position. Taking up residence in a satellite Stark had set up for him, built using other people's technology, War Machine decided to take his fight on a more global scale. Along with Bethany Cabe, the director of Stark's secret Research and Development War Machine facility, former SHIELD agent Jake Oh, cybermancer Suzi Endo, and his one-man pit crew Parnell Jacobs, Rhodey ran a tight ship. He also rescued his former girlfriend, Parnell's wife Dr. Glenda Sandoval, from a run-in with the giant robot Ultimo.

When rescuing his friend Glenda in occupied Aqiria, War Machine was forced to prove his worth to Ares, the Greek god of war.

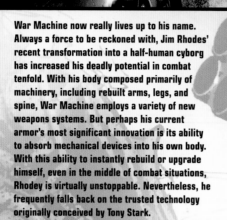

War Machine now really lives up to his name. Always a force to be reckoned with, Jim Rhodes' recent transformation into a half-human cyborg has increased his deadly potential in combat tenfold. With his body composed primarily of machinery, including rebuilt arms, legs, and spine, War Machine employs a variety of new weapons systems. But perhaps his current armor's most significant innovation is its ability to absorb mechanical devices into his own body. With this ability to instantly rebuild or upgrade himself, even in the middle of combat situations, Rhodey is virtually unstoppable. Nevertheless, he frequently falls back on the trusted technology originally conceived by Tony Stark.

main armaments

Barrel deploy mechanism

Breech activator

Left breech

Magnetic lock casing

Electrostatic ammunition feed

Right breech

Round select arm

Ammunition carousel

Variable ammunition cassettes

"All right, you monsters want war? you got it... South Philly style!"

Wrist Cannon

Officially part of Stark's variable threat response suit, the gauntlet cannon possesses a continuous belt-feed of ammunition and an electronic firing mechanism that allows for eight different forms of ammo. An electronic feed device allows War Machine to mix and match the rounds he uses, including spent uranium armor-piercing, high-explosive, concussion-type, high-temperature thermite, tear gas, tracer, flare, and smoke 3.9 mm projectiles.

Rapid-fire barrel

Laser-sighting
guidance system

Spiral-feed
ammunition
cassette

Minigun

The shoulder-mounted minigun is loosely based on conventional electric mini-guns carried by various military aircraft. The weapon was designed by Tony Stark, albeit reluctantly, as he was hesitant to unleash such an efficient and deadly compact machine on any battlefield. Carrying 1,800 caseless, uranium-cored, armor-piercing rounds in its spiral magazine, the minigun is able to fire at impressive speeds. Computer controlled, the gun can fire up to 1,000 rounds per second. The weapon locks into an upright position when not in use or during flight mode.

Standby position

Cooling
vents

One-shot frangible
weather seal

Solid rocket-fuel
chamber

Warhead

Rotational jacks

Lineal motor
housing

Recoil
damper

High-speed
positioning rail

Magnetic
clamping panel

Rotating self-aligning
breach

Protective
shielding

Standby position

Missile Launcher

Constructed with a standby position similar to the minigun, the missile launcher is another deadly accessory in War Machine's arsenal. The launcher fires projectiles about the size of an average road flare at speeds up to Mach 2. Able to achieve pinpoint accuracy due to the laser site built into War Machine's helmet, the missiles pack a punch up to sub-nuke level, exploding with the force of a charge of 1.8 kilotons of TNT. War Machine can fire at eight targets at once, and employ a variety of missiles, including anti-tank, flame-bomb, fire-suppressant, smoke, and tear gas.

Magnetic
clamping panels

Schematics based on the work of Eliot R. Brown

FORCE WORKS

AVENGERS: TERMINATED

It was a tough time to be a West Coast Avenger. Their headquarters lay in ruins, longtime team member Mockingbird had seemingly been brutally murdered, and her husband Hawkeye had suddenly disappeared. So when Vision and the other members of the East Coast team called a meeting to end what they considered a failed experiment in their western branch, the affected heroes were more than a little enraged. But the votes were cast, with Iron Man getting the final say. And soon, the West Coast Avengers were no more.

Iron man was ready to become proactive. The world's foremost futurist read the writing on the wall and realized that in today's changing climate, the best defense was a strong offense.

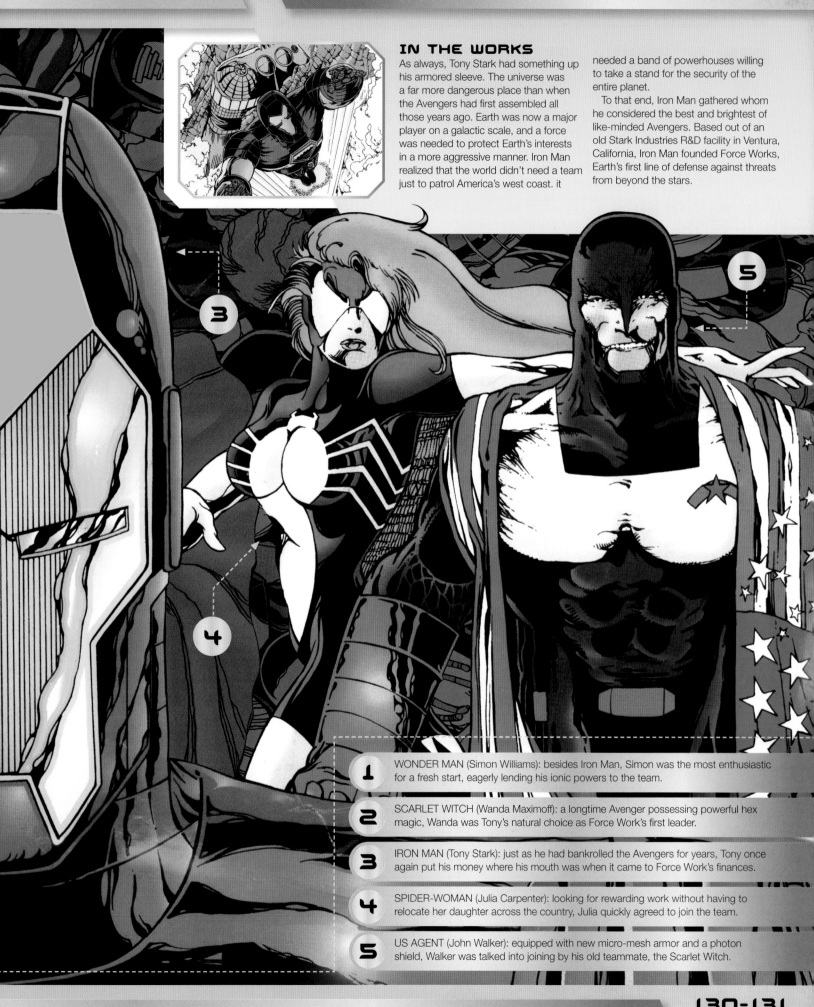

IN THE WORKS

As always, Tony Stark had something up his armored sleeve. The universe was a far more dangerous place than when the Avengers had first assembled all those years ago. Earth was now a major player on a galactic scale, and a force was needed to protect Earth's interests in a more aggressive manner. Iron Man realized that the world didn't need a team just to patrol America's west coast. it needed a band of powerhouses willing to take a stand for the security of the entire planet.

To that end, Iron Man gathered whom he considered the best and brightest of like-minded Avengers. Based out of an old Stark Industries R&D facility in Ventura, California, Iron Man founded Force Works, Earth's first line of defense against threats from beyond the stars.

1 WONDER MAN (Simon Williams): besides Iron Man, Simon was the most enthusiastic for a fresh start, eagerly lending his ionic powers to the team.

2 SCARLET WITCH (Wanda Maximoff): a longtime Avenger possessing powerful hex magic, Wanda was Tony's natural choice as Force Work's first leader.

3 IRON MAN (Tony Stark): just as he had bankrolled the Avengers for years, Tony once again put his money where his mouth was when it came to Force Work's finances.

4 SPIDER-WOMAN (Julia Carpenter): looking for rewarding work without having to relocate her daughter across the country, Julia quickly agreed to join the team.

5 US AGENT (John Walker): equipped with new micro-mesh armor and a photon shield, Walker was talked into joining by his old teammate, the Scarlet Witch.

TIMESLIDE

Tony Stark was no longer a hero. He'd become a murderer, and only one man could stop him: Tony Stark himself.

THE CROSSING

He hadn't been himself for some time. However it was not his physical body that was under threat...Tony Stark was struggling to retain his very sanity, and he was losing the battle. Tony had fallen under the control of the time-traveling despot Immortus, who was currently posing as his younger self, Kang the Conqueror. Under the villain's domination, Tony was becoming not only a traitor to his Avengers teammates, but an apparently emotionless killer. In rapid succession, Tony viciously murdered the heroine Yellowjacket, Force Works' public relations agent Amanda Chaney, and finally Marilla, the nanny tending to Quicksilver's daughter. Tony then critically wounded his old teammate and friend Wasp, triggering her metamorphosis into a human/wasp hybrid. Although Tony tried to resist Kang's mind manipulation, the villain's powers were too strong. Tony had passed the point of no return, and it fell to the Avengers to see that he and his evil master were brought to justice.

Tony killed the nanny Marilla when she discovered him exiting through a mysterious portal that had formed beneath Avengers Mansion.

FALLEN FROM GRACE

Tony's corruption hadn't happened over night. He'd lived a stressful life full of guilt and struggle, constantly battling inner demons caused by a strict childhood and an alcohol addiction. But when his college professor Ted Slaught was trapped in a laboratory explosion and turned into the monstrous Slag, a part of Tony died when he was forced to destroy his old mentor. Suddenly, his mind was ripe for Kang's mental manipulations, and Tony soon began spending more and more time in a new, secret base he had set up in the Arctic.

IMMORTUS' PLAN

Immortus was determined to secure his future. In the guise of Kang, Immortus had induced the former Avenger, Mantis, to follow his every command, and he had also convinced Tony Stark to be his agent on Earth. On Kang's orders, Tony had constructed an Arctic bunker. Locked away from prying eyes, he had then built a chronographic weapon. When enabled, the weapon would cauterize the timeline, erasing all other possible futures and cementing a destiny in which Kang would rule supreme. However, as Tony completed work on this malevolent device, the Avengers were developing their own time-traveling ploy.

YOUNG TONY

With the help of a mystical portal they discovered in the basement of Avengers Mansion, the Avengers journeyed back in time ten years to recruit a younger version of Tony Stark from an alternate timeline. Bringing the youthful Tony back to the future with them, the Avengers planned to confront the adult Stark with his younger counterpart, and hopefully knock some sense into their corrupted friend. Alongside a heroic clone of Madame Masque, the Avengers and young Tony headed to Stark's Arctic bunker. There they discovered Tony's Iron Man armory, showcasing dozens of Iron Man suits past and present. But there was no sign of Stark himself—until one of the Iron Men moved.

Wearing a new suit of powerful armor that featured teleportation capabilities, Tony Stark attacked the Avengers and his younger self. While the battle raged, the younger Tony managed to equip himself with one of Iron Man's unused armors, but then realized he lacked the necessary experience to operate it.

After the elder Stark's death, young Tony stayed in the present and developed his own Iron Man armor, quickly forming a friendship with Jim Rhodes.

IRON MAN IS DEAD...

The Avengers' plan almost worked. Iron Man was nearly swayed by his younger self. But Kang's influence was just too strong. While Iron Man seriously wounded the younger Tony, his boss Kang arrived at the Arctic bunker. It was time to activate Tony's machine. As the Avengers battled Kang, ready to sacrifice their lives to defeat him, Iron Man saw the error of his ways. He threw himself in front of the chronographic weapon's transposer energy, halting the machine's functions, even as he sacrificed his life. It was now up to the younger Tony Stark to carry on the mantle of Iron Man.

He was reborn in a pocket universe very different from the one he used to know. With no memories of his past life and adventures, Tony Stark was forced to discover Iron Man again, as if for the first time.

ONSLAUGHT ATTACKS

He was the darkest halves of two of the world's most powerful mutants. A living creation of the repressed anger of the X-Men's Professor X and their old foe Magneto, Onslaught waged war on all humanity. In a desperate, last-ditch effort to stop the malign entity's rampage, the younger Iron Man, along with several other heroes, leaped into Onslaught's form, even at the cost of their own lives.

HEROES REBORN

However, Iron Man did not die. None of the heroes did. Franklin Richards, the young son of the Fantastic Four's leader, Mr. Fantastic, and his wife, the Invisible Woman, used his vast psionic mutant abilities to save his family and their friends. He did so by creating a pocket universe for them to live in with his mind. While similar to the Earth they came from, this new world had fewer heroes and villains.

In this new dimension, history had been rewritten, and Tony and the others found themselves in the middle of new lives, complete with new memories and, in some cases, new appearances. Tony himself was no longer the youth who had entered Onslaught's nebulous body. He was now back to his proper age, a millionaire playboy once again at the helm of Stark International.

Tony was also part of a group of brilliant friends nicknamed the Atomic Knights. Along with Reed Richards, Victor Von Doom and Tony's new best friend, Conner "Rebel" O'Reilly, Tony was a shining star, with the future firmly in his grasp. However, power corrupts, and somewhere along the way, Tony stopped caring about the common man. From his ivory tower, he bought his way out of any and all legal problems, even when trusted friends like Pepper Potts took issue with his ethics. In fact, Tony went so far as to fire Pepper when she lashed out at him in front of a shocked public.

HEROES REBORN

THE DEATH OF REBEL

Tony Stark had watched his best friend Rebel die. Rebel was the first person Tony turned to when he needed someone to test out his new prototype Iron Man technology. On a test flight, Rebel pushed the suit beyond it's safeguards causing the weapons systems to overload and fire all together. Tony's old friend died in the blast.

"I built you... somehow you and me are responsible. I'm not going to stop until I have the answers."

IRON MAN & HULK

Seeking some hands-on action, Tony insisted on inspecting an emergency signal triggered at his Buffalo annex. He stumbled across a terrorist plot by the criminal organization Hydra to instigate a gamma explosion powerful enough to kill half the population of the eastern seaboard. When top scientist Bruce Banner sacrificed his life to trigger the bomb safely underground, he was transformed into the Hulk, a green-skinnned behemoth. The Hulk attacked Tony's helicopter, critically wounding the multi-millionaire. To survive the night, Tony was forced to don his experimental life-saving Iron Man armor and battle the rampaging Hulk.

Rebel mysteriously returned to attack Tony as a mutilated cyborg, a twisted visage of his former self.

BIRTH OF A HERO

After fighting the Hulk to a standstill atop Niagara Falls, Tony paid a visit to Pepper Potts (a blonde in this brave new world), asking for her help. Pepper hid Tony's injuries from the public, inventing a cover story that Iron man was Tony Stark's bodyguard to explain Iron Man's sudden emergence. Facing the continued threat of Hydra, and new villains like the Mandarin and the wind-controlling Whirlwind, Iron Man soon became a hero in his own right. His life became a virtual rollercoaster as he teamed with the Avengers, watched his friend Happy Hogan die at the hands of a twisted version of his old friend Rebel, and even saw a romance bloom between himself and Pepper. With his powerful Promethium armor, Iron Man was a force to be reckoned with. However, Tony Stark's worst enemy was his own nagging guilt. He continued to be haunted by past failures and his own failings.

When Pepper returned home one evening, she was shocked to find the assassin Whirlwind in her kitchen. Hired by Hydra to murder Stark, Whirlwind was outwitted by Tony and failed miserably in his task.

The heroes had left our world for someplace different. They'd begun new lives, started over. But soon they would have no choice: if they wanted to survive, they would have to return.

HEROES RETURN

Franklin Richards had created a universe. The young son of Mr. Fantastic and the Invisible Woman, and arguably one of the most powerful mutants on the planet, Franklin had created a pocket dimension in order to save his parents and their friends. When the Fantastic Four, the Avengers, and the Hulk threw themselves at the psionic entity Onslaught, seemingly sacrificing their very lives to stop the rampaging villain, Franklin transported them to a world of his own creation. There the heroes lived out new lives and fought new battles, with no memories of their past experiences. Meanwhile, Franklin remained in the regular universe, carrying with him a little blue ball that was the only portal to the brave new world he had imagined.

When the heroes of the pocket universe met with Ashema and Franklin, they were told they would have to leave to save their real home, Earth.

Tony & Pepper

Knowing that he would have to leave the pocket universe, Tony Stark decided to spend his last moments with his assistant, Pepper Potts. Tony knew he would never see this version of her again, and that he would soon return to a world in which he and Pepper might not be together. So before he left, Tony gave his true love one last kiss goodbye.

"WHAT OF YOU, TONY STARK? IS IT NOT GALLING TO HURL YOURSELF INTO THE UNKNOWN... WHEN YOU HAVE ALL A MAN COULD WISH FOR?"

Doctor Doom

Doom's Ride

The heroes of the pocket universe were desperate to persuade Ashema to spare their world. The Celestial reluctantly agreed, but only on condition that they all return to their proper dimension. Fortunately for them, Dr. Doom happened to have a space ship equipped for that very purpose.

Breaking Through

Using Dr. Doom's ship to travel into the other-dimensional Negative Zone, the heroes approached a weak point in the dimensional barrier that the Fantastic Four had previously discovered. In a desperate, last-second bid for power, the megalomaniac Doom grabbed Franklin and headed out into space, determined to steal the boy's abilities for himself. However, Thor rushed to the rescue, saving Franklin by hurling both Doom and himself into a rift in space and another, unknown dimension. Meanwhile, the heroes arrived safely back in their own universe. As they traveled, memories of their true pasts came back to them and they returned to their former homes, the same heroes they always were.

Iron Man Returns

Tony Stark was acting his age again. Now back in the dimension of his birth, Tony Stark was no longer the youth that had leaped into Onslaught in order to save humanity. Tony was back to his proper age, possessing all the memories of his long career as Iron Man, as well as those of his younger counterpart. After digging up his own, now-empty grave, Tony realized that Franklin Richards had restored him as best he could. So finally, Tony Stark was back to his old self again.

IRON MAN
VOL.3 #1

"You want to come after Mr. Stark—you want to hurt him, kill him, stop him from doing what he's setting out to do—you do it over Iron Man's dead body. That's all I've got to say."

IRON MAN

MAIN CHARACTERS: Iron Man (Tony Stark),
MAIN SUPPORTING CHARACTERS: Death Squad; Georgie Avalon; Ms. Denton; Vittorio Silvani; Rosalind Sharpe; Foggy Nelson; Norman Osborn; Sunset Bain; Pepper Potts; Jim Rhodes
MAIN LOCATIONS: Avalon Trading Co.; Stark Tower; Maria Stark Community Center; Baintronics (all New York); AIM hideout

PUBLICATION DATE
February 1998

EDITOR-IN-CHIEF
Bob Harris

COVER ARTIST
Sean Chen & Eric Cannon

WRITER
Kurt Busiek

PENCILER
Sean Chen

INKER
Eric Cannon

COLORIST
Liquid!

BACKGROUND

The heroes were returning, and Marvel fans couldn't be more relieved. After all, Iron Man had been through a lot lately. He had turned evil, died, been replaced by a younger version of himself, died again, and been reborn in a pocket universe as an adult version of himself. Fans were tired of the ever-shifting status quo, and when the *Heroes Return* mini series event catapulted Marvel's famous heroes back to their old familiar selves and realities, they welcomed them back with open arms.

Enter Kurt Busiek. Already a fan-favorite writer for his groundbreaking *Marvels* mini series and his innovative take on super-heroics in the pages of *Thunderbolts*, Busiek set out to not only restore Iron Man to his past glory, but to also control the fate of the Avengers comic. Busiek didn't disappoint. He told consistently classic tales that paid tribute to the past, while always moving forward in new, unexpected directions. The result was a true rebirth for the Golden Avenger, worthy of a new first issue heralding his fresh start.

The Story...

As Iron Man returns to his proper dimension and to his life as a millionaire playboy, he faces new threats hired by old foes, and is forced to adapt and change with the times.

"Wide-beam, shallow-effect repulsor blasts turn the glass fragments to powder. Don't want anyone getting hurt..."

New York City was abuzz. Not only was Tony Stark back from the seeming dead, but so was his fabled bodyguard, the armored hero known as Iron Man **(1)**. And as all of Manhattan wondered if Tony was going to attempt to take back his old company, now merged with the Japanese conglomerate Fujikawa Industries, Iron Man had other priorities on his mind. There was a hostage situation at the Avalon Trading Company that needed the hero's attention **(2)**.

After dealing with the violent mercenary Vittorio Silvani and his hired help, Iron Man headed back to Stark Tower, situated in the heart of Manhattan's flatiron district. After all, the evening was drawing close, and Tony Stark had quite a homecoming gala to attend **(3)**.

With a guest list including such luminaries as the Fantastic Four's Reed Richards and Sue Storm, Daily Bugle founder J. Jonah Jameson, and famous crusading attorney Foggy Nelson, Tony Stark spent the majority of the black tie affair shaking hands and making small talk. After turning down the advancements of the beautiful, and quite available Leah Sheffield, Tony stood outside on Stark Tower's rooftop balcony, reminiscing about a tour of a Southeast Asia plant he went on years ago that went horribly wrong **(4)**. He thought about the guerrilla leader Wong-Chu, and the death of his friend Ho Yinsen. But most of all, Tony thought about donning his Iron Man armor for the first time in order to escape Wong-Chu's custody **(5)**, and about the start of his own long-lasting war on crime that began soon after.

Deciding to get a bit of fresh air from a vantage point other than his ivory tower, Tony walked over to the construction site of a housing development he was spearheading through his charitable Maria Stark Foundation. As he toured the grounds, finding comfort in the bare steel and rivets surrounding him **(6)**, Stark's musings were interrupted by gunfire. Behind him were five heavily armed assailants, calling themselves the Death Squad.

Led by the militant Firefight, and containing members Rocket-Launcher, Airborne, Smokescreen, and Boobytrap, the Death Squad wasted no time in attacking Stark on behalf of their mysterious employer. With his trademark briefcase in hand, Tony sprinted away from the villains until he found a nice deserted hole in the ground, perfect for a quick costume change. And seconds later, the Death Squad was no longer facing a helpless millionaire playboy. Now they were up against the updated and extremely advanced technology of Iron Man **(7)**.

As the fight raged on and Iron Man gained the upper hand, the mercenaries made their getaway with the help of Smokescreen's blackout blast **(8)**. And it wasn't until the villains were safely out of sight that Iron Man realized the damage the battle had cost him. True, Tony Stark was still alive, but the housing project he had worked so hard to construct was now nothing more than expensive smoking rubble. Something had to change. He'd lost too many things that truly mattered to him.

After a sleepless night spent lost in thought **(9)**, Tony Stark called a press conference the following morning. There, to the surprise of friends and enemies, Tony announced the creation of Stark Solutions, a new company offering aid, advice or, appropriately enough, solutions, to any client willing to pay his extremely high fees. Profits would largely be turned over to the Maria Stark Foundation for reconstruction projects to help make the world a better place. And as Tony Stark turned the press conference over to questions from the audience **(10)**, he felt he could rest easier that night. He knew there would be problems yet to face, and foes yet to fight, but at least now he knew where he was going. And for Tony Stark, that was all that mattered.

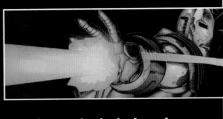

"As dawn starts to break, I make a few decisions."

ASSEMBLED

When Morgan le Fay reared her ugly head, it was time for the return of Earth's mightiest heroes. All of them.

Reunited

The Avengers were under attack. Former members in all corners of the globe suddenly became targets of Morgan le Fay's magic. Led by longtime members Captain America, Iron Man, Giant-Man, and the Wasp, nearly every past member gathered together to defeat the evil sorceress, beginning a stirring new chapter in the Avengers' legacy.

Vision: an artificial creation by the robotic villain Ultron, the Vision has used his density manipulation to aid the Avengers for years, developing his own personality in the process.

Captain America: the living embodiment of the American Dream, Steve Rogers lent his courage, energy shield, and moral character to the team.

Firestar: a mutant possessing microwave-based powers and a former member of the New Warriors, Angelica Jones was one of the Avenger's new recruits.

Justice: Firestar's boyfriend and fellow mutant, Vance Astrovik had always dreamed of using his telekinetic powers to fight alongside his childhood heroes.

Scarlet Witch: the daughter of the notorious mutant Magneto with unique "hex powers," the Scarlet Witch found a new family in the Avengers years ago.

Thor: the Norse god of Thunder, Thor fought his way back from the dimensional void to warn his friends of the dangers that faced them.

Iron Man: joining as an active member, Tony Stark once again took his place in the elite inner circle of the Avengers' founders.

It seems that every incarnation of the Avengers is destined to battle the construction-themed Wrecking Crew, and the current roster was no exception. This time, the Avengers were forced to travel to another dimension to defeat these particularly persistent villains.

After defeating Morgan le Fay and her attempt to alter reality, the Avengers were left with a new problem: what to do with 39 members.

Shaping the Future

There were too many cooks in the kitchen. The Avengers were stumbling over each other in the field—they couldn't even take down the minor villain Whirlwind. Through lack of communication and coordination, they injured each other while the wind-controlling criminal made his escape. It was time to streamline the roster, and who better to do the job than the inner circle of Iron Man, Thor, Captain America, the Wasp, and Giant-Man. Together they painstakingly selected the new line-up, adding the Vision, Scarlet Witch, the archer Hawkeye, powerhouse Warbird (later Ms. Marvel), and newcomers Firestar and Justice to the fold.

This new incarnation fought the likes of the other-dimensional Squadron Supreme, the geological villain Moses Magnum, the robotic Alkema-2, and the Taskmaster, gaining members like the ionic powered Wonder Man, the versatile Triathlon, and the incredible She-Hulk along the way. While their roster continued to change, there was no doubt that the Avengers had reclaimed their mantle as Earth's premier team of heroes.

A thorn in the side of his creator Hank Pym, Ultron returned to capture the people he considered his "family," only to have their true family, the Avengers, come to the rescue.

BETRAYED

All seemed lost. The Avengers were faced with the horror of fighting dead past teammates and the energy version of Wonder Man. But using her love to guide her, the Scarlet Witch was able to restore Wonder Man to his true self, turning the tables on the true mastermind behind the attack, the Grim Reaper.

2000s
AND ON...

Having walked a hard road, Iron Man now flew to new heights of popularity and became the center of attention in the Marvel Universe.

Iron Man was thriving in his new environment: the book store. With newsstand comics nearly a thing of the past, Marvel had largely switched its format to six-issue arcs that could be easily collected into trade paperback form. This approach seemed tailor-made for Iron Man, and the character soon appeared in a few miniseries of his own.

It wasn't long before Tony Stark was attracting top talent in the industry. Luminaries Warren Ellis and Adi Granov relaunched Iron Man's title with a new first issue and revamped origin. Writer Brian Michael Bendis placed Tony in the New Avengers and then at the helm of the Mighty Avengers and the Initiative. Ed Brubaker granted Tony a recurring role in his death of Captain America saga. With the added push of Jon Favreau's 2008 blockbuster *Iron Man* film, starring Robert Downey Jr. as Tony Stark, Iron Man had become one of the most important characters in the Marvel Universe. Iron Man was at the heart of every major event, and continued to star in several miniseries, including Joe Casey's *Enter the Mandarin* and *Inevitable* limited series.

Iron Man would see his title rebooted for the fifth time, this time to spotlight popular new writer Matt Fraction. As the comic became a bestseller, the character of War Machine was given another chance at his own ongoing series. With the release of a new animated series in 2009 and a sequel film in 2010, the future looked brighter than ever for Iron Man and his compelling, endlessly fascinating world.

OVERLEAF *Invincible Iron Man Vol. 3 #76*: Artist Adi Granov helped establish Iron Man's modern look with his popular covers, including this gem from "The Best Defense" storyline.

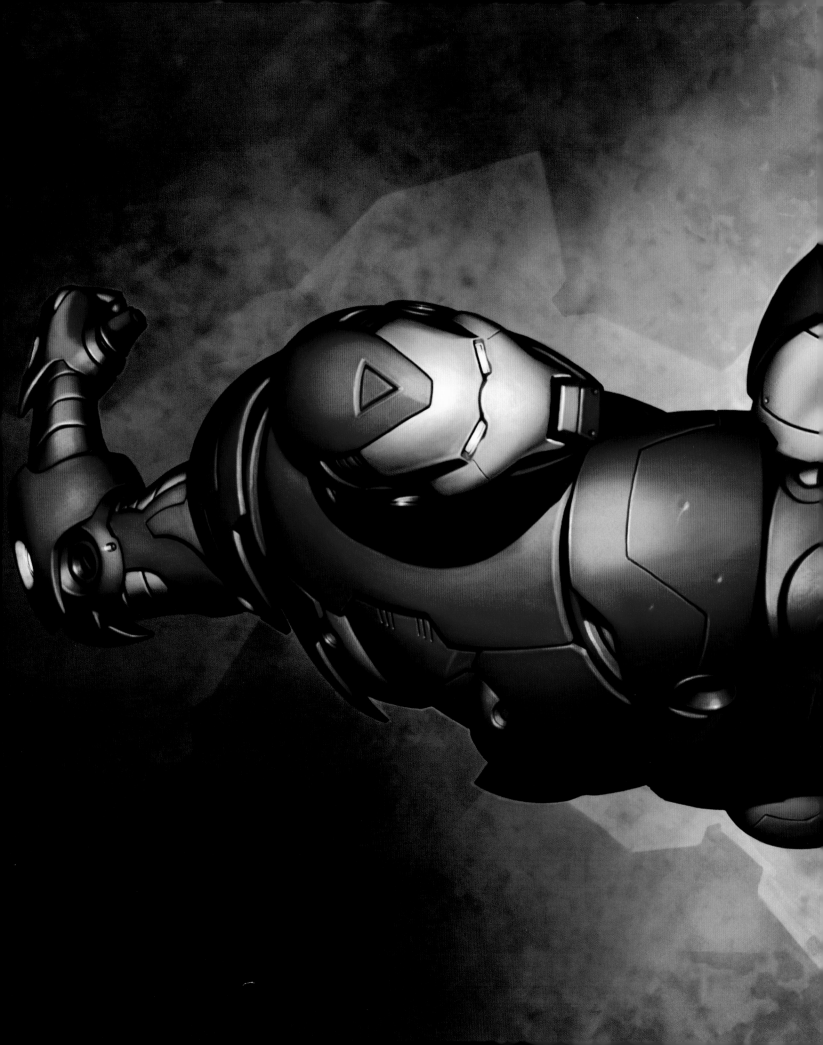

...NO ONE NEED EVER DIE IN WAR AGAIN!

Although he started his career as a weapons manufacturer with thousands of lives on his conscience, Tony Stark campaigned for the United States Secretary of Defense position, proposing a revolutionary, non-lethal approach to war.

Mr. Stark Goes to Washington

Tony Stark had finally gone public. In order to save the life of a mere dog, Tony had changed into Iron Man in the middle of a crowded street, outing his secret identity as Iron Man to an astonished nation. Unfortunately, Tony had no idea of the lasting ramifications that this split-second act of heroism would have on his world.

With Stark's life as a vigilante now a matter of public record, Sonny Burch, the Under-Secretary for Acquisition, Technology, and Logistics was granted the loophole he had been searching for. An appointed official with a less than ethical moral code, Burch had been looking for a way to exploit Stark's advanced weaponry. And now it seemed that every time Stark had denied being Iron Man in the past, he had unwittingly committed fraud and violated the terms of his many patents. This gave Burch the legal right to steal any and all of Stark's Iron Man innovations for the government. Suddenly, Tony Stark had lost control of his own designs, and he desperately wanted to get it back.

SECRETARY OF DEFENSE

Tony Stark knew he couldn't beat the government, so he opted to join them,

using all his power and influence to gain the nomination of Secretary of Defense.

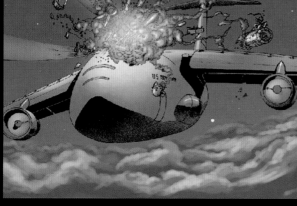

For all his legal shrewdness, Burch lacked patience. Burch conducted trial after dangerous trial of Stark's stolen technology, wanting the Secretary of Defense job as badly as Tony himself.

When overseeing the creation of a new experimental spy plane, Burch watched as the aircraft flew off course and collided with an army transport plane. As Iron Man saved the endangered craft, securing his bid to the Defense seat, Burch took his own life rather than face the repercussions of his actions.

Titanium Man

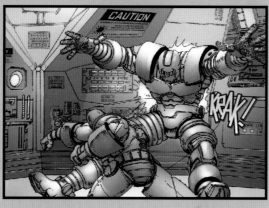

While utilizing his new hypergravity armor to compensate for the extreme pressure during an experimental space flight, Iron Man attempted to destroy a rogue comet that was on a collision course with Earth. But first he had to combat the renegade communist threat of the Titanium Man.

VITRIOL

Discovering that an archaeological team had gone missing in war-torn Iraq, Tony Stark journeyed there to investigate their disappearance. He stumbled across the super-powered leader of a terrorist clan, the acid-controlling would-be goddess Vitriol. With help from his old ally Force, Stark and the US military managed to halt Vitriol's plan to poison Iraq's rivers with a dangerous bio-weapon.

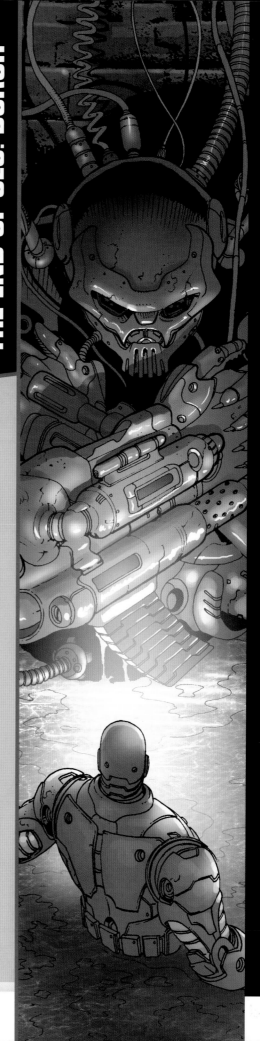

ARSENAL ALPHA

When government officials informed Tony about Arsenal Alpha (a killing machine developed by his father during the Cold War and housed in a secret lab at Stark's old home, Avengers Mansion) Iron Man embarked on a mission to destroy the dangerous device. However, when the robot was accidentally activated, Iron Man and the Avengers were forced to combat Arsenal Alpha in a very public battle on the streets of Manhattan's famed Fifth Avenue.

Maniacal despots, time-traveling bandits, world-conquering alien tyrants—the Avengers had survived them all. But when a teammate turned against them, the Avengers discovered an enemy that they might not all walk away from.

After spying the Latverian Ambassador in attendance at a UN assembly, Stark began to lash out at the official, and his corrupt country.

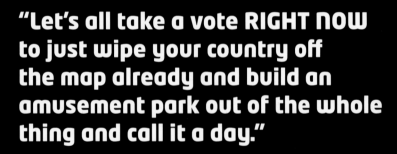

"Let's all take a vote RIGHT NOW to just wipe your country off the map already and build an amusement park out of the whole thing and call it a day."

Outburst at the UN

Tony Stark was perhaps the most widely trusted member of the Avengers. In his position as the US Secretary of Defense, he was the natural choice to speak at a peace conference at the United Nations. But suddenly, he found himself unable to contain his temper while addressing the Latverian Ambassador and ended his rant by storming out of the assembly in a huff. The outburst seemed totally out of character; nevertheless, Tony recognized the way he was feeling. He felt as if he were drunk. Yet he hadn't had a drop of alcohol in years...

Meanwhile at the Mansion ...

The Avengers believed their old teammate Jack of Hearts was dead. They were stunned when, little more than a walking corpse, he staggered through the gates of Avengers Mansion. Moments later their shock turned to horror: Jack of Hearts exploded. The blast killed Ant-Man Scott Lang and demolished the mansion. But this was only the beginning.

Hawkeye was the next to fall when an armada of alien spaceships filled the sky. Then an army of enemies past and present appeared.

UNDER ATTACK?

I WASN'T DRUNK. I DIDN'T *HAVE* A DRINK. I HAVEN'T HAD ONE IN WHO KNOWS HOW LONG. I WAS OVERCOME WITH THE FEELING--THE *FEELING* OF BEING DRUNK--I WASN'T *IN* CONTROL.

THAT'S WHY I THINK THIS IS SOME SORT OF *ATTACK.*

ALL OF THIS.

ALL OF IT HAPPENING AT THE SAME TIME.

THE MANSION. BOOM. SCOTT. BOOM. VISION. BOOM AND BOOM! I'M ASKED TO STEP DOWN AS SECRETARY OF DEFENSE.

As Captain America arrived at the devastated mansion, he was shocked to find the Vision leading an attack of Ultron androids against his former friends. To make matters worse, She-Hulk lost control while fighting the Vision, and literally ripped her old robotic teammate in half. All this tragedy couldn't be a coincidence. It had to be a coordinated attack.

Hex Magic

Dr. Strange, the world's greatest sorcerer, figured it out first. All these apparently random events had the same origin: they had been caused by the magical hex powers of longtime Avenger, the Scarlet Witch. After years of emotional trauma, Wanda Maximoff had finally lost control of her sanity, and was lashing out at the Avengers.

Luckily for the Avengers, Dr. Strange's knowledge of magic knew no rival, and he was able to defeat Wanda by taking away what little remained of her fragile mind.

Her tortured mind shattered beyond repair, Wanda Maximoff, the Scarlet Witch, decided to use her hex powers to remodel existence in her own image. No longer were mutants the despised minority, they were now the overwhelming majority.

In a world where humans fought in an arena for the enjoyment of the mutant population, there was no better showman than Tony Stark.

Father and Son

While Tony Stark enjoyed the spotlight of wearing his Iron Man suit for the entertainment of thousands of mutant fans, he was still no match for his father, Howard Stark, the grand champion of giant robot gladiator fighting. Not only did Howard and Tony fight together, but they also did business together in the most successful, human-run corporation in the world, Stark Industries.

THE GREAT HUMAN HOPE

Tony Stark was living the dream in the Scarlet Witch's House of M world. His father was still alive, he was a successful businessman, and he was adored and envied by millions in the sports arena. But at heart, he was still the same hero who had struggled against opposition and overwhelming odds for his entire life. So when his old friend Henry Pym went missing while running controversial experiments on the mutant genome, Tony donned his most recent Iron Man suit and headed out to find his trusted Stark Industries employee. After doing battle with a fleet of human-hunting giant sentinel robots led by his own father, Tony teamed up with fellow robot fighter Johnny Storm and attacked a human holding facility to free Pym.

Mutants and Madmen

Hank Pym was up to more than just studying the genetic makeup of mutants. He had secretly created dozens of mutant-targeting bombs in an attempt to wipe *homo superior* from the face of the Earth. And as Tony raced to destroy the explosive devices one by one, he discovered that his father was the true mastermind behind the attack, a fact that led to Howard Stark's death at the hands of the leader of the mutants, Magneto.

THE RESISTANCE

Howard Stark had been wrong. Mass murder could never be an acceptable answer. But deep down in his soul, Tony still knew that something about this world was seriously out of kilter. A major wrong needed to be put right... Then the mutant Layla Miller and a band of familiar heroes paid him a visit in his hometown of Chicago to restore his memories to what they were before the Scarlet Witch altered them. Tony immediately joined their underground resistance, which had the sole aim of bringing the tyranny of the House of Magneto to an end.

It was time to take the fight directly to Magneto's front door, the island nation of Genosha.

The Scarlet Witch was responsible for the creation of the parallel reality where Homo Superior ruled and many of her fellow Avengers led happy and contented lives.

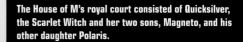

The House of M's royal court consisted of Quicksilver, the Scarlet Witch and her two sons, Magneto, and his other daughter Polaris.

"No More Mutants"

As the heroes invaded Genosha on the back of a reprogrammed sentinel robot, they unlocked Magneto's mind so that he, too, remembered the way the world should be. Enraged to discover that his son Quicksilver had influenced the Scarlet Witch's thinking and had inspired her to create the World of M, Magneto attacked his own son, forcing the Scarlet Witch into action. Seeing the damage her people had caused, Wanda Maximoff restored the world to normal, dramatically reducing the number of powered mutants.

Iron Man fought alongside Spider-Man, Cyclops and other heroes in an attempt to bring down the House of M and restore their reality.

ELECTRO When notorious Spider-Man foe Max Dillon, also known as the costumed villain Electro, was hired to trigger a massive breakout in New York City's maximum-security penitentiary the Raft, he had little idea that the resulting riots would unite several of the world's greatest Super Heroes in battle. No, Dillon was only hired with one goal in mind: to free all the incarcerated villains—especially the prehistorically powered mutant Sauron. The aim was to cause maximum chaos but the result was to bring together a new line-up of the Avengers.

> "We'll find out who our enemies are. We'll find who did this. And then we'll avenge it." IRON MAN

THE NEW AVENGERS

While visiting a prisoner at Ryker's Island's Raft Installation, crusading lawyer Matthew Murdock, his escorting SHIELD agent and former Spider-Woman Jessica Drew, and his bodyguard Luke Cage found themselves in the fight of their lives. When the facility's power suddenly shut off, the deadliest super-powered prisoners New York City had to offer were freed.

BREAKOUT

Joined by Spider-Man, Iron Man, and Captain America, as well as the formerly imprisoned powerhouse the Sentry, the heroes managed to quell the riots, though not before 42 inmates made good their escape. The mission didn't have the best result by any means, but it inspired Captain America, making him realize the need for a team of super-powered crime fighters.

Captain America set out to recruit those that had helped deal with the prison breakout. With Iron Man on board, as well as Spider-Woman, Spider-Man, and Luke Cage, this ragtag team of New Avengers set up a headquarters in the top three floors of Manhattan's Stark Tower skyscraper, and soon added Wolverine, the Sentry, and the mysterious martial artist Ronin to their ranks.

An opportunist by nature, Electro made sure that the Raft prisoners knew that they owed him a favor.

WORLD CLASS

After their first team-up led them to the prehistoric island known as the Savage Land in order to battle Sauron and a renegade faction of SHIELD, the New Avengers would soon grow accustomed to world travel. Before they knew it, they found themselves flying off to Japan to fight the terrorist organization Hydra, and then to Genosha to combat the mutant threat of the Collective. But little did the team know that their most devastating challenge was yet to come, and would occur right in their own backyard.

MEMBERS

1. **IRON MAN**
   Real Name: Tony Stark
2. **RONIN** aka Echo
   Real Name: Maya Lopez
3. **SPIDER-WOMAN**
   Real Name: Jessica Drew
4. **LUKE CAGE**
   Formerly known as Power Man
5. **SPIDER-MAN**
   Real Name: Peter Parker
6. **WOLVERINE** aka Logan
   Real Name: James Howlett
7. **CAPTAIN AMERICA**
   Real Name: Steve Rogers

SENTRY'S STORY

Robert Reynolds was once the Sentry, a hero that no one remembered. When his brain was manipulated by the mutant Mastermind, Reynolds, as well as the world at large, simply forgot his heroic past. Not only did Reynolds suppress his powers, he soon unwittingly manifested a dark second personality he called the Void. With the help of the New Avengers and the X-Men's telepath Emma Frost, Reynolds was able to unlock his hidden memories and finally overcome this dark side.

...I'M FROM THE THIRTIETH CENTURY. THEY CALL ME KANG...

IRON LAD

Soon after recruiting his teenage allies in the Young Avengers, Iron Lad revealed his double identity to Captain America, Iron Man and *Daily Bugle* employee Jessica Jones. From his past trauma of being the target of schoolyard bullies, to his time traveling adventures with his future self, Kang, Iron Lad divulged his entire life story to the heroes.

Iron Lad's costume was made up of neuro-kinetic material that could change its shape with a single thought.

After traveling to the present, Iron Lad broke into Stark Industries in order to locate the living computer program and former Avenger known as the Vision.

IRON LAD & The YOUNG AVENGERS

They appeared out of nowhere. A group of teenage heroes bearing striking resemblances to familiar icons. Although their heroism was immediately obvious, the origins of these Young Avengers were shrouded in mystery.

Back in the Past

Iron Lad was having a heated argument with himself. Growing up in the far-flung future, the boy who was destined to become the Avengers' arch foe Kang the Conqueror was visited one day by his future evil self. Giving this young version of himself a suit of powerful armor, Kang was surprised when his young self rebelled from his teaching, fleeing into the past instead of killing one of his childhood bullies.

Now residing in our present, the young Kang decided to alter his armor in an homage to Iron Man, and began going by the name Iron Lad. He then set out to recruit the Avengers to help him battle his older self. When he discovered that contacting a Super Hero team was a bit more difficult than he had originally thought, Iron Lad formed his own squad of young heroes in anticipation of Kang's arrival. The media soon dubbed this group the Young Avengers.

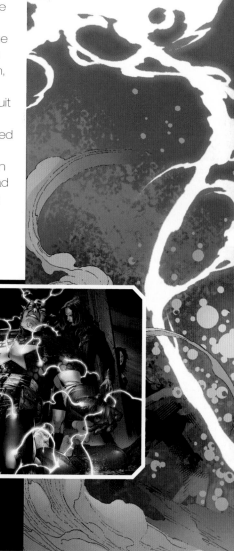

Despite being beaten by the Avengers time and time again, Kang was still a seriously powerful threat.

When Kang returned to the present to kidnap his younger self, the Young Avengers stood against him, united despite having to escape the Avengers' protective custody.

Kang's Spy

Soon after the Young Avengers introduced themselves to their older counterparts, they were attacked by the Growing Man, an old foe of the Avengers and Thor. After being subdued by the heroes, the Growing Man disappeared, sending a beacon to his master Kang to let him know that he'd located Iron Lad.

YOUNG AVENGERS

By downloading Vision's consciousness into his own futuristic armor, Iron Lad was able to track down the next generation of young heroes: Hulkling, the shape-shifting offspring of two alien races; Asgardian, an inexperienced magician with uncanny abilities; and Patriot, the grandson of the original Captain America, Isaiah Bradley. Soon after their public debut, circumstance led to two other teenage crime-fighters joining up: the expert female archer Hawkeye; and Cassie Lang, the size-changing daughter of former Avenger, Ant-Man. The Young Avengers were an impressive team, with plenty of firepower, however, they still weren't a match for Kang's awe-inspiring might. As Kang rewrote time and the landscape shifted around them, the Young Avengers battled their foe to no avail until Iron Lad made a dramatic decision. He would stab his future self in the back. Literally.

The Death and Birth of Kang

With Kang lying dead at his feet, Iron Lad was shocked to see his friends beginning to disappear from reality, one by one. By refusing to travel forward in time to his proper place in the timestream, Iron Lad had dramatically changed the present. Realizing that he had to set things right, Iron Lad kissed his sweetheart Cassie Lang goodbye and headed back to the future to fulfill his horrible destiny.

When all seemed lost, Iron Lad committed a valiant act of suicide, killing his evil future self.

EXTREMIS

The Extremis formula, a super-serum that melded man into machine, seemed like a scientific breakthrough and the next step in human evolution. Until it fell into the wrong hands. Then it was time to call Iron Man.

HURGL

HHRRGAAAHH

Mallen had a tragic past. As a child, he watched helplessly as his mother and father were gunned down during a standoff with police.

During his first encounter with Iron Man, Mallen shorted out Tony's armor with small spikes protruding from his fingertips, and effortlessly tossed him like a rag doll hundreds of feet through the air.

A Man Called Mallen

Fittingly, Mallen gained his powers in a slaughterhouse. He came into possession of a stolen experimental super-serum being developed at Futurepharm labs in Austin, Texas. After injecting himself with the formula in an abandoned slaughterhouse, Mallen was instantly incased in a thick, black cocoon. Waking two days later, he was reborn into a super-strong, fire-breathing monstrosity, with a vendetta to unleash upon the unsuspecting populace.

Futurepharm decided to give Iron Man a call. Extremis developer, Maya Hansen, an old friend of Tony Stark's who had met him at a technology convention years ago, recruited Iron Man into her service soon after the Extremis solution went missing from her laboratory. As he met with Maya and their old mentor, Sal Kennedy, Tony witnessed the televised aftermath of a brutal terrorist attack Mallen had orchestrated on the Houston headquarters of the FBI. Stirred into action, Tony tracked the murderer down and confronted him, only to be severely trounced by the villain's superior strength and power.

In the first stage of the Extremis transformation, Mallen's body was essentially reduced to a giant open wound. Encased in layers of scabs, Mallen's organs were rebuilt from the inside out, making him an extremely dangerous super-being.

With the Extremis solution enhancing his body and mind, Tony could now sense and control machinery around him and command his Iron Man suit at will. He could see through the cameras of satellites and even make cell phone calls with his mind. He was now a true Iron Man, inside and out.

Man Into Machine

Tony had barely escaped with his life. With shattered bones, internal bleeding, and more bruises and injuries than he could count, Tony Stark was airlifted back to Futurepharm after Mallen made his escape. As the villain continued his killing spree across America, Tony asked Maya to inject him with her one remaining dose of the Extremis formula, in order to mend his injuries and allow him to defeat Mallen in their next confrontation. Reluctantly, Maya agreed, not noticing that Tony had made a few of his own modifications to her super-soldier serum. She injected Tony with the solution and watched as her old friend grew his cocoon, only to emerge a day later, much earlier than she had anticipated.

Tony had not only survived the serum's effects, he had thrived on them. Now essentially one with his armor, Iron Man headed back out into the field, determined to track Mallen to Washington DC and defeat the terrorist once and for all.

Suit Integration

Formerly having to ship his bulky armor around in a giant crate, the Extremis solution enabled Tony to store his golden undersheath inside his newly hollow bones. The rest of his suit could be stored in his briefcase until he summoned it to him mentally, using vectored repulsor fields.

Despite utilizing her help to upgrade his armor, Tony was later forced to arrest Maya Hansen when he discovered that she had leaked Extremis on purpose.

IRON MAN
Vol. 4 # 5

PUBLICATION DATE
March 2006

EDITOR-IN-CHIEF
Joe Quesada

COVER ARTIST
Adi Granov

WRITER
Warren Ellis

ARTIST
Adi Granov

COLORIST
Adi Granov

LETTERER
Randy Gentile

> "Maya, I can see through satellites now."
>
> IRON MAN

MAIN CHARACTERS: Iron Man (Tony Stark); Ho Yinsen; Maya Hansen
SUPPORTING CHARACTERS: Various terrorists under Wong-Chu's employ
LOCATIONS: Wong-Chu's insurgent camp, presumably Afghanistan; Maya Hansen's laboratory at Futurepharm, Austin, Texas

BACKGROUND

It was time for Iron Man to get a boost. A major Marvel writer of the 1990s, Warren Ellis had taken a brief respite from mainstream heroes to explore uncharted waters on various successful titles, including Vertigo Comics' *Transmetropolitan* and Wildstorm's *The Authority*. After amassing much critical acclaim, Ellis was triumphantly returning to the comic mainstream with projects like the highly popular *Ultimate Fantastic Four*. Soon, Ellis was tapped to relaunch Iron Man into a fourth series.

Already praised for his distinctive covers for the end of Iron Man's third series, Adi Granov was looking for a new project. He jumped at the chance of drawing six Iron Man issues alongside Ellis. The collaboration brought about not only a best-selling graphic novel, when the issues were collected, but also a startling reinvention of the character, evolving Iron Man to the next level as both man and machine.

The Story...

As Tony Stark's body lies helpless on Maya Hansen's operating table, undergoing the Extremis procedure, his mind flashes back to his first time in an Iron Man suit.

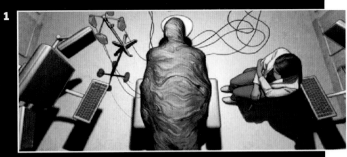

Iron Man needed an upgrade, or he wouldn't survive the night **(1)**. That much was clear to Tony Stark as he lay there on Maya Hansen's operating table in the heart of Futurepharm labs. Maya's experimental super-soldier serum known as Extremis had been stolen from the company, and a man known only as Mallen had injected himself with it. Tony had tracked down the vicious criminal only to receive a severe beating that had badly injured his body inside his Iron Man armor. He'd managed to make it to Maya's doorstep, and even tinker with her computer system a bit, but that took all the life that was left in him. So Maya reluctantly did as he told her. She injected him with the last remaining sample of the Extremis formula, sending Tony's body into a series of convulsions before ceasing all movement. As Maya waited for a sign that Tony had survived the injection, Tony slept. And dreamed. And remembered…

The location was Afghanistan. While on a consultation mission with the US Army, Tony Stark and his military escorts were caught in a vicious attack by insurgent rebels. A stray bullet hit one of Stark Industries' own landmines, knocking Tony unconscious. When he finally regained his senses **(2)**, he found himself in a shabby room with an array of technology stacked in the corner **(3)** and an elderly Asian man looking down at him. The man was Ho Yinsen **(4)**, a brilliant medical innovator, who had been captured by the terrorists and put to work against his will. Tony knew the man's work quite well. He'd even attended a lecture of his once, although he was a bit drunk at the time.

Yinsen explained the current situation. Tony had shrapnel stuck in his chest and was probably going to die within the week. In that time he was expected to create a weapon for the terrorists, however absurd that sounded. Determined to survive, Tony remembered Yinsen's lecture from that night so many years ago. It was about magnetic wound excision. He also recalled the subject of his own speech at that same conference. It was about an exoskeleton suit of armor that he planned to call the Iron Man. Now, Tony was going to build a prototype Iron Man suit, and Yinsen was going to add his magnetic technology into the chest plate.

Meanwhile, back in the present on the operating table, a strange black cocoon had formed around Tony's body. And Maya waited.

Back in Tony's memories, he and Yinsen built their suit of armor, and it worked just like Tony thought it would **(5)**. He easily escaped, killing the very terrorist soldiers who had kidnapped him. And just like that, Iron Man was born.

Maya had been waiting for an hour when the energy shot out of Tony's chest **(6)**. It was a red, unfocused beam, that cracked the cocoon like lava bursting through hardened magma. As the cocoon broke away, Tony sat up. He was alive, and filled with more energy than ever before.

The Extremis serum had rebuilt him. It had regrown his organs and mended his crushed bones. The problem was, according to Maya's calculations, it shouldn't have worked so quickly. But in the time before he passed out, Tony had made his own modifications to the Extremis solution. Now, his crucial undersheath, the golden layer of electronics under his armor **(7)**, was stored in his hollow bones, and formed around his skin as it poured out of his pores on his mental command. He could send electronic signals with his brain, even make telephone calls without saying a word out loud. Even better, he could communicate with machinery remotely **(8)**, like the compressed outer Iron Man armor he kept in his treasured briefcase.

Tony Stark was now a new man. A true Iron Man. And he was ready to take the fight back to Mallen.

"This either saves you or kills you."

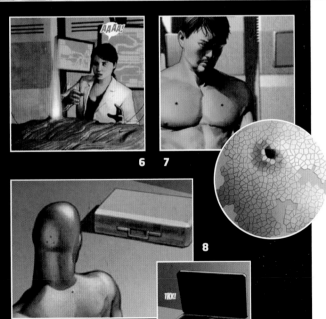

ILLUMINATI

Brought together by a conscious resolve to make the world a better place, the Illuminati were a secret band of brothers, each a hero in his own right, representing the best of man and mutantkind. They formed to prevent an invasion. And they would disband when an invasion occurred...

The Illuminati were a group of leaders gathered together by Iron Man in order to keep the lines of communication open between all the world's superhuman communities. Comprising Iron Man, the Inhuman king Black Bolt, the mutant rights activist and leader of the X-Men Professor X, Namor the Sub-Mariner and king of Atlantis, Dr. Strange, the world's sorcerer supreme, and the Fantastic Four's Mr. Fantastic, the Illuminati was a brain trust that served as a clandestine direct link between the world's greatest super hero teams.

The organization was founded after the Kree/Skrull War. A war between two alien races on a scale so massive it was unheard of, the war shook the Avengers' world and opened Iron Man's eyes to the threats facing the Earth. Tony realized that if there had been better communication between the Earth's super-powered groups, then they would have detected the seeds of war much earlier, and preventative measures could have been taken.

So Iron Man assembled the Illuminati, and also invited the king of Wakanda and former Avenger Black Panther to join its ranks. While the rest of the Illuminati realized that Iron Man might be on to something and embraced his idea, Black Panther opposed the notion. He felt that there would be too much at stake if the group disagreed, and he wanted no part in their self-proclaimed role as protectors of Earth. Panther left the meeting, and the others moved on to their first new order of business.

It wasn't long before the Illuminati took offensive action against the shape-shifting alien Skrulls. After destroying a warship that contained the Skrulls' king, who had refused to listen to reason, the heroes were ambushed and taken prisoner. Although they eventually escaped, the Skrulls had experimented on them, and discerned how to duplicate their powers. The Skrulls started to plan their revenge.

160-161

ILLUMINATI ACTS

The Illuminati convened in times of crisis, acting only when they felt the situation was too dire to ignore.

THE HULK EXILED

When the Hulk's latest destructive outburst resulted in a death count of 26 people, Iron Man could no longer overlook the uncontrollable actions of his friend Bruce Banner's alter ego. Bringing the issue to the attention of the Illuminati, Iron Man was surprised to encounter fierce opposition from Namor. Iron Man and the others voted to exile the Hulk into outer space and onto a deserted planet where the brute could finally find peace, Namor attacked Iron Man until the sea king was restrained by Dr. Strange. The vote was taken and Hulk was sentenced to be sent away for good.

The Illuminati set about tricking Hulk to man a vessel that was to be propelled into deep space. However, the ship happened to pass through a wormhole, and Hulk was sent to a war-torn planet instead of the paradise the Illuminati had intended. Thus a series of events were set in motion that culminated in the seismic conflict known as World War Hulk.

THE INFINITY GAUNTLET

Containing six all-powerful gems that each controlled a different cosmic power, the Infinity Gauntlet granted its wearer control of all of space, matter, and time. Determined that the gems should not fall into the wrong hands, the Illuminati set out to locate them. After traveling the globe to find the stones, each one of the Illuminati became a guardian of a particular gem, to ensure that its power would never be abused.

The Illuminati each became a caretaker of the Infinity gems that controlled reality, the mind, power, space, the soul, and time.

THE BREAKUP

The US government was intent on passing the Superhuman Registration Act that would force all powered individuals to register their abilities with them. Iron Man brought the proposed legislation up with Illuminati, insisting that the members back the act. He was immediately met with opposition from Dr. Strange and Namor. Both members resigned from the group, and it seemed the Illuminati were finished for good. Iron Man called upon the Illuminati one last time to show them evidence of a coming Skrull invasion. Once Black Bolt had revealed himself to be a Skrull sleeper agent, the Illuminati went their separate ways, not knowing whom to trust, and haunted by the realization that their actions years ago had prompted the Skrulls to attack Earth in a clandestine move that came to be known as the Secret Invasion.

CIVIL WAR

It was brother against brother. Friend against friend. The Super Hero Civil War created a rift in the superhuman community that might never heal.

It was the law. Super Heroes, or anyone possessing enhanced abilities for that matter, had to register their powers with the government. Their secret identities would now be a matter of record. Their crime-fighting careers would be regulated, with paid vacations and sick days, just like any other job. Super Heroes were now civil servants. Anyone operating outside of those perimeters would be arrested and locked in an extra-dimensional prison developed by Mr. Fantastic himself in the fabled Negative Zone. There was a definite line drawn in the sand, and it came as no surprise to anyone that Captain America was the first to cross it.

To Captain America, trading in personal freedoms for a government promise of security was totally unacceptable. He was convinced that registering their identities would be like painting targets on the innocent families and friends of some Super Heroes. After all, a hero's life is fraught with peril, and the last thing he or she would want to do would be to bring that danger home at night. So Cap organized his own underground rebellion against the Registration Act and many heroes flocked to him.

STAMFORD

It was one of the worst disasters in human history. When a youthful team of crime fighters called the New Warriors were locked in combat with a group of villains, the ruthless Nitro set off an explosive charge that devastated the town of Stamford, Connecticut, killing more than 600 people. The nation blamed all Super Heroes, and Congress passed the Superhuman Registration Act.

THE RIGHT THING?

Tony Stark wouldn't get a good night's sleep for quite some time. In his heart he knew that regulating the heroes was a necessary step in this day and age. He knew training them and preparing them for a life of fighting crime was a good thing. But he was hunting down his best friends. And he knew no good could come of that.

OH, GOD.
PLEASE LET
US BE DOING
THE RIGHT
THING HERE.

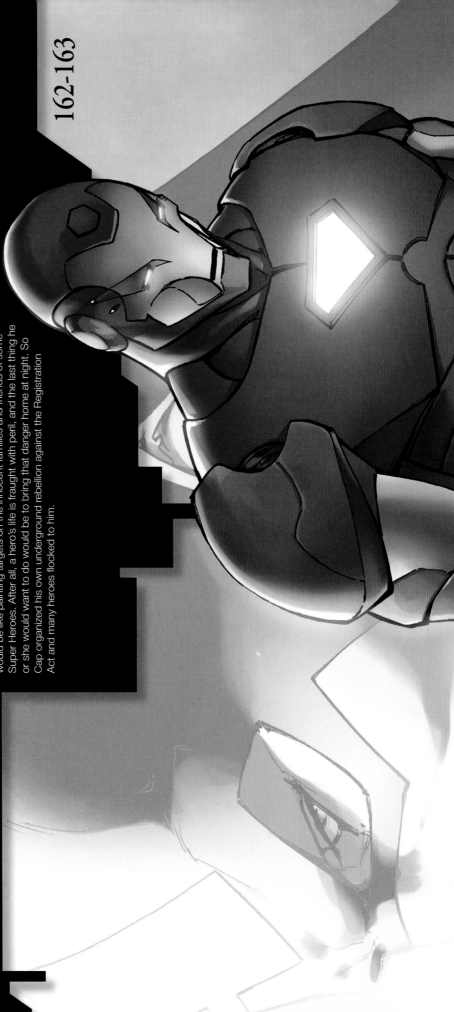

AMERICA'S SACRIFICE

A war was being waged. Lives were being lost. On both sides, ugly decisions were being made. Soon Iron Man and Captain America met face-to-face on the streets of New York City. After the Vision took Tony by surprise and short-circuited his armor, Cap beat his old friend within an inch of his life. A group of rescue workers tore the Captain off Tony's nearly lifeless body, providing the reality check Captain America needed. He looked around and saw the destruction the war had caused his city and he knew that this wasn't the way. Captain America surrendered and ordered his people to stand down. And just like that, the war was over.

I THINK THIS PLAN WILL SETTLE DOWN THE MIDDLE.

I THINK YOU'RE GOING TO HAVE US AT WAR WITH ONE ANOTHER.

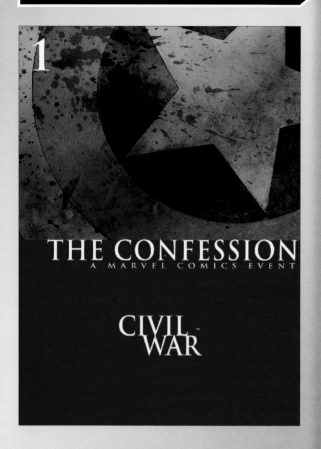

1

THE CONFESSION
A MARVEL COMICS EVENT

CIVIL WAR

PUBLICATION DATE
May 2007

EDITOR-IN-CHIEF
Joe Quesada

WRITER
Brian Michael Bendis

3-D IRON MAN DESIGN
Alex Maleev

PENCILLER
Alex Maleev

INKER
Alex Maleev

COLORIST
Jose Villarrubia

CIVIL WAR: THE CONFESSION #1

> "I—I came here to tell you *why* all this happened. You asked me and I'm going to tell you. It was because of King Arthur."
>
> IRON MAN

MAIN CHARACTERS: Iron Man, Captain America
SUPPORTING CHARACTERS: SHIELD agents, King Arthur and knights, zombies, Dr. Doom, Mr. Fantastic, Magneto, Green Goblin, Spider-Man, Thor, Kingpin, Nick Fury and other heroes
LOCATIONS: SHIELD Helicarrier; Camelot; Stark's lab; the Raft prison

BACKGROUND

Writer Mark Millar rocked the Marvel Universe with his seven-issue mini series *Civil War*, which forced nearly every hero and villain to choose between Iron Man's pro-registration side and Captain America's underground forces. However, fans in the real world wondered why Iron Man made the decision he did. With a long history of clashing with the US government, what would make Tony Stark commit himself so fully to the cause of Super Hero registration?

There was no better writer to explain Tony's stance than Brian Michael Bendis. Known for his realistic dialog and character insights, which had helped to make *Ultimate Spider-Man* and *Daredevil* such successes, Bendis partnered with his longtime Daredevil artist Alex Maleev to relate two poignant conversations between the generals of each side of the Civil War. Born out of these revealing exchanges was a one-shot tie-in special that shed light on the uneasy ramifications of a war between friends.

The Story...

With the Civil War finally over, Iron Man and Captain America share their views with each other in the face of devastating tragedy.

The skies were appropriately cloudy as Iron Man flew to the SHIELD Helicarrier hovering over Washington DC's famous Arlington Cemetery **(1)**. Arriving on Basement Sub-Level 7 of the massive floating fortress, Iron Man continued past the varied faces of his SHIELD subordinates. Although each soldier paid him the professional respect he demanded as Director of the SHIELD global peacekeeping force, Iron Man could sense where their true loyalties rested. They were still the soldiers of SHIELD's former Director, Nick Fury, and to them, Iron Man was an intruder within their proud organization.

Tony Stark soon found the man he was looking for: his old friend and current enemy, Steve Rogers, the flag-wearing icon known to the world as Captain America. As Tony sat down across from his old friend, he took his helmet off **(2)** and began to bare his soul. Earlier, Captain America had asked Tony why all this—the Civil War between the heroes—why it all began… and Tony thought it was finally time to tell him.

Years ago, when Iron Man had battled Dr. Doom in a time-spanning mission that cast the two foes back into the days of King Arthur and the Knights of the Round Table **(3)**, Tony had seen a vision while locked in combat on the field of battle. There amid the blood and the violence, he'd seen his own future. Heroes were fighting heroes **(4)**. Allies were battling each other in a bloody conflict with no clear-cut victor. This image, however brief, stayed with Tony and, upon his return to his proper time, helped him decide to form the Illuminati, a gathering of the leaders of various Super-Hero teams. If this disaster was looming in the future, he would do his best to see to it that it never happened.

Despite his best intentions, Tony began to see the seeds of war all around him. When Nick Fury leaked a copy of the Superhuman Registration Act to him **(5)**, Tony could see a line already forming in the sand. He was a futurist after all. It was what he did for a living. He already knew which side his various friends would choose, and he knew that he had to take a stand. Because if *he* didn't organize the legal side of things, then who would? After all, heroes had to work with the law, and to work against it was nothing short of arrogant.

As Tony sat there, bearing his soul to his old friend, tears formed in his eyes **(6)**. Because recently, Captain America had asked Iron Man if it was worth it. If Tony's stance was worth all the death and destruction that had resulted from brother fighting brother. And as he now looked at the man he'd been talking to all this time, the corpse of Captain America laid out on a cold metal slab in front of him **(7)**, Iron Man knew that he had been wrong. It hadn't been worth it at all.

Before his death, Captain America had been flown to the Raft, the maximum-maximum security penitentiary on Ryker's Island. After being transferred to his cell, Steve Rogers was paid a visit by his captor himself, Iron Man **(8)**. What followed wasn't the friendliest conversation. Captain America accused Iron Man of being sick with power, and Iron Man accused Captain America of being an old man who didn't understand the times he was living in. But Steve Rogers was certain. Despite Iron Man's victory on the battlefield, Stark had lost the fight before it had started. He'd sold his principles and the cause of freedom. So Captain America asked his old friend one last question. He asked him if all of it had been worth it.

Iron Man didn't answer. He just called Rogers a sore loser, and walked away, leaving the living symbol of freedom to sit quietly, alone and behind bars **(9)**.

"Was it worth it?! Tell me!"

I FEEL STRANGE. *WEAK.* AS IF SOMETHING WAS SAPPING MY ENERGY!

Possessing a scientific mind, Peter Parker is always drawn to technology exhibits, despite having gained his powers at one when bitten by a radioactive spider.

KEY DATA

REAL NAME Peter Benjamin Parker

OCCUPATION Freelance photographer, former science teacher, adventurer

AFFILIATIONS New Avengers, Secret Avengers, New Fantastic Four

POWERS/ABILITIES Superhuman strength, reflexes, equilibrium, endurance, and flexibility. Accelerated healing factor. Ability to adhere to flat surfaces. Uncanny extra-sensory "spider-sense." Developed web-shooters and sticky, dissolving web fluid adhesive. Genius level intellect.

Radioactive Man

While attending a New York electronics expo, Tony Stark and Peter Parker felt a chill when walking by the Stane International booth. For Peter, it was his trademark spider-sense warning him of danger. For Tony, it was the lingering memories of his archenemy Obadiah Stane and the damage the ruthless mogul had inflicted on his personal life. However different their origins, both men's instincts proved correct. The mouthpiece for Stane International's presence at the show was none other than Chen Lu, secretly the Radioactive Man, a threat from both heroes' pasts. And when Spider-Man returned to the expo at night, the Radioactive Man showed the wall-crawler exactly how much of a threat he truly was.

As the Radioactive Man experimented on a captive Spider-Man, Iron Man barged in on the scene and freed his fellow hero. With Spidey clad in a radiation suit, the two used ultra-freon to subdue their poisonous adversary.

"What—Spider Man in a radiation suit? ...Ingenious!"

IRON MAN and SPIDER-MAN

Made of heat-resistant Kevlar micro-fiber, Spider-Man's new costume could resist small-caliber bullets, had carbon filters in the mouth to keep out toxins, a short-range GPS system, and three arm-like waldoes that could extend from the back.

The Iron Spider

Years later, when both Spider-Man and Iron Man were members of the New Avengers, Tony took Peter under his wing as his protégé. Not only did Stark allow Peter and his family to live in Avengers Tower, but he also designed a suit of armor specifically created for Spider-Man's abilities. The new Iron Spider costume allowed Peter to glide for short distances, had built-in fire, police, and emergency scanners, as well as infrared and ultraviolet visual amplification.

Peter's Iron Spider suit also possessed chameleon abilities, allowing him to change his appearance to his classic costume, or even street clothes.

Tony warned Peter of the proposed Superhuman Registration Act and Peter agreed to stand by him.

To Washington

Tony Stark doesn't do anything without a reason. Although he enjoyed mentoring Peter Parker, he also needed his help. Tony hired Peter to work for him as his second-in-command, and informed his young friend that the two of them would soon be heading to Washington DC. Congress was preparing to pass a Superhuman Registration Act, a law requiring Super Heroes to register their powers and identities with the US government. Convinced that the Act was timely and sure to become law, Stark reluctantly became a spokesman for it. Tony knew that if Spider-Man—who represented the common man to many in the Super Hero community—came out in support of the Act, many other superhuman individuals would agree to sign up, and the chance of violence erupting would be significantly reduced.

Tony Stark did his best to talk the government out of their proposed Superhuman Registration Act. He even went so far as to stage an attack on his life by the Titanium Man, one Peter valiantly saved him from.

Civil War

Peter Parker was raised to stick by his word. So as a Civil War sparked in the Super Hero community over the recently passed Superhuman Registration Act, Spider-Man stayed by Iron Man's side, despite many of his friends joining the underground opposition. Spider-Man even went so far as to take his mask off in public at a press conference Tony arranged to show his support. But as the war waged on, Spider-Man realized he had chosen the wrong side, and abandoned Tony, joining Captain America's secret forces.

Friends Again?

With the war over and Spider-Man's identity magically restored to its secret status due to the manipulations of a demon named Mephisto, Iron Man and Spider-Man now have a very different relationship. While Spider-Man still respects Tony's intellect and wishes to restore their strained friendship, the weight of his responsibilities and the ramifications of the Civil War still weigh heavily on Iron Man's shoulders. However, Spidey did manage to team up with Iron Man after an explosion wrecked Stark's main facility. Despite Shellhead's protests, Spidey tagged along with his former mentor and helped the Golden Avenger arrest several technology based criminals.

TONY STARK
DIRECTOR OF S.H.I.E.L.D

In the US government's eyes, Iron Man single-handedly ended the Super Hero Civil War. He was a maverick leader, reminiscent of SHIELD directors past, and the perfect spokesman for a bold new era.

Tony Stark revealed his secret identity to an adoring public. That simple action made him a trusted official and a hero of the people.

Timothy "Dum Dum" Dugan was Nick Fury's right-hand man for years. Watching his director lead the government agency in its golden age, Dum Dum had a hard time filling that role for Tony Stark, and even attempted to tender his resignation.

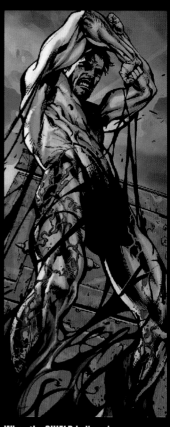

THE NEW BOSS

It was tense for a while, but Stark has a way of putting his employees at ease. Promoted to be the director of the world's foremost peacekeeping agency SHIELD because of his uncompromising, pro-government stance during the Super Hero Civil War, Stark faced plenty of criticism from SHIELD agents still loyal to their legendary past director, Nick Fury. However, one by one, Tony began to win his men over. With simple innovations such as a suggestion box outside the cafeteria, doing away with the exclusive officers' club, hiring an executive chef for the mess hall, and a hands-on work ethic, Stark proved himself to his men, and upped morale at the same time. He even managed to cut operational costs by $19.8 million in the first fiscal quarter alone. It was official. Like everything else in his life that he put his mind to, Stark seemed to have another success on his hands.

Tony Stark's first major operational test soon arrived. Various terrorist splinter groups were getting their hands on highly advanced technology. Masterminded by Tony, SHIELD's investigation pointed to one man, a mysterious terrorist named Karim Mahwash Najeeb, who had been missing for four months.

While inspecting Najeeb's rumored last-known whereabouts, Iron Man and his elite squadron came under attack by mindless undead cyborgs.

When the SHIELD helicarrier was attacked by a living cancer, Tony used the Extremis technology in his own body in order to eradicate the plague.

THE MANDARIN'S PLAN

THE MANDARIN DISCOVERED
Najeeb located Iron Man's old enemy, the Mandarin, and proposed an alliance. However, one of Najeeb's men switched his loyalties and shot his boss in order to aid his new master, the Mandarin.

THE LIVING CANCER
While examining one of the high-tech terrorists, scientist Maya Hansen stumbled upon a living cancer that took over the SHIELD helicarrier. The cancer killed Tony's friend and advisor Sal Kennedy before Iron Man was able to stop it.

MAYA'S FAKED SUICIDE
In order to work in secret on her controversial Extremis technology, Maya Hansen faked her own death and took a job with the mysterious Prometheus Gentech company. Little did Tony's former girlfriend realize that the Mandarin was Prometheus's CEO.

With increasing loyalty from SHIELD mainstays like Maria Hill and Dum Dum Dugan, Stark's directorship was beginning to resemble Nick Fury's. Stark approached everything from a hands-on perspective, despite his colleagues' occasional protests.

168 - 169

THE MANDARIN'S EXTREME AGENDA

Funding the random terror cells, creating the army of undead cyborgs, and releasing the plague on the Helicarrier was all just misdirection. The Mandarin, using the alias Tem Borjigin, really wanted Maya's Extremis technology, and he would stop at nothing to get it.

TONY STARK: SUPERSPY

He was the CEO of Stark Industries, the armored crime fighter Iron Man, the leader of the Mighty Avengers, and the organizer of the 50 State Initiative and the Order. And now, Tony had taken on the role of the ultimate superspy. Never content with the number of pots on his personal fire, Iron Man began to lead covert operations for SHIELD to all corners of the globe, including missions to the corrupt island nation of Madripoor and the eastern European country Kirikhstan.

After discovering Maya was still alive, Iron Man led a successful assault on the Mandarin's headquarters, and halted the warlord's planned Extremis plague. Regardless, the Mandarin once again eluded captivity.

The Mighty Avengers

The Civil War was over, but the world needed its heroes now more than ever. And no one was more aware of this fact than the newly appointed SHIELD Director, Tony Stark.

THE CHOSEN ONES

With his old ally Ms. Marvel at his side as field captain, Iron Man set out to choose a core team of Mighty Avengers to stand as shining examples to the superhuman community. With hundreds of candidates to pick from, Iron Man settled on a roster consisting of the unbalanced powerhouse known as the Sentry, the God of War Ares, super spy Black Widow, the ionic-energy-powered Wonder Man, and the diminutive Wasp.

Mole Man Attacks

Before the team had a chance to train as a group, they were forced to combat the Mole Man and his legions of subterranean monsters, as the villain orchestrated an attack on downtown Manhattan.

In the middle of their violent conflict with the Mole Man, Iron Man's armor suddenly began to liquefy until it had morphed itself into the visage of a female Ultron.

AAGGHHHHH!!!

Familiar Faces

The Mighty Avengers were completely dumbfounded. They had just watched their lauded leader transform into a female version of their greatest android foe, Ultron. And not only that, this Ultron bore a striking resemblance to longtime Avenger, the Wasp. As Ultron shrugged off the most brutal attacks from Ares and the Sentry, SHIELD agents were busy locating Ultron's creator, the scientist and former Avenger, Henry Pym. With Pym's help, the Avengers learned that Ultron had also taken over Tony's experimental weather controlling satellite technology.

In a flash of white light and with the force of an exploding bomb, Iron Man disappeared, and in his place stood the graceful figure of the new Ultron.

Dealing with the Mole Man

With a single thought, Ultron melted Mole Man's servants, eradicating his savage army as easily as swatting a fly. With the villain's threat now extinguished, Ultron turned her attention to her true mission.

Such was Ultron's power, she was able to take down the Mole Man's hordes as well as the Avengers. She also managed to cause a blackout on a global scale.

ATTENTION, AVENGERS.

IF YOU ARE RECEIVING THIS MESSAGE, TONY STARK IS DEAD.

LISTEN CAREFULLY...

Ultron's Agenda

Ultron desired nothing less than the extinction of all of mankind. As she continued to cause freak weather patterns and electrical interference, the old Avengers' foe began to attempt to hack into the launch codes of several nuclear missile stations.

Stark Restored

When Iron Man transformed into Ultron, Tony's contingency plan was activated, summoning a robot aide in order to assist the crisis at hand. But despite Tony's help, seemingly beyond the grave, Ultron commandeered hundreds of other Iron Man suits, and pit them against the Avengers. Finally, thanks to Ares' brute strength and Hank Pym's Ant-Man technology, Ultron was defeated, restoring Tony Stark to his normal, human form.

50-STATE INITIATIVE

Iron Man had a dream for a secure nation. A team of government-regulated Super Heroes in every state, trained and ready to tackle any emergency.

A SUPER ARMY

It was high time America's heroes were made accountable. In Tony Stark's eyes, every hero should carry a license and commit to the same amount of training that other public protectors, such as the military or police, are required to undergo. He hoped that, with the right amount of guidance and instruction, tragedies like the explosion at Stamford, Connecticut, could be avoided altogether.

As the newly appointed director of the peacekeeping force SHIELD, Tony began creating teams of experienced heroes and setting up a training camp for new recruits. Establishing the Stamford-based Camp Hammond as headquarters, Tony appointed several trusted allies to train the next generation of heroes, including his best friend, War Machine Jim Rhodes, longtime Avenger ally Yellowjacket Hank Pym, drill sergeant the Gauntlet, and former New Warrior and Avenger, Justice.

SCARLET SPIDERS

After Spider-Man had abandoned Stark's forces during the Super Hero Civil War, he had also given up wearing the Iron Spider costume that Tony had developed for him. Never one to let a good idea go to waste, the secretive Henry Peter Gyrich, head of the Initiative's splinter organization, the Shadow Initiative, co-opted the Iron Spider uniform. Gyrich outfitted a group of special soldiers with the ingenious costumes and named them the Scarlet Spiders. Alongside trusted field leaders like War Machine and high-testing new recruits, the Scarlet Spiders proved a valuable asset, tracking down individual heroes and villains that had violated the terms of the Superhuman Registration Act.

DIRECTOR RHODES

Jim Rhodes has nearly always followed Tony into battle, despite often being left out of the loop. Installed as the Director of Camp Hammond and prime field commander, Rhodey was the only man Tony could trust to build his army. However, when Rhodes discovered that part of the reason Stark created the Initiative was to ward off an inevitable attack by the Hulk, War Machine felt just as ill-informed as ever.

STARK'S CONFESSION

Tony's true goal all along was to reunite the Super Hero community. So when the Hulk returned from exile in outer space and demanded the surrender of several of the Super Hero elite, Iron Man hoped that this would be the big event that would see old friends forgetting their differences and fighting side-by-side once more. After admitting all this to Rhodey, Tony strapped on his latest Hulkbuster armor and rushed into battle, knowing War Machine and his personal army in the Initiative would have his back in the war to come.

War Machine wouldn't allow his untested new recruits on the front line against a rampaging Hulk.

The ORDER

For heroic deeds in their personal lives, the Order was given the chance to be super-heroic in the public's eyes.

The crowning achievement of Iron Man's 50 State Initiative program, the Order was a select group chosen to protect the state of California. Criticized by some as being the "American Idol" of Super Hero teams, the Order was nevertheless a well-trained group of brave individuals, famous for their charitable work, who were granted superpowers by technology devised by Hank Pym. Leading the Order was none other than Tony Stark's longtime assistant and friend Pepper Potts, who, as their coordinator, Hera, was given telepresence enhancements to maintain communication with the group. Along with operations leader Henry Hellrung, who was endowed with the electrical powers of a thunderstorm and dubbed Anthem, Pepper ran the new team with an iron hand.

Patterned after the ancient Greek gods of myth, the Order was composed of a wide variety of personality types.

Star Secrets

Based in Los Angeles, the Order was very much in the public eye. And with ex-actor Henry Hellrung (who had once played Tony Stark in a TV series) leading the team, that attention wasn't going to fade. So Tony hired PR expert Kate Kildare to help hide any scandals, such as a risqué video Aralune had once made.

KEY MEMBERS

- **IRON MAN (Tony Stark)** Although he rarely had much time to deal with the Order's day-to-day operations, Tony Stark was the brains behind the Order, and was always there for the team if they truly needed him.
- **HERA (Pepper Potts)** Keeping in constant contact with her team on the field, Pepper Potts aided them with instruction and background information on their enemies. She also began a flirtation with the Order's field leader, Anthem.
- **ANTHEM (Henry Hellrung)** Back when he was TV's Iron Man, Henry began a friendship with Tony Stark that involved plenty of partying and drinking. He finally kicked his bad habits, and sponsored Tony when he enrolled in AA years later.
- **VEDA (Magdalena Marie Neuntauben)** An actress/martial artist/model, Magdalena was selected to join the Order because of her dedication to charity work. She was given the ability to create and control humanoid creatures out of organic material.
- **HEAVY (Dennis Murray)** A military hero, Sergeant Major Dennis Murray had been gravely wounded in the same insurgent attack that had led to Tony Stark becoming Iron Man. Before his death, he used his tactical genius and enhanced armor to aid the team.
- **Mulholland Black** Opting not to adopt a Super Hero name, Mulholland's latent mutant abilities were mimicked by Stark's technology, allowing her to once again to share her psychokinetic link with the city of LA and control its various energies.
- **CALAMITY (James Wa)** James was a college baseball and track star when his car was blindsided by a drunk driver. He developed his own revolutionary prosthetic legs in order not only to walk again, but to run at speeds up to Mach 3.
- **ARALUNE (Becky Ryan)** A former teen singing sensation, Becky had been in the spotlight since her youth. Her evolution into the shape-shifting Aralune seemed the next logical step.
- **SUPERNAUT (Milo Fields)** Taken hostage during a humanitarian mission while a US Marine, Milo was later paralyzed during a protest. The Order granted him mobility as the robotic Supernaut.

TRIAL BY FIRE

After a few of the original members were expelled due to breaching the Order's code of conduct, the roster was finally in place when a few new recruits were added to the mix. The final line-up of the team included: super-speedster Calamity, team tactician Heavy, the Golem-creating Veda, robotic ex-soldier Supernaut, and the psychokinetic Mulholland Black. The assembled team had no time to rest on its laurels and enjoy the adulation of fans. During the very press conference that announced their formation, Anthem received an emergency call about an attack near Catalina Island.

Awakened by a disturbance on land, a group of Soviet Super-Soldiers, including an older Crimson Dynamo model, had been unfrozen from their cryogenic status. They set out to destroy all things American.

The ORDER

Tony Stark
IRON MAN

Pepper Potts
HERA

Henry Hellrung
ANTHEM

Magdalena Marie
VEDA

Dennis Murray
HEAVY

Mulholland Black

James Wa
CALAMITY

Becky Ryan
ARALUNE

Milo Fields
SUPERNAUT

ATLANTIS ATTACKS

After defeating the Soviet Super-Soldiers, an army of undead cyborgs, and the red-hot threat known as the Infernal Man, the Order was starting to gain respect and trust. Unfortunately, raised public expectations put more pressure on the team when Atlantis chose to attack the US by positioning a wall of ocean water around San Francisco that threatened to engulf the city. Luckily, Anthem negotiated with Atlantis's ruler Namor, and averted this catastrophe by outwitting the arrogant monarch.

Not recognizing Tony Stark's authority, Namor surrendered to Anthem instead.

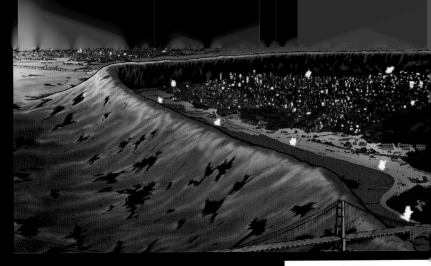

BLACK DAHLIAS

A brutal street gang from Mulholland Black's past, the super-powered Black Dahlias soon emerged in the Order's lives. Working with the clandestine operation SHADOW, Mulholland's former friends began targeting past members of the Order. The Dahlias helped SHADOW kidnap Mulholland Black, and shut off her powers. But Mulholland had been born a mutant, and tampering with her artificial powers, simply activated her dormant natural abilities. More powerful than before, Mulholland attempted to free herself, until she was rendered unconscious by SHADOW's true mastermind.

Mulholland was taken captive by her ex-girlfriend who still had an axe to grind with her former lover.

THE MEN FROM SHADOW

General Sam Softly, the man supposedly in charge of SHADOW actually died in 1957, allowing Ezekiel Stane to co-opt his old base.

It was becoming a predictable pattern. Everywhere the Order went, the MEN from SHADOW would appear. Posing as a government-sponsored program, SHADOW attacked the Order's members on several fronts. Only after he had prevented Mulholland Black's escape did the SHADOW's mastermind stand revealed as Ezekiel Stane, the son of Iron Man's most deadly enemy.

Created in Softly's image, the robotic life model decoys of the deceased general served as Stane's henchmen, allowing him to remain hidden from the public.

A CITY IN CHAOS

Ezekiel Stane wanted nothing less than to destroy everything Tony Stark had ever touched. And the Order was high on his list. Augmenting Mulholland Black's link to the city of Los Angeles so that she wreaked havoc, Stane sat back and watched the Order struggle to save their city. After Heavy died in the chaos, Anthem was forced to take Mulholland's life in order to restore the peace. LA was safe, and the surviving members of the Order were given extensions to their crime fighting careers. But Ezekiel Stane was still out there.

WORLD WAR HULK

They thought they could get away with sending the Hulk into space. They were dead wrong.

PLANET HULK

The madder the Hulk gets, the stronger he gets—and the greater his potential threat. The Green Goliath was just too unpredictable to be allowed to roam free, and too powerful to cage. Working with the rest of the elite heroes known as the Illuminati, and with the participation of Nick Fury and SHIELD, Iron Man helped to exile the Hulk to another planet. But after claiming this exotic new world for himself, and taking a queen there, Hulk's spaceship suddenly exploded, killing the love of his life. Now, he wanted revenge on the Illuminati, and on Earth and its people.

The Hulk and his allies, the Warbound, arrived in Manhattan aboard a giant stone spaceship. The Hulk ordered the surrender of the remaining Illuminati, or else he would destroy the entire planet.

ENTER IRON MAN

Tony had planned for this day, but that didn't mean he didn't dread it. When Hulk broadcast his demands to the people of Earth, Stark headed to Long Island to retrieve his newest Hulkbuster suit of armor. Secure inside the equivalent of a flying tank, Iron Man flew to Manhattan (now mostly evacuated) and charged Hulk head-on. The shockwave of their collision shattered windows and knocked rescue workers off their feet. But the battle had only just begun.

"I need you to keep everybody clear of the combat zone. This is MY fight."

Iron Man

The Hulk wanted revenge on the four core members of the Illuminati: Iron Man, Mr. Fantastic, Dr. Strange, and Black Bolt. After stopping on the moon to defeat and capture Black Bolt, the Hulk's next stop was Manhattan, where he was greeted by Iron Man in appropriate fashion.

Iron Man injected the Hulk with power-suppressing nanobots, but Hulk's rage was too overpowering for any human, no matter how well armed.

LOSING THE WAR

In a moment of overwhelming rage, the Hulk leaped at Iron Man, knocking the two of them into Avengers Tower. There Hulk pounded away at Stark, hammering the Sentry's watchtower straight through the center of Tony's impressive skyscraper [1]. It was a demonstration of pure might and unrestrained will. The Hulk had won. He had defeated Iron Man, mankind's protector.

But the Hulk wasn't through yet. After besting the Avengers [2], Mr. Fantastic and his entire Fantastic Four [3], the Hulk set his sights on Earth's sorcerer supreme, Dr. Strange [4]. The struggle was soon over. The Hulk had taken his captives, and even conquered the US military [5]. Now it was time for the Illuminati to pay.

One by one, the Hulk forced the captured Illuminati members to battle each other in a makeshift gladiatorial arena in New York's Madison Square Garden. But even as an armor-less Iron Man fought Mr. Fantastic, his mind was elsewhere, working on a plan. And luckily for Tony, the cavalry arrived, giving him enough time to bring it about.

Before Iron Man had gone off to battle the Hulk, he'd petitioned the powerful hero Sentry for help. The Sentry had finally made up his mind. He attacked the Hulk with the strength of hundreds of exploding stars. After a violent display, the Sentry succeeded in transforming the Hulk back into Bruce Banner by the sheer force of his impacting fists [6]. Given enough time to act, Iron Man then fired a satellite weapon at the Hulk, taking the brute down for good.

Clad in the garb of his conquered planet, the Hulk sought revenge for the death of his queen. However when the Hulk finally learned that Iron Man and the Illuminati weren't responsible for the explosion of his spaceship and his wife's death, the fight was finally taken out of him.

[1]　　　　[2]　　　　[3]　　　　[4]　　　　[5]　　　　[6]

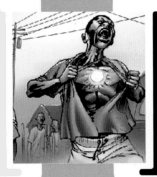

EZEKIEL STANE

21ST-CENTURY TERRORISM

In the African town of Tabora, Tanzania, a group of girls happily played with their first cell phone. Soon their excitement turned to terror when three young men ran into the center of town, yelling and exposing repulsor technology embedded in their chests. And then they promptly exploded.

MONEY TO BURN

Ezekiel Stane was working for Big Tobacco. Or rather, he had Big Tobacco working for him. After agreeing to develop a new weight-loss cigarette, this brilliant, cutthroat inventor took an advance from his greedy clients in order to turn himself into a living weapon. At a business meeting with tobacco executives, Ezekiel then used his body's excess energy to murder everyone in the room.

TAKING AIM AT TONY

Ezekiel Stane hated Tony Stark and everything he stood for, and he was determined to take it all away from him. The son of Tony's former rival Obadiah Stane, Ezekiel had already spent much time and energy making the members of Tony's pet project the Order (California's hero team in the 50 State Initiative) run the proverbial gauntlet. Now he was ready to stop messing around and go for the jugular.

Having successfully used reverse-engineered Stark technology to convert his own body into a deadly weapon, Stane had begun selling the same dangerous tech to any terrorist willing to pay his rather hefty bill. Responsible not only for the tragedy in Tabora, but for other outrages all over the globe, Ezekiel headed to Taiwan, to personally observe his men bombing a Starkdynamics gala. He introduced himself to Tony at the gala moments before the bomb went off.

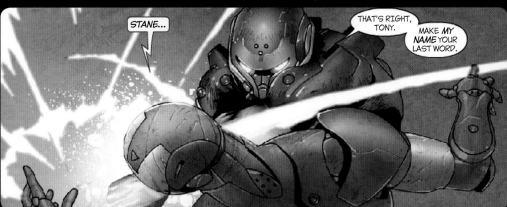

Having shunned Pepper in favor of a bevy of beautiful socialites just minutes before the explosion at Starkdynamics, Tony felt horribly guilty for her injuries. When it came to her recovery, he spared absolutely no expense.

At Death's Door

Tony saved himself from the explosion at the gala by summoning his Iron Man armor just in time. Unfortunately, his assistant Pepper Potts didn't fair as well. Although she survived the attack, Pepper was critically injured, forcing Tony to implant a device in her chest that would prevent shrapnel from piercing her heart.

To save Pepper's life, Tony had to use similar state of the art magnetic technology that had once saved his own.

STANE...

THAT'S RIGHT, TONY.

MAKE *MY* NAME YOUR LAST WORD.

Not only did Stane survive the explosion as well, but he began to develop a body armor to help supplement his enhanced abilities.

Ezekiel was younger, more ambitious, and utilized technology even more advanced than Tony's. He was Iron Man 2.0.

Ezekiel Stane vs. Stark Industries

Starkdynamics had just been an appetizer. Now it was time for Ezekiel's main course. While hiding in plain sight on a tour of Stark's Long Island facility, Stane wandered away from the group. After attacking an empty Iron Man suit operated by remote control, Stane found himself surrounded by some of Tony's newest Iron Man models. Joining his remote armors in person, Tony overpowered Stane, and nearly succumbed to his darker impulses by ending his young enemy's life. However, Stark's true colors showed through, and he pulled his punches just enough so that Stane could be taken into SHIELD custody, very much alive—and already plotting his revenge.

HE'S DEAD! TONY STARK IS DEAD!

Ezekiel Stane was not only a haunting reminder of Tony Stark's tragic past, but also a terrifying glimpse into a future that lurked just around the corner.

SECRET INVASION

A race of warlike shape-shifters, the alien Skrulls were masters of espionage. They set their sights on Earth and strategically placed covert sleeper agents among the populace. They believed that the battle for the planet was almost won before a shot had been fired.

The Skrulls were everywhere. They had all but conquered Earth, and humanity didn't even know it yet.

REED DISCOVERS THE KEY

Who do you trust? That was the question on every hero's mind. Famed martial-arts assassin Elektra had been unmasked as a Skrull sleeper agent and the Avengers were determined to find out just how many more members of the superhuman community had been replaced by Skrulls. After many hours of study, Reed Richards of the Fantastic Four devised a sure-fire way to detect these shape-shifting aliens.

FSHAMMM

HE EVEN LOVES YOU.

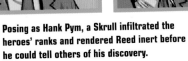

Posing as Hank Pym, a Skrull infiltrated the heroes' ranks and rendered Reed inert before he could tell others of his discovery.

HE
LOVES
YOU...

JARVIS THE SKRULL

A Skrull invasion was in full force. All over the world, Skrulls carried out their allotted roles in the elaborate plan. At Avengers Tower, Tony Stark's faithful butler Jarvis revealed himself to be a Skrull by sabotaging the Avengers' computer system with an alien virus. The bug shut down all of Stark's electronic devices—even Iron Man's armor.

UNDER SIEGE

After luring both the government-sponsored Mighty Avengers and the underground Secret Avengers far away to the Savage Land, the Skrulls sent a ship full of doppelgangers to keep the heroes busy. Meanwhile, an armada of Skrulls with amalgamated super powers attacked Times Square, with only the novice heroes of the Initiative and the Young Avengers to keep them at bay.

TONY GETS THE BUG

All over the world, Stark electronic devices were shutting down. The mammoth SHIELD helicarrier fell out of the sky, satellites drifted out of their orbits, prisons' security systems went offline. Tony Stark was arguably the most powerful man in the world, but he'd gotten that way because of technological genius. As his inventions failed, so did the augmented Extremis tech flowing through his body. Iron Man shut down, and Tony Stark had a seizure.

SECRET WARRIORS
When things seemed most bleak in the battle for Times Square, disgraced former SHIELD Director Nick Fury appeared in public for the first time in months. Along with a ragtag team of Secret Warriors, Fury rescued the defeated Young Avengers.

THE WAR IS OVER

As Tony lay alone in pain, the Skrull Queen paid him a visit in the form of Spider-Woman. Failing to convince Tony that he was a Skrull in disguise, the Queen departed for Manhattan to meet the rest of her forces. As the heroes of Earth assembled for a last battle and Iron Man freed the Skrulls' prisoners, Norman Osborn, formerly the villain, Green Goblin, killed the Skrull Queen. He thus ended the Skrull invasion and cunningly stole the spotlight from Tony Stark.

I'M NOT A SKRULL!

I KNOW THAT'S WHAT YOU THINK.

STOP!

THAT'S WHAT YOU WERE *TRAINED* TO THINK!

After commandeering an Iron Man suit of armor, Norman Osborn repainted it to reflect Captain America's colors in a bid to gain public support.

Comprised of villains in disguise and two of the Mighty Avengers' more easily manipulated former members, Osborn's twisted perversion of the Avengers was born.

He was a killer, kidnapper, and Super Villain. But that was before the Secret Invasion. Now Norman Osborn was America's favorite son.

Iron Patriot

Iron Patriot

To the general public, Norman Osborn was mankind's savior: the hero who swooped in, stared death in the face, and ended the Secret Invasion—the attempt by the alien shape-changing Skrulls to conquer Earth—with a single bullet. Osborn had restored the natural order of things to the planet, and been rewarded for his loyal service to his country with the job of heading a new government peacekeeping agency HAMMER. The man with more money than God now had nearly as much power. Norman Osborn had everyone fooled.

Well, not *quite* everyone. Every political appointee has his share of naysayers, and though Osborn was well regarded in most households, a handful of people remained skeptical of his credentials. Counted among that number was the majority of the Super Hero community, for they had witnessed Osborn's true colors firsthand.

Years ago, before he became a "reformed" government employee at the helm of the Thunderbolts program, Norman Osborn used to slip on a green mask and tights and, calling himself the Green Goblin, leave a trail of chaos and destruction in his wake. He had frequently clashed with Spider-Man—even throwing the hero's girlfriend off a bridge. As the Green Goblin, Norman Osborn had achieved infamy as one of the most brilliant criminal masterminds ever to plague Manhattan.

But that was before the Secret Invasion, and before Osborn had led the Thunderbolts into a well-publicized battle against the Skrull invaders. It was Norman Osborn who made the kill shot heard around the world, taking down the Skrull's Queen. And so Norman Osborn was a hero. And America couldn't be less safe.

Osborn was able to convince the mentally unbalanced Sentry to fight by his side.

KEY DATA

REAL NAME Norman Osborn

OCCUPATION Director of HAMMER, CEO of Oscorp, "former" criminal

AFFILIATIONS Dark Avengers, Thunderbolts, The Cabal, Sinister Twelve

POWERS/WEAPONS As the Iron Patriot, Osborn presumably has all of Iron Man's technology at his disposal, possessing the same powers and abilities as the original Golden Avenger. Genius-level criminal intellect. Enhanced strength, increased speed, reflexes, and endurance owing to signature Goblin Formula. Access to the advanced weaponry of the Green Goblin, including grenades and "goblin-glider."

Dark Avengers

Promoted to essentially the same position Tony Stark held when he was Director of SHIELD, Norman Osborn set out to corrupt the programs Tony had set in motion. Taking advantage of Stark's well-meaning 50 State Initiative, Osborn formed his own group of government-sponsored heroes, dubbed the Dark Avengers by the Super Hero community. Breaking into Stark Industries with the help of Ghost, Osborn stole an Iron Man suit for his own use, renaming himself the Iron Patriot. He then gathered Mighty Avengers Ares and Sentry, loose cannon Marvel Boy (declaring him Captain Marvel), Wolverine's murderous son Daken (declaring him Wolverine), the villainous Bullseye (declaring him Hawkeye), former Thunderbolt Moonstone (declaring her Ms. Marvel), and the symbiotic Venom (declaring him Spider-Man), presenting the whole team as the newest incarnation of the Avengers.

When he merged with the Extremis virus, Stark's mind became a living computer. With the only record of the Super Hero Registration database locked in his brain, Stark was forced to run from the law.

IRON MAN: FUGITIVE

The Secret Invasion was over and the villainous Norman Osborn had surprisingly saved the day. Already a trusted government employee for his work with the Super Hero team known as the Thunderbolts, Osborn easily outshined Iron Man in what was arguably Earth's greatest crisis. Amoral and chemically unbalanced, Osborn replaced Tony Stark as Director of the newly formed agency HAMMER. It wasn't long before he began ruthlessly exploiting his power. But before Osborn could get his hands on the database that contained all the Initiative's records of Super Hero secret identities, Stark destroyed the file and went into hiding.

Iron Man Against the World

Tony Stark had lost everything but his friends. As the result of the alien Skrulls infecting all Stark technology with a disabling virus, Stark Industries was on the verge of financial ruin. The public considered Iron Man little more than a bumbling incompetent, and the Super Hero community was still divided about his uncompromising stance during the Civil War. Besides his former SHIELD colleague Maria Hill and friend Pepper Potts, Tony didn't seem to have many allies left. But Jim Rhodes, alias War Machine, proved his loyalty to his old friend by staging a fight with Iron Man and allowing him to escape.

A NO-BRAINER

As always, Tony Stark had a plan. He would travel to his different bases all over the globe, destroying his own technology to ensure Norman Osborn wouldn't be able to commandeer it. And what's more, at each stop, Tony would delete a piece of his brain, to erase the database, and the records of all his personal technology from his mind. Tony knew he was destroying his intellect, but it was the only way to protect his legacy.

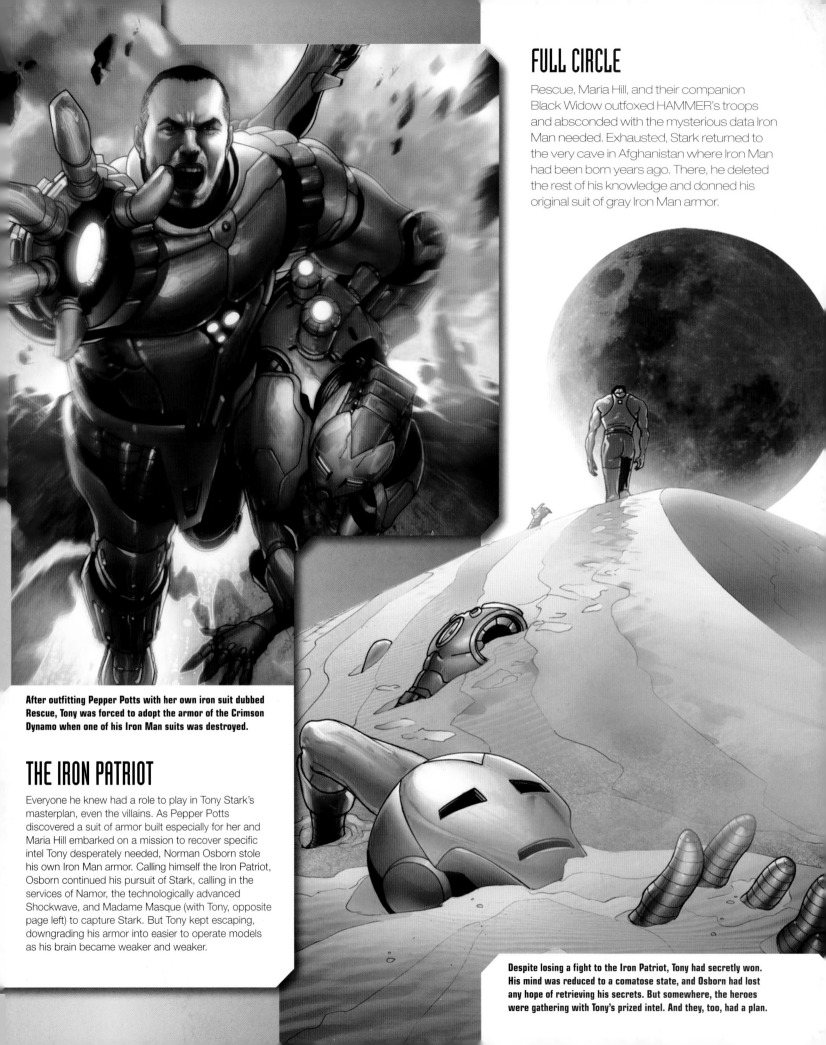

FULL CIRCLE

Rescue, Maria Hill, and their companion Black Widow outfoxed HAMMER's troops and absconded with the mysterious data Iron Man needed. Exhausted, Stark returned to the very cave in Afghanistan where Iron Man had been born years ago. There, he deleted the rest of his knowledge and donned his original suit of gray Iron Man armor.

After outfitting Pepper Potts with her own iron suit dubbed Rescue, Tony was forced to adopt the armor of the Crimson Dynamo when one of his Iron Man suits was destroyed.

THE IRON PATRIOT

Everyone he knew had a role to play in Tony Stark's masterplan, even the villains. As Pepper Potts discovered a suit of armor built especially for her and Maria Hill embarked on a mission to recover specific intel Tony desperately needed, Norman Osborn stole his own Iron Man armor. Calling himself the Iron Patriot, Osborn continued his pursuit of Stark, calling in the services of Namor, the technologically advanced Shockwave, and Madame Masque (with Tony, opposite page left) to capture Stark. But Tony kept escaping, downgrading his armor into easier to operate models as his brain became weaker and weaker.

Despite losing a fight to the Iron Patriot, Tony had secretly won. His mind was reduced to a comatose state, and Osborn had lost any hope of retrieving his secrets. But somewhere, the heroes were gathering with Tony's prized intel. And they, too, had a plan.

IRON MAN
Vol. 5 #10

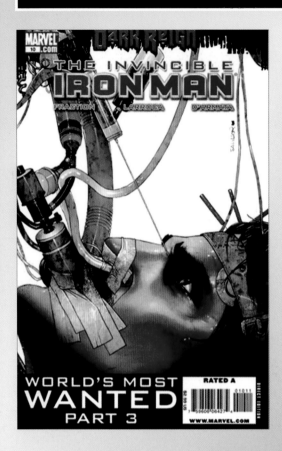

"And while you're there doing your thing… and Pepper is at Stark doing her thing… I'm doing my thing and running like hell."

TONY STARK

MAIN CHARACTERS: Iron Man; Maria Hill; Pepper Potts; Iron Patriot (Norman Osborn)
SUPPORTING CHARACTERS: Kat Farrell; Victoria Hand; HAMMER employees
LOCATIONS: Stark Industries; Funtime, Inc.; Restoration Park, NYC; Chicago; Los Angeles; Rome; Berlin; Hong Kong; Seattle

PUBLICATION DATE
April 2009

EDITOR-IN-CHIEF
Joe Quesada

COVER ARTIST
Salvador Larroca

WRITER
Matt Fraction

ARTIST
Salvador Larroca

COLORIST
Frank D'Armata

LETTERER
Joe Caramagna

BACKGROUND

Following his support of the Superhuman Registration Act that helped spark the Civil War between heroes, Iron Man was almost being regarded as a villain by the majority of the heroes in the Marvel Universe. As such, it was growing harder and harder for writers to create sympathy for the character, or to paint him in a heroic light. Tony Stark was in need of an adventure or two that would restore his previous status as a modern-day knight in shining armor. So when writer Matt Fraction helped relaunch Iron Man's fifth series, he looked to Tony's long and storied history, charm, and good nature to restore the hero to his former glory. By turning Iron Man from a government employee to a noble fugitive from that same institution, Fraction superbly achieved his aim. Fraction also fleshed out Tony's supporting cast, giving new prominence to longtime love interest Pepper Potts, and also the most recent villain to challenge Tony's legacy, Norman Osborn.

The Story...

With her boss, Tony Stark, on the run from Norman Osborn and his newly-formed HAMMER organization, Pepper Potts stumbles upon an Iron Man suit tailor-made just for her.

Blamed for not anticipating the recent invasion of the alien Skrulls, Tony Stark had been proclaimed a criminal by Norman Osborn, the Director of a new government security organization named HAMMER. He was now on the run, and his former, computer-based Iron Man powers had been shut down. Furthermore, Tony possessed the only copy of the Superhuman Registration data files, a directory of every hero's secret identity, downloaded into his brain, and was forced to slowly delete his intelligence in order to make sure that Osborn never got his villainous hands on them. And yet, despite all this mayhem, Tony Stark had a plan, and he was determined to see it out.

While Norman Osborn engaged in the latest of a number of press conferences regarding Iron Man's fugitive status **(1)**, Pepper Potts was doing her best to figure out why Tony Stark had just recently placed her in charge of Stark Industries **(2)**. The former multi-billion-dollar national conglomerate had been reduced to a virtually bankrupt shell staffed by a skeleton crew. Tony's company was dying, and it seemed that Pepper's job was simply to pull the plug.

Meanwhile, at one of Tony Stark's subsidiaries, Funtime, Inc., Tony and his former right-hand woman at SHIELD, Maria Hill, were discussing their plans now that Osborn had made both of them into wanted criminals. Tony needed Maria to break into his Futurepharm plant in Austin, Texas and, using a jump drive **(3)** locate a hard drive containing crucial information. She should then take the hard drive to Captain America. Maria agreed and, knowing that she might be embarking on her very last mission, kissed Tony. Overcome by passion, Tony and Maria forgot grim reality for a few brief moments.

Back at Stark Industries, Pepper was growing ever more frustrated with the responsibilities of her new position **(4)**. In a fit of rage, she threw her chair across the room, knocking a framed picture askew. And that's when she discovered just why Tony had placed her in charge of his company. She had accidentally tripped a trigger that opened a panel to a secret room. Inside this futuristic chamber was a female version of the Iron Man armor, made to fit Pepper's body **(5)**.

But Pepper wouldn't be the only person trying out an Iron Man suit that day. Across town, in the newly christened Restoration Park, Norman Osborn was hosting yet another press conference, this time clad in a suit of armor appropriated from Stark Tower: a red, white, and blue version of Iron Man's own suit **(6)**. With the public now referring to him as the Iron Patriot, Osborn announced that since Tony had failed to meet him at this public forum, he had ordered the seizure of all of Tony's companies all over the world. He was going to bring Tony Stark to justice **(7)**.

Of course, Osborn wouldn't get everything. Back at Funtime, Inc., Maria Stark was busy blowing up the main building, ensuring that dozens of Iron Man suits wouldn't fall into the wrong hands **(8)**. And as Tony Stark flew through the sky in one of his older suits of armor to continue his mission, yet another Iron Man suit was escaping Osborn's clutches. Because back on Long Island, on the rooftop of Stark Industries, Pepper Potts stood in her new suit of armor, about to take to the skies for the first time, realizing that there would truly be no turning back now **(9)**.

> ## "Oh, I think going bonkers is completely imperative."
>
> **Tony Stark**

Iron Man 2093

Tony Stark is the world's premier futurist. But when a mystical artifact transported him alongside Doctor Doom into the future and the year 2093, even Tony couldn't have predicted what life would be like in that possible future reality. Summoned by Merlin, the ancient magician of Arthurian lore, Iron Man headed out into space to check on a malfunctioning satellite that Merlin claimed was at the heart of the world's current troubles. With his armor augmented by advanced technology from a local shopping mall, Iron Man came into conflict with his future descendant, Andros Stark. The grandson of Arno Stark, the Iron Man of the year 2020, Andros was using a neutron cannon to thin the population of Earth. As Tony trailed Arno back to his lair, he realized that his murderous descendant was no more than a lackey to a much older version of Doctor Doom.

With the help of the legendary sword Excalibur, Iron Man prevailed over his evil future counterpart even as a younger Doctor Doom destroyed his future self. The two men were then sent back to their own present, with no memory of their adventures.

AND NASTIER!

SHATTERED THE TELE-OPTICS! STARTING TO PRESS ON MY HELMET LENSES!

ANDROS MUST BE A FUTURE VERSION OF ME! BUT MUCH STRONGER!

MARVEL ADVENTURES

In the myriads of dimensions and possible timelines, there are many other Iron Men. Some exist in futures that may yet come to pass, others in alternate realms similar to the world we know. In the simpler universe of Marvel Adventures, Tony Stark's life is a bit less complicated. In that world, Tony's heart was damaged not in an explosion caused by insurgent forces, but when he was flying an experimental plane that was brought down by AIM. While the result was still the birth of Iron Man, the Tony of the Marvel Adventures universe isn't tormented by the alcohol addiction that plagues his more familiar counterpart.

The Iron Man of the Marvel Adventures universe once made a completely steam-powered suit of armor when facing a Super Villain named Jolt in a technology-free village.

The Iron Man of 2020 was haunted by his inability to live up to the legends of his predecessor, Tony Stark.

Iron Man 2020

In a not-too-distant future, Arno Stark was the heir to the legacy of the original Iron Man. The son of Tony's cousin Morgan, Arno sullied the Stark name by causing Stark International to teeter on the brink of financial ruin. He also spoiled Iron Man's heroic image by becoming an armored mercenary for hire. After losing a battle with the more noble Machine Man, Arno's perspective began to change, and he later rebelled against a corrupt client named Wellington Marcus in order to save an innocent woman's life.

> **"Great—you've turned yourself into the mightiest Super Hero of the nineteenth century!"** Jolt

THE END

Tony Stark was falling asleep at the wheel. Too old to pull all-nighters at the drawing board, Tony began to wonder if he wasn't obsolete as Iron Man as well. When his slower reaction time led to him losing a battle with the Ultra-Dynamo, he began to search for an heir to carry on his legacy. Finding an ideal candidate in his employee Nick Travis, Tony passed the torch on to the reluctant young man. Tony then retired from the spotlight, ready for a well-earned rest with his lovely wife Bethany Cabe.

Before Tony retired from his life of fighting crime, he kept his armor as state-of-the-art as possible. It would transform around his body from a normal looking briefcase, and was capable of morphing into a supersonic configuration.

Ultimate Iron Man

Separate from the world of the Tony Stark we know, there's a different Earth with a different Tony Stark. It's the Ultimate Universe, home of the Ultimate Iron Man.

In this alternate take on the lives of Earth's mightiest heroes, there's no such thing as the Avengers. In this dimension, the government assembled a familiar team of heroes to be the US's protectors. Spearheaded by SHIELD Director Nick Fury, the team operated out of a heavily fortified think tank off the coast of Manhattan called the Triskelion.

The Ultimates

The original roster of Nick Fury's Ultimates consisted of familiar heroes given modern updates and struggles in a world very much like our own: the often-drunk, playboy-turned-jet-setting Super Hero, Iron Man; the World War II hero struggling to find his place in the modern world, Captain America; the mutant shrinking hero, the Wasp; the abusive, tormented genius Giant-Man; the possibly delusional theoretical god of thunder, Thor; and the scientist with the world's most dangerous weapon living inside him, the Hulk.

The Ultimates wore costumes that reflected a more contemporary mindset, from Captain America's "wingless" cowl, to Iron Man's yellow, gray, and red armor.

The Never-ending Battle

From large-scale alien invasions, to an angry Hulk loose in Manhattan, to the machinations of the god Loki, the Ultimates proved worthy of their moniker on many occasions. The group expanded, adding members like the sharp-shooter Hawkeye, former criminals Quicksilver and the Scarlet Witch, and traitor spy, Black Widow. Established as heroes in the eyes of the public, the team dropped their government status in favor of being independent, backed by the near-limitless finances of Tony Stark.

The Origin of Ultimate Iron Man

When scientist Maria Stark was contaminated by a lab monkey infected with a skin growing virus, she also discovered that she was pregnant. Inside her womb, the virus mutated her child, allowing him to grow neural tissue all over his body. So when Antonio Stark was born, the majority of his makeup was brain. Unfortunately, the virus also caused him constant agony.

Liquid Blue Armor

A genius inventor years before his time, Howard Stark had developed a bacteria armor that made the wearer nearly invulnerable. After his son was born and his wife died during labor, he burst into the hospital room and coated his boy in the experimental liquid.

> Let our son live.

Howard worked tirelessly to perfect the liquid armor that would relieve his son of the pain of daily life.

Zebediah Stane

Howard Stark had a way of making enemies. When Howard outmaneuvered an attempted takeover of his company by his rival businessman Zebediah Stane, Stane never forgot the slight. Years later, Stane kidnapped a four-year-old Tony in order to steal information about the protective liquid armor the boy was still required to wear. Howard soon tracked Stane down, but only after a brave Tony had been tortured at the criminal's hands.

Just the simple act of washing Tony's head with antibacterial soap caused the boy excruciating pain, similar to that of third-degree burns. Even contact with the air and with dust particles was too much for his sensitive neural tissue.

> Call 9-1-1!
>
> Tony! I swear I didn't think you could burn!
>
> Don't...call... doctor...

Passage to Manhood

Tony tried his hardest to live a normal childhood. He enrolled in school, wearing new flesh-colored liquid armor, and did his best to fit in. However, with his firm moral conscience and willingness to stand up for the little guy, Tony found himself the victim of constant bullying. On one occasion, he even had his legs burned off when a fight got out of hand. However, Tony's liquid armor also allowed him to regenerate lost body parts, so despite the pain, he made a full recovery and was able to continue his studies. All the while, Tony was working on a pet project. A better suit of armor. Something more along the lines of Iron…

AFTERWORD

I didn't know much about Iron Man when I was growing up. In fact, my knowledge of Tony Stark was limited to a beaten up Secret Wars action figure and the contents of *Iron Man #214*, a story that focused more on Spider-Woman than it did the title character. Iron Man was just another face in a crowd of intriguing heroes that my extremely limited allowance prohibited me from pursuing. To be perfectly honest, I probably would have delved into his adventures a bit sooner, had the Distinguished Competition not released a feature film starring a certain Caped Crusader. But they did, and I was quickly drawn into the world of Gotham City, leaving Iron Man and his Avenger companions behind in favor of a less sunny coast.

Like many fans, I was reintroduced to Iron Man with Kurt Busiek's revamp of the character in 1998. And I finally started to realize what I'd been missing. This unique character, who had somehow stayed beneath my radar for so many years, had a wealth of great stories seemingly hidden from view. I'd missed work by some of comicdom's greatest writers. Creative minds like Denny O'Neil, Archie Goodwin and even Barry Windsor-Smith had lent their storytelling prowess to the Golden Avenger throughout his career, not to mention the classic work of David Michelinie and Bob Layton. I had a lot of catching-up to do.

Writing this book has given me the perfect excuse to delve even further into the life and times of Tony Stark. I'd like to thank the great design staff at DK and the patient folks in editorial who helped make this book the complete package that it is. Thanks also go to Matt Fraction for giving me a sneak peak into what's happening next, as well as to Mark Beazley, for continued access to his dangerously teetering stack of back issues. And, as always, I'd like to thank my wife Dorothy for her continued love and support, and for allowing me to work through the occasional evening's dinner.

In 2008, the first Iron Man feature film was released, stimulating the imagination and curiosity of thousands of new potential comic-book readers. Although *Iron Man* wasn't the only comic-book movie that came out that summer, it was easily my favorite. Nobody tell a certain Caped Crusader.

MATTHEW K. MANNING
September 2009

INDEX

A

Abbott, Sinclair 45
Ablative armor 22
Advanced Genocide Mechanics 47
AIM 47, 189
Airborne 139
Alkema-2 141
Anders, Gretl 100–1
Anders, Timothy 100–1
Angel 51
Ant-Man 10, 32, 48–9, 55, 68, 110, 148, 155, 171
Anthem 33, 174–5
Aqiria 127
Aralune 174–5
Arbogast, Bambi 29, 56
Ares 127, 170–1, 183
Armor Wars 19, 32, 57, 66–7, 81, 109, 110–11
Armor Wars II 114–15
Arsenal Alpha 147
Arthur, King 56, 93, 164–5, 188
Ashema 136–7
Askew Electronics 25
Askew Labs 58
Astrovik, Vance 140
Atlanta, Dr. Theron 43, 79
Atlantis 51, 175
Atlas 51
Atom Smasher 125
Atomic Knights 134
Avalon, Georgie 138–9
Avalon Trading Company 139
Avengers 29, 48–9, 55, 56, 57, 66, 68, 72, 83, 92, 104, 136
    Dark 59, 183
    disassembled 148–9
    East Coast 130
    Mighty 59, 143, 169, 170–1, 181, 182
    New 59, 143, 152–3, 166, 167
    Operation Galactic Storm 122–3
    reunited 140–1
    Secret 166, 181
    West Coast 39, 58–9, 108–9, 130
    Young 154–5, 181
Avenger's Crossing 117
Axxon-Karr 76–7
Ayers, Dick 64, 76

B

Bain, Sunset 40
Banner, Bruce 68–9, 135, 161, 177
Barnett, Philip 90–1
Battleworld 57, 101, 104–5
Beetle 50, 51, 110, 125
Benchley, Mr. 88–9
Bendis, Brian Michael 143, 164
Benning, Veronica 41
Beyonder 57, 104
Big M 78
Big Wheel 50
Binary 50
Bishop 106
Black Bolt 56, 160–1, 176
Black Dahlias 175
Black Knight 122
Black, Mulholland 174–5
Black Panther 29, 160
Black Widow 51, 55, 61, 72, 170, 185, 190
Blacklash 45, 125
Blake, Dr. Donald 48
Blizzard 45, 51, 56, 86, 125
Boobytrap 139
Borjigin, Tem 75
Bradley, Isaiah 155
Brodsky, Sol 64
Brubaker, Ed 143
Bukharin, Dimitri 45, 73
Bullseye 183
Bullski, Boris 45, 73
Burch, Sonny 53, 146–7
Busiek, Kurt 138

C

Cabal 183
Cabe, Bethany 33, 40, 42–3, 52, 56, 79, 86–9, 127, 189
Cable 126
Cage, Luke 152–3
Calamity 174–5
Camelot 56, 93, 164–5
Camp Hammond 39, 127, 172–3
Cannon, Eric 138
Cap's shield 29
Captain America 49, 55, 56, 59, 61, 66–7, 76, 87, 88, 90, 100–1, 143, 149, 154, 190
    Armor Wars 66–7
    Avengers 140–1
    Civil War 67, 162–5, 187
    New Avengers 152–3
    Operation Galactic Storm 122–3
Captain Marvel 39, 100–1, 105, 183
Caramagna, Joe 186
Carnelia 90
Carpenter, Julia 129
Casey, Joe 143
Celestials 136

C (cont.)

Champions 51
Chaney, Amanda 132
Charcoal 51
Chen Hsu 115, 120–1
Chen Lu 166
Chen, Sean 138
Chessmen 98–9, 106
Circuits Maximus 25, 28, 44, 57, 103, 107, 108
Civil War 49, 50, 59, 67, 162–5, 167, 168, 172
Cobalt Man 51
Cold War 72–3, 114
Collective 153
Colletta, Vince 76
Controller 46, 56, 110
Cord, Edwin 46, 47, 56, 111
Cord, Janice 40, 56
Costanza, John 88
Crimson Dynamo 40, 45, 55, 56, 61, 73, 110, 111
Crystal 122
Cyclops 151

D

Daken 183
Daniels, Brie 41
Danvers, Carol 50
Dare, Kathy 41, 57, 124
Dark Avengers 59, 183
D'Armata, Frank 186
De La Spirosa, Countess Stephanie 41
Dearbom, Arthur 47
Death Squad 139
Deathick 126
Deathtoll 126
DeFalco, Tom 112
Demonicus, Dr. 53, 109
Dennison, Rick 46
Denton, Ms. 138–9
DeWitt, Kearson 114–15, 120, 124
Dillon, Max 152
Ditko, Steve 10, 64
Doctor Demonicus see Demonicus, Dr.
Doctor Doom see Doom, Victor Von
Doll, Mr. 55, 64–5
Doom, Victor Von (Doctor Doom) 47, 56, 92–3, 104, 134, 137, 164–5, 188
Dragon Seed 57, 74, 120–1
Drew, Jessica 152
Dugan, Timothy "Dum Dum" 32, 168–9

E

Echo 153
Electro 152
Elektra 180
Eliopoulos, Chris 164
Ellis, Warren 143, 158
Encephalo-circuitry 29
encephalo-controlled armor 114–15
Endo, Suzi 127

Enervation Intensifier 37
Erwin, Clytemnestra 29, 103
Erwin, Morley 29, 100–1, 102–3
Espionage Elite 56
Evader 29
Excalibur 188
Extremis 75, 156–7, 159, 168–9, 181, 184
Extremis armor 23, 59

F

Fantastic Four 10, 12, 50, 104, 136–7, 177
  New 166
Fantastic, Mr. 50, 56, 57, 134, 136, 162, 164–5,
  176–7
Farrell, Kat 186–7
Favreau, Jon 143
Fields, Milo 174
Fifty-State Initiative 39, 59, 127, 169, 172–5, 178,
  183
Fin Fang Foom 45, 57, 115, 121
Firebrand 40, 46, 56, 58, 103
Firefight 139
Firepower 46, 110–11, 125
Firestar 140
Fixer 51, 52
Flying Prowler 29
Force 33, 57, 110, 147
Force Works 58, 126, 130–1, 132
Fraction, Matt 143, 186
Freak 36–7
Friday-Virtual 29
Frost, Byron 78
Frost, Emma 153
Frost, Jack 55, 56
Frost, Whitney 40, 46, 47, 78–9
Frostbite 40
Fujikawa, Rumiko 28, 41, 58
Fury, Nick 32, 55, 80–1, 164–5, 168, 176, 181, 190
Futurepharm 156–9, 187

G

Galactus 104
gamma armor 69
Gauntlet 172
Gavrilov, Gennady 73
Genghis Khan 44, 77
Genosha 151, 153
Gentile, Randy 158
Ghost 32, 45, 47, 57, 183
Ghost Rider 51
Giant-Man 123, 141, 190
Gilbert, Gary 46
Gilbert, Roxanne 40
Gill, Donald 45
Glenn, Heather 40
Goodwin, Archie 83
Granov, Adi 143, 158
Graviton 108

gray armor 10, 18
Green Goblin 35, 47, 59, 79, 164–5, 181, 182
Gremlin 73, 111
Grim Reaper 141
Grimm, Ben 50
Growing Man 155
Guardsmen 29, 33, 56, 110
Gyrich, Henry Peter 172

H

HAMMER 59, 73, 79, 182–7
Hammer, Justin 44, 45, 50, 56, 87, 88–9, 90–1,
  110
Hancock, Calista 41
Hand ninja 50
Hand, Victoria 186–7
Hansen, Maya 41, 59, 75, 156–9, 168–9
Harris, Bob 138
Hawkeye 29, 49, 55, 61, 72, 100–1, 108, 123, 130,
  141, 149, 155, 183, 190
Heavy 174–5
Heck, Don 11, 12, 76
Hellrung, Henry 33, 174
Hera 34, 174–5
Hercules 51, 122
Heroes Return 117, 136–7, 138
Hex Ships 29
High-G armor 23
Hill, Maria 33, 169, 184–7
Hogan, Clay 34
Hogan, Happy 33, 36–7, 52, 55, 59, 61, 64–5, 72,
  135
Holo-Comminicator 29
HOMER 20, 29
Homo Superior 150–1
Hood 79
Horgan, Bruno 46, 55
House of M 150–1
Hulk 10, 21, 48–9, 55, 59, 68–71, 135, 136, 161, 173,
  176–7, 190
Hulkbuster 20, 23, 58, 68, 70–1, 173
Hulkling 155
Human Torch 50
Hydra 50, 135, 153
hydro armor 19, 23, 57
Hypervelocity armor 23

I

Iceman 51
Illuminati 50, 59, 160–1, 165, 176–7
Immortus 21, 28, 46, 58, 132
Inevitable 143
Infernal Man 175
Infinity Gauntlet 117, 161
Inhuman 160–1
Initiative 25, 143
Invisible Woman 50, 136
Iron Lad 46, 154–5

Iron Legion 43
Iron Man II 102–5, 112–13, 179
Iron Man's suit 13, 14–23, 25, 54–5
Iron Monger 44
Iron Patriot 47, 59, 182–7
Iron Spider 29, 59, 167

J

Jack of Hearts 33, 148
Jacobs, Parnell 127
Jameson, J. Jonah 138–9
Jarvis, Edwin 33, 87, 88–9, 181
jet boots 14–15
Jocasta 29
Jolt 51, 189
Jones, Angelica 140
Jones, Jessica 154
Jones, Rick 83, 122
Joystick 51
Jupiter Landing Vehicle 29
Justice 140, 172

K

Ka-Zar 51
Kakaranthara 121
Kang the Conqueror 46, 58, 104, 132, 154–5
Kennedy, Sal 33, 156, 168
Kildare, Kate 174
Kingpin 164–5
Kirby, Jack 10–11, 12, 64, 76
Klein, Abraham 29
Knight 106
Koto 77
Kotznin, Ambassador 86, 87
Kree 57, 67, 122–3
Kree/Skrull War 56, 83, 160

L

Lacoste, Rae 39, 41, 125, 126
Lang, Cassie 155
Lang, Scott 32, 110, 148
Larroca, Salvador 186
Latveria 92–3, 148
Laughton, Ebenezer 47
Layton, Bob 83, 88
Le Fay, Morgan 58, 93, 140–1
Lee, Stan 10–11, 12, 64, 76
Lemon, Nathan 45
Lieber, Larry 11, 12
Life Model Decoys 29, 80
Living Laser 47, 56, 57, 115, 125
LMD 47
Lobo 117
Loki 48, 55, 68, 190

M

McCall, Meredith 40, 54
McDonnell, Steve 100
Machine Man 98, 112, 189
Madame Masque 40, 43, 46, 47, 56, 78–9, 133, 185
Madison, Dr. Maria 138–9
Madripoor 169
Magma 102
Magneto 109, 134, 140, 150–1, 164–5
Magnum, Moses 141
Maleev, Alex 164
Mallen 156–7, 159
Mandarin 33, 44, 45, 47, 55, 57, 58, 74–7, 103, 115, 126, 135, 168–9
   Dragon Seed Saga 120–1
   rings 74, 121
Mandroids 29, 81, 110
March, Eddie 32, 52, 56, 83
Marcus, Wellington 189
Maria Stark Foundation 25, 28, 58, 139
Marilla 132
Marion 40
Marrs, Desmond 114–15
Marrs, Phoebe 114–15
Marvel Boy 183
Marvel, Ms. 50, 170, 183
Masaryk, Milos 46
Masque, Madame *see* Madame Masque
Mastermind 153
Masters of Evil 51
Masters of Silence 20, 91
Mauler 110
Maximoff, Wanda 129, 149–51
   see also Scarlet Witch
Melter 46, 55, 86
Mephisto 167
Merlin 188
Michelinie, David 83, 88, 112
Midas, Mordecai 47, 56, 76–9
Millar, Mark 164
Miller, Layla 151
Missile Gun 29
MIT 24, 54
Mitchell, Steve 100
Mjölnir 22
Mockingbird 108, 130
MODOK 46, 51
modular armor 20
Mole Man 170–1
Moomji, Indries 40, 99
Moonstone 51, 183
Murdock, Matthew 152
Murray, Dennis 174

N

Najeeb, Karim Mahwash 75, 168
Namor the Sub-Mariner 49, 51, 56, 114, 160–1, 175, 185
Nefaria, Count 46, 78
Nega-Bomb 123
Negative Zone 137, 162
Nelson, Foggy 139
neo-classic armor 19
New Warriors 140, 162
Nitro 53, 162
Nivena, Joanna 40, 54, 55
NTU 58

O

Oakley, Bill 112
O'Brien, Kevin 29, 33, 56
O'Brien, Michael 33, 52, 56
Oh, Jake 127
O'Neill, Dennis 95, 100
Onslaught 51, 58, 117, 134, 136–7
Operation Galactic Storm 57, 122–3
Order 59, 159, 174–5, 178
O'Reilly, Conner 134
Osborn, Norman 35, 47, 59, 73, 79, 127, 181, 182–7
Oscorp 183

P

Parker, Peter 50, 64, 166–7
Parks, Arthur 47
Patriot 155
Pawns 106
Pearson, Mary 29, 39
Pithins, Artemis 29
Plato 29
Plunder, Lord Kevin 51
Polaris 151
Potts, Pepper 25, 32, 34–7, 41, 54, 55, 59, 61, 64–5, 72, 79, 134–5, 137, 179, 184–7
Hera 174–5
Rescue 35, 59
Professor X 56
prometheum armor 21
Prometheus Gentech 75, 168
Punisher 117
Pym, Hank 40, 109, 141, 150–1, 170–1, 172, 174, 180

Q

Quesada, Joe 158, 164, 186
Quicksilver 132, 151
Quinjet 29, 49

R

Radioactive Man 50, 51, 166
Raft 59, 152, 164–5
Raiders 47, 56, 110
Rebel 135

recovery armor 19
Red Skull 67
red/gold armor 18, 64
repulsors 14–15
Rescue 35, 59
retro armor 21
Reynolds, Robert 153
Rhodes, Jim 19, 20, 25, 33, 38–9, 54, 56, 83, 87, 88–9, 91, 95, 98–9, 100–1, 133
   Armor Wars II 114–15
   Dragon Seed Saga 120–1
   Iron Man 38–9, 52, 57, 102–5, 108–9, 112–13
   War Machine 39, 43, 58–9, 117, 124–9, 172–3, 184
   West Coast Avengers 39, 58–9, 108–9
Richards, Franklin 134, 136–7
Richards, Nathaniel 46
Richards, Reed 50, 134, 139, 180
Richards, Sue 50
Richlen, Buck 81
Roberts, Chess 138–9
Rocket-Launcher 139
Rodgers, Marianne 40, 56
Rogers, Steve 29, 66, 140, 165
Rogue 50
Romanova, Natalia 40, 72 *see also* Black Widow
Romita, John 88
Ronin 153
Rosen, Sam 64, 76
Roxxon Oil 24, 51, 56
Ryan, Becky 174
Ryker's Island 152, 165

S

Saboteur 55
Sandhurst, Basil 46
Sandoval, Glenda 39, 127
Santini, Dr. Jose 56
Savage Land 51, 181
Scarecrow 47, 55
Scarlet Spiders 172
Scarlet Witch 32, 58, 59, 109, 129, 140–1, 149–51, 190
Scarlotti, Mark 45
Sea Tank 29
Secret Invasion 32, 33, 59, 127, 161, 180–1, 182, 184
Secret Wars 104–5, 108
sentient armor 21
Sentinel 29
Sentinel ONE 126
Sentry 92, 152–3, 170, 177, 183
Sersi 122
SHADOW 175
Shadow Initiative 172
Shanna 51
Sharen, Bob 88, 100
She-Hulk 41, 141, 149
Sheffield, Leah 138–9

Shepanka, Gregor 45
Shi'ar 57, 122–3
SHIELD 25, 29, 55, 59, 74, 80–1, 86, 89, 127, 152–3, 164–5, 176, 179
   helicarrier 29, 80–1, 164–5, 168–9, 181
   Tony Stark as Director 168–9, 172
Shockwave 185
Shooter, Jim 88, 100
Shroud 108
Silvani, Vittorio 138–9
Silver Centurion 19, 107, 108
Sinister Twelve 183
Sitwell, Jasper 78, 80
SK-1 29
SKIN armor 22
Skrulls 28, 32, 33, 51, 59, 123, 160–1, 180–1, 182, 184
Slaught, Ted 54, 132
Smokescreen 139
Softly, Sam 175
Songbird 51
Soviet Super Soldiers 73, 174–5
space armor 19, 22, 56
Space Phantom 49
Spare Parts Man 53
Speed Demon 51
Spider-Man 10, 12, 50, 59, 64, 104, 151, 152–3, 164–5, 166–7, 172, 182, 183
Spider-Woman 129, 152–3, 181
Spymaster 33, 37, 45, 56, 81, 84–5, 110, 125
Squadron Supreme 141
Stane, Ezekiel 28, 47, 59, 175, 178–9
Stane International 106, 166
Stane, Obadiah 28, 40, 43, 44, 56, 57, 79, 91, 98–9, 100–1, 102, 106–7, 178
Stane, Zebediah 106, 191
Stark, Andros 188
Stark, Arno 188–9
Stark, Edward 25
Stark Enterprises 25, 28, 57
Stark, Howard 24, 25, 28, 54, 150–1, 191
Stark Industries 24, 25, 28–9, 34, 54, 90
Stark International 25, 28, 86, 88–9, 90–1, 110
Stark, Isaac 25, 28
Stark, Maria 24, 25, 28, 54, 191
Stark, Morgan 25, 47, 189
Stark Solutions 25, 28, 58, 139
Stark, Tony 9, 10, 24–7, 30–1, 54
   Secretary of Defense 146–9
   SHIELD Director 168–9, 172
   telepresence armor 125
Stark-Fujikawa 28, 39, 58
Starkdynamics 178–9
stealth armor 19, 22, 56, 73
Stilt Man 110
Stingray 110–11
Stockpile 32, 72
Stone, Tiberius 58
Storm, Johnny 50, 150
Storm, Sue 139

Strange, Dr. 56, 149, 160–1, 176–7
Strucker, Baron 80
Sunturion 47
Superhuman Registration Act 59, 67, 161, 162, 165, 167, 172, 186–7
Supernaut 174–5
Supreme Intelligence 67, 122–3

T

Tales of Suspense 61, 76–7
   #39 9, 10–13
   #48 64–5
   #50 62–3
   #62 76–7
Taskmaster 141
T'Challa 29
telepresence armor 125
Temujin 47
Terrible Thinker 50
Thing 50
Thor 10, 12, 22, 48–9, 55, 68, 100–1, 140–1, 164–5, 190
Thorbuster Armor 22, 58
Thunderball 103
Thunderbolts 47, 51, 182, 183, 184–5
Tigra 108
timeline 54–9
Timeslide 132–3
Tin Man Armor 22
Titanium Man 36, 37, 45, 55, 73, 110–11, 147, 167
Amor Wars II 114–15
Travis, Nick 189
Triskelion 190
Turgenov, Boris 45
Tuska, George 83

U

Ultimate Iron Man 190–1
Ultimates 190
Ultimo 47, 52, 55, 58, 127, 149
Ultra-Dynamo 189
Ultron 104, 140–1, 170–1
unibeam 14–15
Unicorn 46, 72
Uranus II 29
USAgent 109, 122–3, 129

V

Valley of the Sleeping Dragon 115
Valley of Spirits 76–7
Van Dyne, Janet 40
van Tilberg, Alexander 42, 88–9
Vane, Roger 78
Vanko, Professor 55, 73
Vault 33, 66–7
Veda 174–5
Venk, Anton 45

Venom 183
Venom Bomb 92
Vibereaux, Alton 47
Vibro 47, 57
Villarrubia, Jose 164
Vision 109, 130, 140–1, 149, 154–5, 162
Vitriol 147
Void 153
VR mask 20
Vroom Room 29

W

Wa, James 174
Wakanda 160
Walker, Carl 33, 52
Walker, John 129
War Machine 20, 33, 39, 43, 57, 58–9, 91, 109, 124–9, 172–3, 184
weapon spec 128–9
War Machine magazine 117
Warbird 50, 141
Warbound 176
Ward, Clarence 58
Warwagon 29
Wasp 40, 48–9, 55, 67, 68, 109, 132, 141, 170, 190
Whiggins, Mrs. 88–9
Whiplash 45, 55, 61, 78, 86
Whirlwind 135, 141
Williams, Simon 129
Wilson, Clayton 33
Windsor-Smith, Barry 112
Winter Guard 73
Wolverine 53, 72, 112, 152–3, 183
Wonder Man 108, 129, 141, 170
Wong-Chu 12–13, 44, 47, 139, 158–9
The Works 29
World War Hulk 161, 176–7
Worldwatch 39, 126
Wrecking Crew 104, 141
wrist cannon 128

X

X, Professor 134, 160–1
X-Force 126
X-Men 51, 72, 104, 112, 134, 153, 160

Y

Yellow Claw 80
Yellowjacket 132, 172
Yin, Dr. Su 41, 120
Yinsen, Professor Ho 12–13, 33, 54, 139, 158–9

Z

Zimmer, Abe 20, 29, 32, 110, 125
zombies 154–5

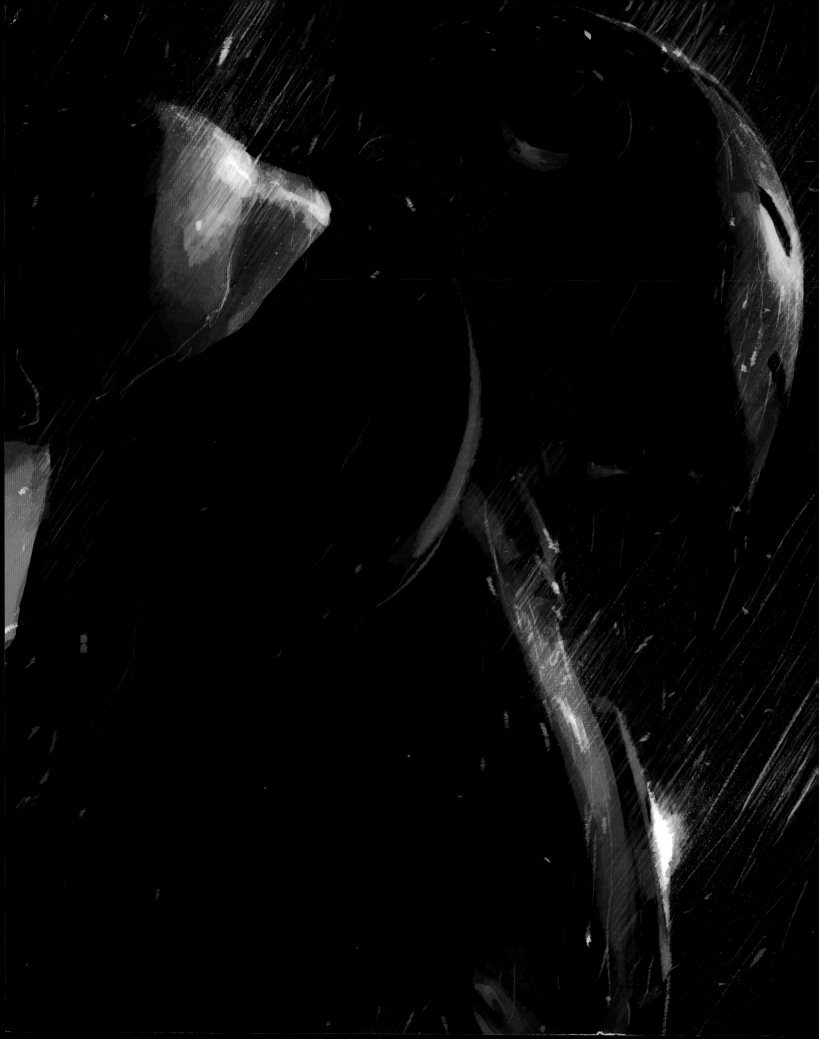